Microsoft® Windows™
Multimedia
Programmer's Reference

*Written, edited, and produced by
Microsoft Corporation*

Distributed by Microsoft Press

MICROSOFT®
WINDOWS™
PROGRAMMER'S
REFERENCE
LIBRARY

PUBLISHED BY
Microsoft Press
A Division of Microsoft Corporation
One Microsoft Way, Redmond, Washington 98052-6399

Library of Congress Cataloging-in-Publication Data

Microsoft Windows multimedia programmer's reference / Microsoft
    Corporation.
        p.   cm. -- (Microsoft Windows multimedia programmer's
    reference library)
    Includes index.
    ISBN 1-55615-389-9
    1. Computer animation.   2. Computer sound processing.
3. Microsoft Windows (Computer program)   I. Microsoft.   II. Series.
TR897.5.M535   1991
006.6'76 -- dc20   91-15490
                                                      CIP

Printed and bound in the United States of America.

1 2 3 4 5 6 7 8 9 MLML 6 5 4 3 2 1

Distributed to the book trade in Canada by Macmillan of Canada, a division of Canada Publishing Corporation.

Distributed to the book trade outside the United States and Canada by Penguin Books Ltd.

Penguin Books Ltd., Harmondsworth, Middlesex, England
Penguin Books Australia Ltd., Ringwood, Victoria, Australia
Penguin Books N.Z. Ltd., 182-190 Wairau Road, Auckland 10, New Zealand

British Cataloging-in-Publication Data available.

Document Number: MM20347-0691

Contents

Chapter 3   Function Directory

Chapter 4   Message Overview

Chapter 5   Message Directory

Chapter 6   Data Types and Structures

Chapter 7   MCI Command Strings

Chapter 8   Multimedia File Formats

Appendixes

A MCI Command String Syntax Summary

B Manufacturer ID and Product ID Lists

Index

Introduction

This manual provides reference information for the application programming interface (API) of Microsoft® Multimedia Extensions 1.0. The Multimedia extensions work with Microsoft Windows™ to provide an operating environment for multimedia personal computers.

The Multimedia extensions API includes functions, messages, data structures, data types, and file formats you can use along with the Windows 3.0 API to create Windows with Multimedia applications. For information on the Windows 3.0 API, see the *Microsoft Windows Programmer's Reference*, *Volume 1* and *Volume 2* provided with the Microsoft Windows Software Development Kit.

Multimedia Extensions Features

The Multimedia extensions API offers different types of services you can use to add features such as sound, animation, and external-device control to your applications. Multimedia extensions provide the following services:

- Audio—The audio services provide a device-independent interface to computer-audio hardware, providing sound for multimedia applications.

- The Media Control Interface (MCI)—MCI provides a high-level generalized interface to control media devices such as audio hardware, movie players, and videodisc and videotape players.

- Multimedia File I/O—The multimedia file I/O services provide buffered and unbuffered file I/O, as well as support for standard Resource Interchange File Format (RIFF) files. These services are extensible with custom I/O procedures that can be shared among applications.

- Movie Playback—The movie playback services provide high-level and low-level support for playing multimedia movie files.

- Video, joystick, and timer—These services provide support for joysticks, special video modes and operations, and high-resolution event timing.

- Screen saver—The screen saver services provide support for creating, configuring, and registering screen savers.

Multimedia Extensions Naming Conventions

The Multimedia extensions API uses certain conventions for naming functions, messages, and parameters. This section describes these conventions.

Function Names

Most multimedia functions are named with a prefix-verb-noun model to help you remember and become familiar with the function.

Name Element	Description
Prefix	Indicates the software module the function belongs to. All prefixes are lowercase.
Verb	Defines what the function does. Verbs begin with an uppercase letter.
Noun	Describes the target of the action. Nouns, like verbs, begin with an uppercase letter.

Note   No spaces or underscores separate the words in a function name.

The following are samples of function names:

waveOutGetVolume

The prefix (*waveOut*) indicates that this is a waveform output function. The verb (*Get*) defines the purpose of the function. The noun (*Volume*) describes the target of the action. This function is used to get the volume of a waveform audio device.

joySetThreshold

The prefix (*joy*) identifies the function as a joystick-control function. The verb (*Set*) and the noun (*Threshold*) describe the purpose of the function and the target of the action, respectively. This function is used to set the movement threshold of a joystick.

Message Names

Message names, like function names, begin with a prefix. Related messages are grouped together with a common prefix. An underscore character (_) follows the prefix in each message name. One or more words describing the purpose of the message appear after the underscore. Message names use only uppercase letters.

The following is an example of a message name:

WOM_CLOSE

The prefix (*WOM*) indicates that the message is a waveform output message. The descriptive portion of the message (*CLOSE*) indicates the purpose of the message. This message is sent whenever a waveform output device is closed.

Parameter Names

Most parameter and local-variable names consist of a lowercase prefix followed by one or more capitalized words. The prefix indicates the general type of the parameter, while the words that follow describe the contents of the parameter. The standard prefixes used in parameter and variable names are defined as follows:

Prefix	Description
b	Boolean (a non-zero value specifies TRUE, zero specifies FALSE)
ch	Character (a one-byte value)
dw	Long (32-bit) unsigned integer
h	Handle
l	Long (32-bit) integer
lp	Far pointer
np	Near pointer
pt	x and y coordinates packed into an unsigned 32-bit integer
rgb	An RGB color value packed into a 32-bit integer
w	Short (16-bit) unsigned integer

Note If no lowercase prefix is given, the parameter is a short integer with a descriptive name.

The following are some examples of parameter and variable names:

Parameter/Variable	Description
bResult	A boolean parameter
dwEvent	A long, unsigned integer parameter
hWaveOut	A handle to a waveform audio device
lParam	A long integer parameter
wFlags	A short, unsigned integer parameter

Multimedia Extensions Calling Convention

Like Windows, the Multimedia extensions use the Pascal calling convention, which operates as follows:

- Parameters are pushed onto the stack in the order in which they appear in the function call.

- The code that restores the stack is part of the called function (rather than the calling function).

This convention differs from the calling convention used in some languages, such as C. In C, parameters are pushed onto the stack in reverse order, and the calling function is responsible for restoring the stack.

When developing applications using the Multimedia extensions in C (or any other language that doesn't ordinarily use the Pascal calling convention), use the Pascal calling convention for any Multimedia extensions functions called by your application. In C, use the **PASCAL** keyword when declaring the function, as shown in the following example:

```
BOOL FAR PASCAL midiOutGetNumDevs()
```

The WINDOWS.H header file declares prototypes for all standard Windows functions. The MMSYSTEM.H, MMP.H, and DISPDIB.H header files declare prototypes for all Multimedia extensions functions. The declarations in these header files use the Pascal calling convention.

Contents of This Reference

This reference provides important reference information for application developers and multimedia authors. It includes complete informatoin on the functions, message, data types, file formats, and MCI command sets provided with the Multimedia extensions. For information and examples on how to use the Multimedia extensions, see the *Programmer's Workbook* in the Multimedia Development Kit.

The following information is included in this reference:

- Chapter 2, "Function Overview," summarizes all the functions provided with the Multimedia extensions. Functions are grouped by the software module that contains them and are further grouped by use.

- Chapter 3, "Function Directory," alphabetically lists all the functions provided with the Multimedia extensions. The documentation for each function describes the function, shows the correct syntax, and describes input parameters, appropriate flags, and return values. Most function descriptions include a list of related functions and messages.

- Chapter 4, "Message Overview," summarizes the messages associated with the Multimedia extensions. Messages are grouped by the software module that uses them.

- Chapter 5, "Message Directory," alphabetically lists the messages associated with the Multimedia extensions. The documentation for each message describes the message, shows the correct syntax, and describes the parameters and any return values. Groups of messages use similar prefixes, so they are listed together in the chapter.

- Chapter 6, "Data Types," describes the data types and structures exclusive to the Multimedia extensions. The first part of the chapter describes each data type. The second part of the chapter describes each data structures, including the fields within each structure.

- Chapter 7, "MCI Command Strings," describes command strings for the Media Control Interface (MCI). It describes how to use MCI command strings and describes each command string recognized by MCI. Commands are grouped by device type.

- Chapter 8, "File Formats," describes the file formats used with the Multimedia extensions.

- Appendix A, "MCI Command String Summary," presents a summary of the syntax of the MCI command strings.

- Appendix B, "Manufacturer ID and Product ID Lists," lists the constants that identify multimedia product manufacturers and products used with the Multimedia extensions.

Conventions

The following section explains the document conventions used throughout this manual:

Type Style	Used For
bold	Bold letters indicate a specific term intended to be used literally: functions (such as **waveOutGetNumDevs**), messages (such as **WIM_OPEN**), and structure fields (such as **dwReturn**). You must enter these terms exactly as shown.
italic	Words in italics indicate a placeholder; you are expected to provide the actual value. For example, the following syntax for the **timeGetSystemTime** function indicates that you must substitute values for the *lpTime* and *wSize* parameters: **timeGetSystemTime**(*lpTime,wSize*)
monospace	Code examples are displayed in a monospaced typeface.
brackets [ ]	Optional items.
Horizontal ellipsis ...	An ellipsis shows that one or more copies of the preceding item may occur. Brackets followed by an ellipsis means that the item enclosed within the brackets may occur zero or more times.
Angle brackets < >	Indicates the name and position of a field within a file format definition.
Arrow →	In a file format definition, the item to the left of the arrow is equivalent to the item to the right.

Related Documentation

This manual provides you with an overview and alphabetical reference of the functions, messages, command strings, data types, and file formats for the Multimedia extensions. Other MDK documentation describes additional aspects of the software-development process. In addition to the *Programmer's Reference*, the MDK includes the following manuals:

- The *Getting Started* manual is intended for both multimedia application programmers and multimedia authors. It describes the MDK and other software required to develop multimedia applications and explains how to install the MDK software.

- The *Programmer's Workbook* explains in detail how to use the services of the Multimedia extensions to create multimedia applications. This workbook is intended for multimedia application programmers.

- The *Data Preparation Tools User's Guide* describes the data-preparation tools provided with the MDK. These tools allow authors to edit media elements, such as bitmaps and waveforms, and to convert data files.

- The *Multimedia Authoring Guide* describes the authoring process for multimedia titles. This guide describes how to acquire and prepare data for multimedia titles.

- The *Multimedia Viewer Developer's Guide* describes how to build titles for the Multimedia Viewer software.

If you're an application programmer, you will find this reference and the *Programmer's Workbook* to be most useful in learning about programming for Windows with Multimedia. Also, multimedia authors will find the information on file formats and the descriptions of the MCI command strings useful.

The Online References

When you install the MDK, you have the option of installing the following online reference files:

Filename	File Type	Description
MDKREF.MVB	Viewer	Provides complete information on all of the functions, messages, and data structures in the Multimedia extensions. The full-text search capability of Viewer allows you to quickly find information.
MDKREF.HLP	Windows Help	Provides the same contents as MDKREF.MVB, but in Windows Help format. This version lacks the full-text indexing.
MCISTR.MVB	Viewer	Provides complete information on the MCI command strings used with the Multimedia extensions. The full-text search capability of Viewer allows you to quickly find information.
MCISTR.HLP	Windows Help	Provides the same contents as MCISTR.MVB, but in Windows Help format. This version lacks the full-text indexing.

Chapter 2
Function Overview

This chapter provides an overview of the functions in the Multimedia extensions to Windows. The functions are organized into the following categories, some of which contain smaller groups of related functions:

- High-level audio services
- Low-level waveform audio services
- Low-level MIDI audio services
- Auxiliary audio device services
- Multimedia movie-playback services
- File I/O services
- Media Control Interface (MCI) services
- Joystick services
- Timer services
- Screen-saver services
- Bitmap display services
- Debugging services

For detailed information on the functions listed in this chapter, see Chapter 3, "Function Directory," which is an alphabetical listing of the functions in the Multimedia extensions to Windows.

High-Level Audio Services

High-level audio services allow applications to play audio files directly, while the Multimedia extensions system software manages audio playback. Use the following functions to play memory-resident waveform sounds specified by filename, system-alert level, or WIN.INI entries:

MessageBeep

Plays the sound that corresponds to a given system alert level.

sndPlaySound

Plays the sound that corresponds to the given filename or WIN.INI entry.

In addition to these two functions, the Media Control Interface provides high-level audio services. For an overview of the MCI functions, see the section "Media Control Interface Services," later in this chapter.

Low-Level Waveform Audio Services

Low-level waveform audio services allow applications to manage waveform audio playback and recording. Low-level waveform audio services are divided into the following categories:

- Querying waveform devices
- Opening and closing waveform devices
- Getting the device ID of waveform devices
- Recording waveform data
- Playing waveform data
- Handling waveform errors
- Getting the current position of waveform devices
- Controlling waveform playback
- Controlling waveform recording
- Changing pitch and playback rate
- Changing playback volume

Querying Waveform Devices

Before playing or recording a waveform, you must determine the capabilities of the waveform hardware present in the system. Use the following functions to retrieve the number of waveform devices and the capabilities of each device:

waveInGetNumDevs

Retrieves the number of waveform input devices present in the system.

waveInGetDevCaps

Retrieves the capabilities of a given waveform input device.

waveOutGetNumDevs

Retrieves the number of waveform output devices present in the system.

waveOutGetDevCaps

Retrieves the capabilities of a given waveform output device.

Opening and Closing Waveform Devices

You must open a device before you can begin waveform playback or recording. Once you finish using a device, you must close it so that it will be available to other applications. Use the following functions to open and close waveform devices:

waveInOpen

Opens a waveform input device for recording.

waveInClose

Closes a specified waveform input device.

waveOutOpen

Opens a waveform output device for playback.

waveOutClose

Closes a specified waveform output device.

Getting the Device ID of Waveform Devices

Using a waveform device handle, you can retrieve the device ID for an open waveform device. Use the following functions to get the device ID:

waveInGetID

Gets the device ID for a waveform input device.

waveOutGetID

Gets the device ID for a waveform output device.

Playing Waveform Data

After opening a waveform output device, you can begin sending data blocks to the device. Before sending data blocks to the device, each data block must be prepared. Use the following functions to prepare data blocks and send them to a waveform output device:

waveOutPrepareHeader

Informs the waveform output device driver that the given data block should be prepared for playback.

waveOutWrite

Writes a data block to a waveform output device.

waveOutUnprepareHeader

Informs the waveform output device driver that the preparation performed on the given data block can be cleaned up.

Recording Waveform Data

After opening a waveform input device, you can begin recording waveform data. To record waveform data, you must supply the waveform input device with data buffers. These data buffers must be prepared before being sent to the waveform device. Use the following functions to prepare data buffers and send them to waveform input devices:

waveInAddBuffer

Sends a data buffer to a waveform output device. The data buffer is filled with recorded waveform data and sent back to the application.

waveInPrepareHeader

Informs the waveform input device driver that the given data buffer should be prepared for recording.

waveInUnprepareHeader

Informs the waveform input device driver that the preparation performed on the given data buffer can be cleaned up.

Getting the Current Position of Waveform Devices

While playing or recording waveform audio, you can query the device for the current playback or recording position. Use the following functions to determine the current position of a waveform device:

waveInGetPosition

Retrieves the current recording position of a waveform input device.

waveOutGetPosition

Retrieves the current playback position of a waveform output device.

Controlling Waveform Playback

Waveform playback begins as soon as you begin sending data to the waveform output device. Use the following functions to pause, restart, or stop playback and to break loops on a waveform device:

waveOutBreakLoop

Breaks a loop on a waveform output device.

waveOutPause

Pauses playback on a waveform output device.

waveOutRestart

Resumes playback on a paused waveform output device.

waveOutReset

Stops playback on a waveform output device. Marks all pending data blocks as done.

Controlling Waveform Recording

When recording waveform audio, you can control when recording starts and stops. Use the following functions to start and stop recording on a waveform input device:

waveInStart

Starts recording on a waveform input device.

waveInStop

Stops recording on a waveform input device.

waveInReset

Stops recording on a waveform input device. Marks all pending data blocks as done.

Changing Pitch and Playback Rate

Some waveform output devices can scale the pitch and the playback rate when playing a waveform. Both of these operations have the effect of changing the pitch of the waveform. Use these functions to query and set waveform pitch and playback rate scale factors:

waveOutGetPitch

Queries the pitch scale factor for a waveform output device.

waveOutGetPlaybackRate

Queries the playback rate scale factor for a waveform output device.

waveOutSetPitch

Sets the pitch scale factor for a waveform output device.

waveOutSetPlaybackRate

Sets the playback rate scale factor for a waveform output device.

Changing Playback Volume

Some waveform output devices support changes to the playback volume level. Use these functions to query and set the volume level of waveform output devices:

waveOutGetVolume

Queries the current volume level of a waveform output device.

waveOutSetVolume

Sets the volume level of a waveform output device.

Handling Waveform Errors

Most of the low-level waveform audio functions return error codes. Use these functions to convert the error codes returned from waveform functions into a textual description of the error:

waveInGetErrorText

Retrieves a textual description of a specified waveform input error.

waveOutGetErrorText

Retrieves a textual description of a specified waveform output error.

Low-Level MIDI Audio Services

The low-level MIDI audio services allow applications to communicate directly with device drivers to manage MIDI audio playback and recording. The low-level MIDI audio services are divided into the following categories of functions:

- Querying MIDI devices
- Opening and closing MIDI devices
- Getting the device ID of MIDI devices
- Sending MIDI messages
- Receiving MIDI messages
- Controlling MIDI input
- Changing MIDI volume and caching patches
- Handling MIDI errors

Querying MIDI Devices

Before playing MIDI audio, you must determine the capabilities of the MIDI hardware that is present in the system. Use the following functions to get the number of MIDI devices and the capabilities of these devices:

midiInGetNumDevs

Retrieves the number of MIDI input devices present in the system.

midiInGetDevCaps

Retrieves the capabilities of a given MIDI input device.

midiOutGetNumDevs

Retrieves the number of MIDI output devices present in the system.

midiOutGetDevCaps

Retrieves the capabilities of a given MIDI output device.

Opening and Closing MIDI Devices

After getting the MIDI capabilities, you must open a MIDI device to play or record MIDI messages. After using the device, you should close it to make it available to other applications. Use the following functions to open and close MIDI devices:

midiInOpen

Opens a MIDI input device for recording.

midiInClose

Closes a specified MIDI input device.

midiOutOpen

Opens a MIDI output device for playback.

midiOutClose

Closes a specified MIDI output device.

Getting the Device ID of MIDI Devices

Using a MIDI device handle, you can retrieve the device ID for an open MIDI device. Use the following functions to get the device ID:

midiInGetID

Gets the device ID for a MIDI input device.

midiOutGetID

Gets the device ID for a MIDI output device.

Sending MIDI Messages

Once you have opened a MIDI output device, you can send it MIDI messages. MIDI system exclusive messages are sent in data blocks that must be prepared before being sent to an output device. Use the following functions to send MIDI messages to output devices and to prepare system exclusive data blocks:

midiOutLongMsg

Sends a buffer containing MIDI data to a specified MIDI output device.

midiOutShortMsg

Sends any MIDI message other than a system exclusive message to the specified MIDI output device.

midiOutPrepareHeader

Informs the MIDI output device driver that the given MIDI data buffer should be prepared for playback.

midiOutReset

Turns off all notes on all channels for a specified MIDI output device.

midiOutUnprepareHeader

Informs the MIDI output device driver that the preparation performed on the given MIDI data buffer can be cleaned up.

Receiving MIDI Messages

Once you have opened a MIDI input device, you can begin receiving MIDI input. MIDI messages other than system exclusive messages are sent directly to a callback. To receive system exclusive messages, you must pass data buffers to the input device. These data buffers must be prepared before being sent to the device. Use the following messages to prepare system exclusive data buffers and pass these buffers to a MIDI input device:

midiInAddBuffer

Sends an input buffer for system exclusive messages to a specified MIDI input device. The buffer is sent back to the application when it is filled with system exclusive data.

midiInPrepareHeader

Informs a MIDI input device that the given data buffer should be prepared for recording.

midiInUnprepareHeader

Informs a MIDI input device that the preparation performed on the given data buffer can be cleaned up.

Controlling MIDI Input

When receiving MIDI input, you can control when the input starts and stops. Use the following functions to start and stop input on a MIDI input device:

midiInStart

Starts input on a MIDI input device.

midiInStop

Stops input on a MIDI input device.

midiInReset

Stops input on a MIDI input device. Marks all pending data buffers as being done.

Changing MIDI Volume and Caching Patches

Some internal MIDI synthesizers support volume level changes and patch caching. Use the following functions to query and set the volume level and to cache and uncache patches with internal MIDI synthesizer devices:

midiOutCacheDrumPatches

Requests that an internal MIDI synthesizer device preload a specified set of key-based percussion patches.

midiOutCachePatches

Requests that an internal MIDI synthesizer device preload a specified set of patches.

midiOutGetVolume

Queries the current volume level of an internal MIDI synthesizer device.

midiOutSetVolume

Sets the volume level of an internal MIDI synthesizer device.

Handling MIDI Errors

Most of the low-level MIDI audio functions return error codes. Use the following functions to convert the error codes returned from MIDI functions into a textual description of the error:

midiInGetErrorText

Retrieves a textual description of a specified MIDI input error.

midiOutGetErrorText

Retrieves a textual description of a specified MIDI output error.

Auxiliary Audio Services

Auxiliary audio devices are audio devices whose output is mixed with the output of waveform and MIDI synthesizer devices. Use the following functions to query the capabilities of auxiliary audio devices and to query and set their volume level:

auxGetDevCaps

Retrieves the capabilities of a given auxiliary audio device.

auxGetNumDevs

Retrieves the number of auxiliary audio devices present in a system.

auxGetVolume

Queries the volume level of an auxiliary audio device.

auxSetVolume

Sets the volume level of an auxiliary audio device.

Multimedia Movie Playback Services

The multimedia movie playback services provide support for playing Multimedia Movie files. The movie playback services are divided into the following categories:

- Loading the Multimedia Movie Player
- Handling movie files
- Getting movie information
- Animating the movie
- Controlling the playback window
- Controlling playback

Loading the Multimedia Movie Player

Before playing a movie, you must open an instance of the Multimedia Movie Player. Use the following functions to start and stop the Movie Player:

mmpClose

Closes a Movie Player instance.

mmpOpen

Initializes a Movie Player instance.

Handling Movie Files

After opening a Movie Player instance, you can load a movie file. Use the following functions to load and unload movie files:

mmpFileLoaded

Determines whether a movie file has been loaded into the Movie Player instance.

mmpFreeFile

Frees a movie file previously loaded by **mmpLoadFile**.

mmpLoadFile

Loads a movie file and specifies playback options.

Getting Movie Information

The Movie Player provides functions to get error information and to retrieve Movie Player data structures and movie file information. Use the following functions to get error information about a Movie Player instance and to retrieve and set Movie Player data structures:

mmpError

Returns error information and optionally fills a text buffer with error-message text.

mmpGetFileInfo

Returns information about a movie file on disk.

mmpGetInfo

Allows access to the movie file label-list and script-channel entries.

mmpGetMovieInfo

Returns information about the currently loaded movie file.

mmpGetPaletteHandle

Returns a handle to the palette of the currently loaded movie file.

mmpSetInfo

Allows an application to change values for the movie file label-list and script-channel entries.

Animating the Movie

After starting the Movie Player and loading a movie file, you can start the animation. Use the following functions to start and stop the animation and advance the frames:

mmpAnimate

Performs the transition to the next movie frame.

mmpAnimStatus

Returns information about the playback status.

mmpAnimStopped

Determines whether the movie is stopped.

mmpStartAnimating

Starts playback of a movie.

mmpStopAnimating

Stops playback of a movie.

Controlling the Playback Window

The Movie Player provides various functions for controlling the playback window. The following functions assign a playback window and specify the position of the animation within the window, update an invalid rectangle on the playback window, and return information about the playback window:

mmpGetStage

Returns information about the stage window for a Movie Player instance.

mmpSetDC

Assigns a device context to a Movie Player instance.

mmpSetStage

Assigns a playback window to a Movie Player instance and specifies the position and size of the playback area within the window.

mmpUpdate

Updates an invalid rectangle on the stage window, generally in response to a WM_PAINT message.

Controlling the Playback

The following functions allow you to control various aspects of the playback:

mmpGetCurFrame

Returns the current frame number in the movie.

mmpGetFrameHook

Returns a pointer to the most recently attached frame-callback function.

mmpGetMute

Determines whether the sound track of the movie is enabled or disabled.

mmpGetRepeat

Determines whether the movie will repeat.

mmpGoToFrame

Jumps to a specified frame number.

mmpIsLastFrame

Determines whether the movie is at the last frame.

mmpSetMute

Disables or enables the playback of audio cast members.

mmpSetFrameHook

Allows an application to be notified of frame advances and script-channel commands.

mmpSetRepeat

Specifies whether the movie should continuously repeat.

File I/O Services

The multimedia file I/O services provide buffered and unbuffered file I/O, and support for standard Resource Interchange File Format (RIFF) files. The services are extensible with custom I/O procedures that can be shared among applications.

The file I/O services are divided into the following categories:

- Performing Basic File I/O
- Performing Buffered File I/O
- Working with RIFF Files
- Using Custom I/O Procedures

Performing Basic File I/O

Using the basic file I/O services is very similar to using other file I/O services such as the C runtime file I/O services. Files must be opened before they can be read or written. After reading or writing, the file must be closed. You can seek to a specified position in an open file. Use the following functions for basic file I/O:

mmioClose

Closes an opened file.

mmioOpen

Opens a file for reading and/or writing, and returns a handle to the opened file.

mmioRead

Reads a specified number of bytes from an opened file.

mmioSeek

Changes the current position for reading and/or writing in an opened file.

mmioWrite

Writes a specified number of bytes to an opened file.

Performing Buffered File I/O

Using the basic buffered file I/O services is very similar to using the unbuffered services. Specify the MMIO_ALLOCBUF option with the **mmioOpen** function to open a file for buffered I/O. The file I/O manager will maintain an internal buffer which is transparent to the application.

You can also change the size of the internal buffer, allocate your own buffer, and directly access a buffer for optimal I/O performance. Use the following functions for I/O buffer control and direct I/O buffer access:

mmioAdvance

Fills and/or flushes the I/O buffer of a file set up for direct I/O buffer access.

mmioFlush

Writes the contents of the I/O buffer to disk.

mmioGetInfo

Gets information about the file I/O buffer of a file opened for buffered I/O.

mmioSetBuffer

Changes the size of the I/O buffer, and allows applications to supply their own buffer.

mmioSetInfo

Changes information about the file I/O buffer of a file opened for buffered I/O.

Working with RIFF Files

The preferred format for multimedia files is the Microsoft Resource Interchange File Format (RIFF). The RIFF format is based on a tagged-file structure using chunks identified by four-character codes. You can use the multimedia file I/O services to open, read, and write RIFF files the same way as you would any other type of file. You can also use the following functions to create chunks, convert characters and strings to four-character codes, and navigate between chunks in RIFF files:

mmioAscend

Ascends out of a RIFF file chunk to the next chunk in the file.

mmioCreateChunk

Creates a chunk in a RIFF file.

mmioDescend

Descends into a RIFF file chunk starting at the current file position, or searches for a specified chunk.

mmioFOURCC

Converts four individual characters into a FOURCC code.

mmioStringToFOURCC

Converts a NULL-terminated string into a FOURCC code.

Using Custom I/O Procedures

The multimedia file I/O services use I/O procedures to handle the physical input and output associated with reading and writing different types of storage systems. I/O procedures know how to open, close, read, write, and seek a particular type of storage system. Applications can supply custom I/O procedures for accessing unique storage systems such as databases or file archives. Use the following functions for working with custom I/O procedures:

mmioInstallIOProc

Installs, removes, or locates an I/O procedure.

mmioSendMessage

Sends a message to an I/O procedure associated with a specified file.

Media Control Interface Services

The Media Control Interface (MCI) provides a high-level generalized interface for controlling both internal and external media devices. MCI uses device handlers to interpret and execute high-level MCI commands. Applications can communicate with MCI device handlers by sending messages or command strings.

MCI also provides macros for working with the time and position information encoded in a packed DWORD.

Communicating with MCI Devices

You can communicate with MCI devices using messages or command strings. Messages are used directly by MCI; MCI converts command strings into messages that it then sends to the device handler. Use these functions to send messages or command strings to MCI, to get the ID assigned to a device, and to get a textual description of an MCI error:

mciSendCommand

Sends a command message to MCI.

mciSendString

Sends a command string to MCI.

mciExecute

A simple version of **mciSendString**. Errors are displayed automatically in a dialog box.

mciGetDeviceID

Returns the device ID assigned when the device was opened.

mciGetErrorString

Returns the error string corresponding to an MCI error return value.

Most of the MCI functionality is expressed in its command set. See Chapter 4, "Message Overview," and Chapter 5, "Message Directory," for an overview and reference to all MCI command messages. MCI command messages are prefixed with **MCI**.

In addition to its message-based interface, MCI has a string-based interface. Chapter 7, "MCI Command Strings," describes the MCI command strings.

MCI Macros for Encoding and Decoding Time Data

MMSYSTEM.H defines a set of macros that extract information from the packed DWORD that MCI uses to encode time information. Use these macros to extract time and position information from the DWORD:

MCI_HMS_HOUR

Returns the hours field of an argument packed with hours, minutes, and seconds.

MCI_HMS_MINUTE

Returns the minutes field of an argument packed with hours, minutes, and seconds.

MCI_HMS_SECOND

Returns the seconds field of an argument packed with hours, minutes, and seconds.

MCI_MSF_FRAME

Returns the frames field of an argument packed with minutes, seconds, and frames.

MCI_MSF_MINUTE

Returns the minutes field of an argument packed with minutes, seconds, and frames.

MCI_MSF_SECOND

Returns the seconds field of an argument packed with minutes, seconds, and frames.

MCI_TMSF_FRAME

Returns the frames field of an argument packed with tracks, minutes, seconds, and frames.

MCI_TMSF_MINUTE

Returns the minutes field of an argument packed with tracks, minutes, seconds, and frames.

MCI_TMSF_SECOND

Returns the seconds field of an argument packed with tracks, minutes, seconds, and frames.

MCI_TMSF_TRACK

Returns the tracks field of an argument packed with tracks, minutes, seconds, and frames.

MMSYSTEM.H also defines the following macros that combine separate time and position values into the packed DWORD format:

MCI_MAKE_HMS

Creates a DWORD time value in hours/minutes/seconds format from the given hours, minutes, and seconds values.

MCI_MAKE_MSF

Creates a DWORD time value in minutes/seconds/frames format from the given minutes, seconds, and frames values.

MCI_MAKE_TMSF

Creates a DWORD time value in tracks/minutes/seconds/frames format from the given tracks, minutes, seconds, and frames values.

Joystick Services

The joystick services provide support for up to two joystick devices. Use the following functions to get information about joystick devices, to control joystick sensitivity, and to receive messages related to joystick movement and button activity:

---

joyGetDevCaps

Returns the capabilities of a joystick device.

joyGetNumDevs

Returns the number of devices supported by the joystick driver.

joyGetPos

Returns the position and button state of a joystick.

joyGetThreshold

Returns the movement threshold of a joystick.

joyReleaseCapture

Releases the joystick captured with **joySetCapture**.

joySetCapture

Causes periodic joystick messages to be sent to a window.

joySetThreshold

Sets the movement threshold of a joystick.

Timer Services

The timer services allow applications to schedule asynchronous timed periodic or one-time events at a higher resolution than is available through the standard Windows timer services. Use the following functions to request and receive timer messages:

timeBeginPeriod

Establishes the timer resolution an application intends to use.

timeEndPeriod

Clears a previously set timer resolution.

timeGetDevCaps

Returns the capabilities of the timer driver.

timeGetSystemTime

Fills an MMTIME structure with the system time in milliseconds.

timeGetTime

Returns the system time in milliseconds.

timeKillEvent

Cancels a timer event previously created with **timeSetEvent**.

timeSetEvent

Creates a timer event which will call a specified function at periodic intervals or after a single period.

Screen Saver Services

The screen saver services provide support for creating screen saver applications. Screen saver applications temporarily replace the screen display of an inactive application. Use the following function in screen saver applications to process default actions:

DefScreenSaverProc

Provides default message processing for any messages that a screen saver application does not process.

Bitmap Display Services

The bitmap display services provide a function for displaying bitmaps:

DisplayDib

Displays a 256-color bitmap on a standard VGA display.

Debugging Services

The debugging services provide support for debugging applications. Use the following functions to get the current version of the Multimedia extensions and to send debugging messages from an application:

mmsystemGetVersion

Gets the version number of the Multimedia extensions.

OutputDebugStr

Sends a debug string to either the COM1 port or to a monochrome display adapter.

C h a p t e r   3
Function Directory

This chapter contains an alphabetical list of the functions in the Multimedia extensions to Windows. For information about standard Windows functions, see the *Microsoft Windows Software Development Kit Reference—Volume 1*.

For each function, this chapter lists the following items:

- The syntax for the function

- The purpose of the function

- A description of input parameters

- A description of return values

- Optional comments on using the function

- Optional cross references to other functions, messages, and data structures

This chapter also lists the macros defined with the Multimedia extensions. Macros are documented similarly to functions. Each description begins by identifying the routine as a function or a macro (For example, This *function*... or This *macro*...).

Function Prefixes

Groups of related functions in the multimedia extensions are identified by a prefix in the function names. The following table summarizes groups of related functions and the prefixes for each group:

Function Prefix	Description
aux	Auxiliary audio functions
joy	Joystick functions
mci	Media Control Interface functions
midi	Low-level MIDI audio functions
mmio	Multimedia file I/O functions
mmp	Movie playback functions
snd	High-level sound functions
time	Timer event functions
wave	Low-level waveform audio functions

Function Descriptions

This section lists functions and macros in the Multimedia extensions to Windows. The functions and macros are presented in alphabetical order.

auxGetDevCaps

Syntax   WORD   **auxGetDevCaps**(*wDeviceID*, *lpCaps*, *wSize*)

This function queries a specified auxiliary output device to determine its capabilities.

Parameters   WORD   *wDeviceID*
Identifies the auxiliary output device to be queried.

LPAUXCAPS   *lpCaps*
Specifies a far pointer to an AUXCAPS structure. This structure is filled with information about the capabilities of the device.

WORD   *wSize*
Specifies the size of the AUXCAPS structure.

Return Value   Returns zero if the function was successful. Otherwise, it returns an error number. Possible error returns are:

MMSYSERR_BADDEVICEID
    Specified device ID is out of range.

MMSYSERR_NODRIVER
    The driver failed to install.

Comments   Use **auxGetNumDevs** to determine the number of auxiliary output devices present in the system. The device ID specified by *wDeviceID* varies from zero to one less than the number of devices present.

See Also   **auxGetNumDevs**

auxGetNumDevs

Syntax   WORD   **auxGetNumDevs**()

This function retrieves the number of auxiliary output devices present in the system.

Parameters   None

Return Value   Returns the number of auxiliary output devices present in the system.

See Also   **auxGetDevCaps**

auxGetVolume

Syntax   WORD   **auxGetVolume**(*wDeviceID*, *lpdwVolume*)

This function returns the current volume setting of an auxiliary output device.

Parameters   WORD   *wDeviceID*
    Identifies the auxiliary output device to be queried.

LPDWORD   *lpdwVolume*
    Specifies a far pointer to a location to be filled with the current volume setting. The low-order word of this location contains the left channel volume setting, and the high-order word contains the right channel setting. A value of 0xFFFF represents full volume, and a value of 0x0000 is silence.

    If a device does not support both left and right volume control, the low-order word of the specified location contains the volume level.

    The full 16-bit setting(s) set with **auxSetVolume** are returned, regardless of whether the device supports the full 16 bits of volume level control.

Return Value Returns zero if the function was successful. Otherwise, it returns an error number. Possible error returns are:

MMSYSERR_BADDEVICEID
> Specified device ID is out of range.

MMSYSERR_NODRIVER
> The driver failed to install.

Comments Not all devices support volume control. To determine whether the device supports volume control, use the AUXCAPS_VOLUME flag to test the **dwSupport** field of the **AUXCAPS** structure (filled by **auxGetDevCaps**).

To determine whether the device supports volume control on both the left and right channels, use the AUXCAPS_LRVOLUME flag to test the **dwSupport** field of the **AUXCAPS** structure (filled by **auxGetDevCaps**).

See Also **auxSetVolume**

auxSetVolume

Syntax WORD **auxSetVolume**(*wDeviceID*, *dwVolume*)

This function sets the volume in an auxiliary output device.

Parameters WORD *wDeviceID*
> Identifies the auxiliary output device to be queried. Device IDs are determined implicitly from the number of devices present in the system. Device ID values range from zero to one less than the number of devices present. Use **auxGetNumDevs** to determine the number of auxiliary devices in the system.

DWORD *dwVolume*
> Specifies the new volume setting. The low-order word specifies the left channel volume setting, and the high-order word specifies the right channel setting. A value of 0xFFFF represents full volume, and a value of 0x0000 is silence.

> If a device does not support both left and right volume control, the low-order word of *dwVolume* specifies the volume level, and the high-order word is ignored.

Return Value Returns zero if the function was successful. Otherwise, it returns an error number. Possible error returns are:

MMSYSERR_BADDEVICEID
> Specified device ID is out of range.

MMSYSERR_NODRIVER
> The driver failed to install.

Comments   Not all devices support volume control. To determine whether the device supports volume control, use the AUXCAPS_VOLUME flag to test the **dwSupport** field of the **AUXCAPS** structure (filled by **auxGetDevCaps**).

To determine whether the device supports volume control on both the left and right channels, use the AUXCAPS_LRVOLUME flag to test the **dwSupport** field of the **AUXCAPS** structure (filled by **auxGetDevCaps**).

Most devices do not support the full 16 bits of volume level control and will use only the high-order bits of the requested volume setting. For example, for a device that supports 4 bits of volume control, requested volume level values of 0x4000, 0x4fff, and 0x43be will all produce the same physical volume setting, 0x4000. The **auxGetVolume** function will return the full 16-bit setting set with **auxSetVolume**.

Volume settings are interpreted logarithmically. This means the perceived volume increase is the same when increasing the volume level from 0x5000 to 0x6000 as it is from 0x4000 to 0x5000.

See Also   **auxGetVolume**

DefScreenSaverProc

Syntax   LONG   **DefScreenSaverProc**(*hWnd*, *msg*, *wParam*, *lParam*)

This function performs the default actions for screen saver windows.

Parameters   HWND   *hWnd*
Specifies a handle to the screen saver window.

unsigned   *msg*
Specifies the message number. The **DefScreenSaverProc** function responds to messages that affect screen saver operation as follows:

WM_ACTIVATE, WM_ACTIVATE_APP
If *wParam* is FALSE, the window is losing its focus and the screen saver shell terminates.

WM_ERASEBKGND
Paints the screen background black.

WM_LBUTTTONDOWN, WM_RBUTTONDOWN, WM_MBUTTONDOWN
The screen saver shell changes the mouse coordinates. The screen saver shell terminates in response to the resulting WM_MOUSEMOVE message.

WM_KEYDOWN, WM_SYSKEYDOWN
The screen saver shell terminates on this message.

WM_MOUSEMOVE

The shell determines if the mouse has moved, or if it is just being placed on the window again. If the mouse has moved, the screen saver shell terminates.

WM_DESTROY

When the window gets closed, the program should terminate, and the screen saver shell terminates when it receives this message.

If your screen saver needs to perform a different action in response to any of these messages, your **ScreenSaverProc** function should process the message and not call **DefScreenSaverProc** for that message.

WORD   *wParam*

Specifies additional message-dependent information.

LONG   *lParam*

Specifies additional message-dependent information.

Return Value   The return value specifies the result of the message processing and depends on the actual message sent.

Comments   In the **ScreenSaverProc** window procedure of your screen saver, use **DefScreenSaverProc** in place of **DefWindowProc**. The **DefScreenSaverProc** function passes any messages that do not affect screen saver operation to **DefWindowProc**.

DisplayDib

Syntax   WORD   **DisplayDib**(*lpbi, lpBits, wFlags*)

This function displays a 256-color bitmap on a standard VGA display. It reduces the display resolution to 320-by-200 or 320-by-240 and uses the full screen to display the bitmap, clipping and centering it as necessary. The function normally does not return to the application until the user presses a key or clicks a mouse button.

To call **DisplayDib**, an application must be the active application. All inactive applications and GDI screen updates are suspended while **DisplayDib** temporarily reconfigures the display.

Parameters   LPBITMAPINFO   *lpbi*

Specifies a pointer to a **BITMAPINFO** header describing the bitmap to be displayed.

LPSTR   *lpBits*

Specifies a pointer to the bitmap bits. If this parameter is NULL, the bits are assumed to follow the **BITMAPINFO** structure pointed to by *lpbi*.

WORD   *wFlags*

Specifies options for displaying the bitmap. Use the following flags:

DISPLAYDIB_MODE_DEFAULT

Use the default mode (320 by 240) to display the bitmap.

DISPLAYDIB_MODE_320x200x8

Use 320-by-200 mode to display the bitmap.

DISPLAYDIB_MODE_320x240x8

Use 320-by-240 mode to display the bitmap. This is the default.

DISPLAYDIB_NOWAIT

Return immediately after displaying the bitmap; don't wait for a key
press or mouse click before returning.

DISPLAYDIB_NOPALETTE

Ignore the palette associated with the bitmap. You can use this flag
when displaying a series of bitmaps that use a common palette.

DISPLAYDIB_NOCENTER

Don't center the image. The function displays the bitmap in the lower-left
corner of the display.

DISPLAYDIB_BEGIN

Switch to the low-resolution display mode and set the palette. The bitmap is
not displayed.

If you are displaying a series of images that use the same palette, you can call
DisplayDib with this flag to prepare the display for the bitmaps, then make a
series of **DisplayDib** calls with the DISPLAYDIB_NOPALETTE flag. This
technique eliminates the screen flicker that occurs when the display is switched
between the low-resolution and standard VGA modes. To return the display to
standard VGA mode, subsequently call **DisplayDib** with the
DISPLAYDIB_END flag.

DISPLAYDIB_END

Switch back to standard VGA mode and return without displaying a bitmap.
Signifies the end of multiple calls to **DisplayDib**. With this flag, you can
specify NULL for the *lpbi* and *lpBits* parameters.

Return Value   Returns zero if successful, otherwise returns an error code. Error codes are as follows:

DISPLAYDIB_NOTSUPPORTED

DisplayDib is not supported in the current mode.

DISPLAYDIB_INVALIDDIB

The bitmap specified by *lpbi* is not a valid bitmap.

DISPLAYDIB_INVALIDFORMAT

The bitmap specified by *lpbi* specifes a type of bitmap that is not supported.

DISPLAYDIB_INVALIDTASK

The caller is an inactive application. **DisplayDib** can only be called by an active application.

Comments   The **DisplayDib** function displays bitmaps described with the Windows 3.0 **BITMAPINFO** data structure in either BI_RGB or BI_RLE8 format; it does not support bitmaps described with the OS/2 **BITMAPCOREHEADER** data structure.

When **DisplayDib** switches to a low-resolution display, it disables the current display driver. As a result, you cannot use GDI functions to update the display while **DisplayDib** is displaying a bitmap.

joyGetDevCaps

Syntax   WORD   **joyGetDevCaps**(*wId*, *lpCaps*, *wSize*)

This function queries a joystick device to determine its capabilities.

Parameters   WORD   *wId*

Identifies the device to be queried. This value is either JOYSTICKID1 or JOYSTICKID2.

LPJOYCAPS   *lpCaps*

Specifies a far pointer to a **JOYCAPS** data structure. This structure is filled with information about the capabilities of the joystick device.

WORD   *wSize*

Specifies the size of the **JOYCAPS** structure.

Return Value   Returns JOYERR_NOERROR if successful. Otherwise, returns one of the following error codes:

MMSYSERR_NODRIVER

The joystick driver is not present.

JOYERR_PARMS

The specified joystick device ID *wId* is invalid.

Comments   Use **joyGetNumDevs** to determine the number of joystick devices supported by the driver.

See Also   **joyGetNumDevs**

joyGetNumDevs

Syntax   WORD   **joyGetNumDevs**()

This function returns the number of joystick devices supported by the system.

Parameters   None

Return Value   Returns the number of joystick devices supported by the joystick driver. If no driver is present, the function returns zero.

Comments   Use **joyGetPos** to determine whether a given joystick is actually attached to the system. The **joyGetPos** function returns a JOYERR_UNPLUGGED error code if the specified joystick is not connected.

See Also   **joyGetDevCaps, joyGetPos**

---

joyGetPos

Syntax   WORD   **joyGetPos**(*wId, lpInfo*)

This function queries for the position and button activity of a joystick device.

Parameters   WORD   *wId*
                   Identifies the joystick device to be queried. This value is either JOYSTICKID1 or JOYSTICKID2.

                   LPJOYINFO   *lpInfo*
                   Specifies a far pointer to a **JOYINFO** data structure. This structure is filled with information about the position and button activity of the joystick device.

Return Value   Returns JOYERR_NOERROR if successful. Otherwise, returns one of the following error codes:

                   MMSYSERR_NODRIVER
                   The joystick driver is not present.

                   JOYERR_PARMS
                   The specified joystick device ID *wId* is invalid.

                   JOYERR_UNPLUGGED
                   The specified joystick is not connected to the system.

joyGetThreshold

Syntax	WORD **joyGetThreshold**(*wId, lpwThreshold*)

This function queries the current movement threshold of a joystick device.

Parameters   WORD   *wId*

Identifies the joystick device to be queried. This value is either JOYSTICKID1 or JOYSTICKID2.

LPWORD   *lpwThreshold*

Specifies a far pointer to a WORD variable that is filled with the movement threshold value.

Return Value   Returns JOYERR_NOERROR if successful. Otherwise, returns one of the following error codes:

MMSYSERR_NODRIVER

The joystick driver is not present.

JOYERR_PARMS

The specified joystick device ID *wId* is invalid.

Comments   The movement threshold is the distance the joystick must be moved before a WM_JOYMOVE message is sent to a window that has captured the device. The threshold is initially zero.

See Also   **joySetThreshold**

joyReleaseCapture

Syntax   WORD   **joyReleaseCapture**(*wId*)

This function releases the capture set by **joySetCapture** on the specified joystick device.

Parameters   WORD   *wId*

Identifies the joystick device to be released. This value is either JOYSTICKID1 or JOYSTICK2.

Return Value   Returns JOYERR_NOERROR if successful. Otherwise, returns one of the following error codes:

MMSYSERR_NODRIVER

The joystick driver is not present.

JOYERR_PARMS

The specified joystick device ID *wId* is invalid.

See Also   joySetCapture

joySetCapture

Syntax   WORD **joySetCapture**(*hWnd*, *wId*, *wPeriod*, *bChanged*)

This function causes joystick messages to be sent to the specified window.

Parameters   HWND *hWnd*

Specifies a handle to the window to which messages are to be sent.

WORD *wId*

Identifies the joystick device to be captured. This value is either JOYSTICKID1 or JOYSTICKID2.

WORD *wPeriod*

Specifies the polling rate, in milliseconds.

BOOL *bChanged*

If this parameter is set to TRUE, then messages are sent only when the position changes by a value greater than the joystick movement threshold.

Return Value Returns JOYERR_NOERROR if successful. Otherwise, returns one of the following error codes:

MMSYSERR_NODRIVER

The joystick driver is not present.

JOYERR_PARMS

The specified window handle *hWnd* or joystick device ID *wId* is invalid.

JOYERR_NOCANDO

Cannot capture joystick input because some required service (for example, a Windows timer) is unavailable.

JOYERR_UNPLUGGED

The specified joystick is not connected to the system.

Comments   This function fails if the specified joystick device is currently captured. You should call the **joyReleaseCapture** function when the joystick capture is no longer needed. If the window is destroyed, the joystick will be released automatically.

See Also   **joyReleaseCapture**, **joySetThreshold**, **joyGetThreshold**

joySetThreshold

Syntax	WORD **joySetThreshold**(*wId*, *wThreshold*)
	This function sets the movement threshold of a joystick device.
Parameters	WORD *wId*
	Identifies the joystick device. This value is either JOYSTICKID1 or JOYSTICKID2.
	WORD *wThreshold*
	Specifies the new movement threshold.
Return Value	Returns JOYERR_NOERROR if successful. Otherwise, returns one of the following error codes:
	MMSYSERR_NODRIVER
	The joystick driver is not present.
	JOYERR_PARMS
	The specified joystick device ID *wId* is invalid.
Comments	The movement threshold is the distance the joystick must be moved before a WM_JOYMOVE message is sent to a window that has captured the device.
See Also	**joyGetThreshold, joySetCapture**

MCI_HMS_HOUR

Syntax	BYTE **MCI_HMS_HOUR**(*dwHMS*)
	This macro returns the hours field from a DWORD argument containing packed HMS (hours, minutes, seconds) information.
Parameters	DWORD *dwHMS*
	Specifies the time in HMS format.
Return Value	The return value is the hours field of the given argument.
Comments	Time in HMS format is expressed as a DWORD with the least significant byte containing hours, the next least significant byte containing minutes, and the next least significant byte containing seconds. The most significant byte is unused.
See Also	**MCI_HMS_MINUTE, MCI_HMS_SECOND, MCI_MAKE_HMS**

MCI_HMS_MINUTE

Syntax BYTE **MCI_HMS_MINUTE**(*dwHMS*)

This macro returns the minutes field from a DWORD argument containing packed HMS (hours, minutes, seconds) information.

Parameters DWORD *dwHMS*
  Specifies the time in HMS format.

Return Value The return value is the minutes field of the given argument.

Comments Time in HMS format is expressed as a DWORD with the least significant byte containing hours, the next least significant byte containing minutes, and the next least significant byte containing seconds. The most significant byte is unused.

See Also **MCI_HMS_HOUR, MCI_HMS_SECOND, MCI_MAKE_HMS**

MCI_HMS_SECOND

Syntax BYTE **MCI_HMS_SECOND**(*dwHMS*)

This macro returns the seconds field from a DWORD argument containing packed HMS (hours, minutes, seconds) information.

Parameters DWORD *dwHMS*
  Specifies the time in HMS format.

Return Value The return value is the seconds field of the given argument.

Comments Time in HMS format is expressed as a DWORD with the least significant byte containing hours, the next least significant byte containing minutes, and the next least significant byte containing seconds. The most significant byte is unused.

See Also **MCI_HMS_HOUR, MCI_HMS_MINUTE, MCI_MAKE_HMS**

MCI_MAKE_HMS

Syntax DWORD **MCI_MAKE_HMS**(*hours*, *minutes*, *seconds*)

This macro returns a time value in HMS (hours, minutes, seconds) format from the given hours, minutes, and seconds values.

Parameters BYTE *hours*
Specifies the number of hours.

BYTE *minutes*
Specifies the number of minutes.

BYTE *seconds*
Specifies the number of seconds.

Return Value The return value is a DWORD value containing the time in packed HMS format.

Comments Time in HMS format is expressed as a DWORD with the least significant byte containing hours, the next least significant byte containing minutes, and the next least significant byte containing seconds. The most significant byte is unused.

See Also **MCI_HMS_MINUTE, MCI_HMS_SECOND, MCI_HMS_FRAME**

MCI_MAKE_MSF

Syntax DWORD **MCI_MAKE_MSF**(*minutes*, *seconds*, *frames*)

This macro returns a time value in MSF (minutes, seconds, frames) format from the given minutes, seconds, and frames values.

Parameters BYTE *minutes*
Specifies the number of minutes.

BYTE *seconds*
Specifies the number of seconds.

BYTE *frames*
Specifies the number of frames.

Return Value The return value is a DWORD value containing the time in packed MSF format.

Comments Time in MSF format is expressed as a DWORD with the least significant byte containing minutes, the next least significant byte containing seconds, and the next least significant byte containing frames. The most significant byte is unused.

See Also **MCI_MSF_MINUTE, MCI_MSF_SECOND, MCI_MSF_FRAME**

MCI_MAKE_TMSF

Syntax   DWORD   **MCI_MAKE_TMSF**(*tracks*, *minutes*, *seconds*, *frames*)

This macro returns a time value in TMSF (tracks, minutes, seconds, frames) format from the given tracks, minutes, seconds, and frames values.

Parameters   BYTE   *tracks*
Specifies the number of tracks.

BYTE   *minutes*
Specifies the number of minutes.

BYTE   *seconds*
Specifies the number of seconds.

BYTE   *frames*
Specifies the number of frames.

Return Value   The return value is a DWORD value containing the time in packed TMSF (tracks, minutes, seconds, frames) format.

Comments   Time in TMSF format is expressed as a DWORD with the least significant byte containing tracks, the next least significant byte containing minutes, the next least significant byte containing seconds, and the most significant byte containing frames.

See Also   **MCI_TMSF_MINUTE, MCI_TMSF_SECOND, MCI_TMSF_FRAME**

MCI_MSF_FRAME

Syntax   BYTE   **MCI_MSF_FRAME**(*dwMSF*)

This macro returns the frames field from a DWORD argument containing packed MSF (minutes, seconds, frames) information.

Parameters   DWORD   *dwMSF*
Specifies the time in MSF format.

Return Value   The return value is the frames field of the given argument.

Comments   Time in MSF format is expressed as a DWORD with the least significant byte containing minutes, the next least significant byte containing seconds, and the next least significant byte containing frames. The most significant byte is unused.

See Also   **MCI_MSF_MINUTE, MCI_MSF_SECOND, MCI_MAKE_MSF**

MCI_MSF_MINUTE

Syntax   BYTE   **MCI_MSF_MINUTE**(*dwMSF*)

This macro returns the minutes field from a DWORD argument containing packed MSF (minutes, seconds, frames) information.

Parameters   DWORD   *dwMSF*
Specifies the time in MSF format.

Return Value   The return value is the minutes field of the given argument.

Comments   Time in MSF format is expressed as a DWORD with the least significant byte containing minutes, the next least significant byte containing seconds, and the next least significant byte containing frames. The most significant byte is unused.

See Also   **MCI_MSF_SECOND, MCI_MSF_FRAME, MCI_MAKE_MSF**

MCI_MSF_SECOND

Syntax   BYTE   **MCI_MSF_SECOND**(*dwMSF*)

This macro returns the seconds field from a DWORD argument containing packed MSF (minutes, seconds, frames) information.

Parameters   DWORD   *dwMSF*
Specifies the time in MSF format.

Return Value   The return value is the seconds field of the given argument.

Comments   Time in MSF format is expressed as a DWORD with the least significant byte containing minutes, the next least significant byte containing seconds, and the next least significant byte containing frames. The most significant byte is unused.

See Also   **MCI_MSF_MINUTE, MCI_MSF_FRAME, MCI_MAKE_MSF**

MCI_TMSF_FRAME

Syntax   BYTE   **MCI_TMSF_FRAME**(*dwTMSF*)

This macro returns the frames field from a DWORD argument containing packed TMSF (tracks, minutes, seconds, frames) information.

Parameters   DWORD   *dwTMSF*
Specifies the time in TMSF format.

Return Value   The return value is the frames field of the given argument.

Comments   Time in TMSF format is expressed as a DWORD with the least significant byte containing tracks, the next least significant byte containing minutes, the next least significant byte containing seconds, and the most significant byte containing frames.

See Also   **MCI_TMSF_TRACK, MCI_TMSF_MINUTE, MCI_TMSF_SECOND, MCI_MAKE_TMSF**

MCI_TMSF_MINUTE

Syntax   BYTE **MCI_TMSF_MINUTE**(*dwTMSF*)

This macro returns the minutes field from a DWORD argument containing packed TMSF (tracs, minutes, seconds, frames) information.

Parameters   DWORD   *dwTMSF*
                    Specifies the time in TMSF format.

Return Value   The return value is the minutes field of the given argument.

Comments   Time in TMSF format is expressed as a DWORD with the least significant byte containing tracks, the next least significant byte containing minutes, the next least significant byte containing seconds, and the most significant byte containing frames.

See Also   **MCI_TMSF_TRACK, MCI_TMSF_SECOND, MCI_TMSF_FRAME, MCI_MAKE_TMSF**

MCI_TMSF_SECOND

Syntax   BYTE   **MCI_TMSF_SECOND**(*dwTMSF*)

This macro returns the seconds field from a DWORD argument containing packed TMSF (tracks, minutes, seconds, frames) information.

Parameters   DWORD   *dwTMSF*
                    Specifies the time in TMSF format.

Return Value   The return value is the seconds field of the given argument.

Comments   Time in TMSF format is expressed as a DWORD with the least significant byte containing tracks, the next least significant byte containing minutes, the next least significant byte containing seconds, and the most significant byte containing frames.

See Also   **MCI_TMSF_TRACK, MCI_TMSF_MINUTE, MCI_TMSF_FRAME, MCI_MAKE_TMSF**

MCI_TMSF_TRACK

Syntax	BYTE **MCI_TMSF_TRACK**(*dwTMSF*)

This macro returns the tracks field from a DWORD argument containing packed TMSF (tracks, minutes, seconds, frames) information.

Parameters   DWORD   *dwTMSF*
         Specifies the time in TMSF format.

Return Value   The return value is the tracks field of the given argument.

Comments   Time in TMSF format is expressed as a DWORD with the least significant byte containing tracks, the next least significant byte containing minutes, the next least significant byte containing seconds, and the most significant byte containing frames.

See Also   **MCI_TMSF_MINUTE, MCI_TMSF_SECOND, MCI_TMSF_FRAME, MCI_MAKE_TMSF**

---

mciExecute

Syntax   BOOL   **mciExecute**(*lpstrCommand*)

This function is a simplified version of the **mciSendString** function. It does not take a buffer for return information, and it displays a message box when errors occur.

Parameters   LPSTR   *lpstrCommand*
         Specifies an MCI command string.

Return Value   TRUE if successful, FALSE if unsuccessful.

Comments   This function provides a simple interface to MCI from scripting languages.

See Also   **mciSendString**

---

mciGetDeviceID

Syntax   WORD FAR PASCAL   **mciGetDeviceID**(*lpstrName*)

This function retrieves the device ID corresponding to the name of an open MCI device.

Parameters   LPSTR   *lpstrName*
         Specifies the device name used to open the MCI device.

Return Value   Returns the device ID assigned when the device was opened. Returns zero if the device name isn't known, if the device isn't open, or if there was insufficient memory to complete the operation. Each compound device element has a unique device ID. The ID of the "all" device is MCI_ALL_DEVICE_ID

See Also   MCI_OPEN

mciGetErrorString

Syntax   WORD   **mciGetErrorString**(*dwError*, *lpstrBuffer*, *wLength*)

This function returns a textual description of the specified MCI error.

Parameters   DWORD *dwError*
Specifies the error code returned by **mciSendCommand** or **mciSendString**.

LPSTR *lpstrBuffer*
Specifies a pointer to a buffer that is filled with a textual description of the specified error.

WORD *wLength*
Specifies the length of the buffer pointed to by *lpstrBuffer*.

Return Value   Returns TRUE if successful. Otherwise, the given error code was not known.

mciSendCommand

Syntax   DWORD   **mciSendCommand**(*wDeviceID*, *wMessage*, *dwParam1*, *dwParam2*)

This function sends a command message to the specified MCI device.

Parameters   WORD *wDeviceID*
Specifies the device ID of the MCI device to receive the command. This parameter is not used with the **MCI_OPEN** command.

WORD *wMessage*
Specifies the command message.

DWORD *dwParam1*
Specifies flags for the command.

DWORD *dwParam2*
Specifies a pointer to a parameter block for the command.

Return Value   Returns zero if the function was successful. Otherwise, it returns error information. The low-order word of the returned DWORD is the error return value. If the error is device-specific, the high-order word contains the driver ID; otherwise the high-order word is zero.

To get a textual description of **mciSendCommand** return values, pass the return value to **mciGetErrorString**.

Error values that are returned when a device is being opened are listed with the MCI_OPEN message. In addition to the MCI_OPEN error returns, this function can return the following values:

MCIERR_BAD_TIME_FORMAT
> Illegal value for time format.

MCIERR_CANNOT_USE_ALL
> The device name "all" is not allowed for this command.

MCIERR_CREATEWINDOW
> Could not create or use window.

MCIERR_DEVICE_LOCKED
> The device is locked until it is closed automatically.

MCIERR_DEVICE_NOT_READY
> Device not ready.

MCIERR_DEVICE_TYPE_REQUIRED
> The device name must be a valid device type.

MCIERR_DRIVER
> Unspecified device error.

MCIERR_DRIVER_INTERNAL
> Internal driver error.

MCIERR_FILE_NOT_FOUND
> Requested file not found.

MCIERR_FILE_NOT_SAVED
> The file was not saved.

MCIERR_FILE_READ
> A read from the file failed.

MCIERR_FILE_WRITE
> A write to the file failed.

MCIERR_FLAGS_NOT_COMPATIBLE
> Incompatible parameters were specified.

MCIERR_HARDWARE
> Hardware error on media device.

MCIERR_INTERNAL
Internal error.

MCIERR_INVALID_DEVICE_ID
Invalid device ID.

MCIERR_INVALID_DEVICE_NAME
The device is not open or is not known.

MCIERR_INVALID_FILE
Invalid file format.

MCIERR_MULTIPLE
Errors occurred in more than one device.

MCIERR_NO_WINDOW
There is no display window.

MCIERR_NULL_PARAMETER_BLOCK
Parameter block pointer was NULL.

MCIERR_OUT_OF_MEMORY
Not enough memory for requested operation.

MCIERR_OUTOFRANGE
Parameter value out of range.

MCIERR_UNNAMED_RESOURCE
Attempt to save unnamed file.

MCIERR_UNRECOGNIZED_COMMAND
Unknown command.

MCIERR_UNSUPPORTED_FUNCTION
Action not available for this device.

The following additional return values are defined for MCI sequencers:

MCIERR_SEQ_DIV_INCOMPATIBLE
Set Song Pointer incompatible with SMPTE files.

MCIERR_SEQ_PORT_INUSE
Specified port is in use.

MCIERR_SEQ_PORT_MAPNODEVICE
Current map uses non-existent device.

MCIERR_SEQ_PORT_MISCERROR
    Miscellaneous error with specified port.

MCIERR_SEQ_PORT_NONEXISTENT
    Specified port does not exist.

MCIERR_SEQ_PORTUNSPECIFIED
    No current MIDI port.

MCIERR_SEQ_TIMER
    Timer error.

    The following additional return values are defined for MCI waveform audio devices:

MCIERR_WAVE_INPUTSINUSE
    No compatible waveform recording device is free.

MCIERR_WAVE_INPUTSUNSUITABLE
    No compatible waveform recording devices.

MCIERR_WAVE_INPUTUNSPECIFIED
    Any compatible waveform recording device may be used.

MCIERR_WAVE_OUTPUTSINUSE
    No compatible waveform playback device is free.

MCIERR_WAVE_OUTPUTSUNSUITABLE
    No compatible waveform playback devices.

MCIERR_WAVE_OUTPUTUNSPECIFIED
    Any compatible waveform playback device may be used.

MCIERR_WAVE_SETINPUTINUSE
    Set waveform recording device is in use.

MCIERR_WAVE_SETINPUTUNSUITABLE
    Set waveform recording device is incompatible with set format.

MCIERR_WAVE_SETOUTPUTINUSE
    Set waveform playback device is in use.

MCIERR_WAVE_SETOUTPUTUNSUITABLE
    Set waveform playback device is incompatible with set format.

Comments   Use the **MCI_OPEN** command to obtain the device ID specified by *wDeviceID*.

See Also   **mciGetErrorString, mciSendString**

mciSendString

Syntax

DWORD **mciSendString**(*lpstrCommand, lpstrReturnString, wReturnLength, hCallback*)

This function sends a command string to an MCI device. The device that the command is sent to is specified in the command string.

Parameters

LPSTR *lpstrCommand*
Specifies an MCI command string.

LPSTR *lpstrReturnString*
Specifies a buffer for return information. If no return information is needed, you can specify NUL for this parameter.

WORD *wReturnLength*
Specifies the size of the return buffer specified by *lpstrReturnString*.

HANDLE *hCallback*
Specifies a handle to a window to call back if "notify" was specified in the command string.

Return Value

Returns zero if the function was successful. Otherwise, it returns error information. The low-order word of the returned DWORD contains the error return value.

To get a textual description of **mciSendString** return values, pass the return value to **mciGetErrorString**.

The error returns listed for **mciSendCommand** also apply to **mciSendString**. The following error returns are unique to **mciSendString**:

MCIERR_BAD_CONSTANT
Unknown value for parameter.

MCIERR_BAD_INTEGER
Invalid or missing integer in command.

MCIERR_DUPLICATE_FLAGS
A flag or value was specified twice.

MCIERR_MISSING_COMMAND_STRING
No command was specified.

MCIERR_MISSING_DEVICE_NAME
No device name was specified.

MCIERR_MISSING_STRING_ARGUMENT
A string value was missing from the command.

MCIERR_NEW_REQUIRES_ALIAS

An alias must be used with the "new" device name.

MCIERR_NO_CLOSING_QUOTE

A closing quotation mark is missing.

MCIERR_NOTIFY_ON_AUTO_OPEN

The "notify" flag is illegal with auto-open.

MCIERR_PARAM_OVERFLOW

The output string was not long enough.

MCIERR_PARSER_INTERNAL

Internal parser error.

MCIERR_UNRECOGNIZED_KEYWORD

Unknown command parameter.

See Also   **mciExecute, mciGetErrorString, mciSendCommand**

mciSetYieldProc

Syntax   WORD FAR   **mciSetYieldProc**(*wDeviceID*, *fpYieldProc*, *dwYieldData*)

This function sets the address of a callback procedure to be called periodically when an MCI device is completing a command specified with the WAIT flag.

Parameters   WORD   *wDeviceID*

Specifies the device ID of the MCI device to which the yield procedure is to be assigned.

YIELDPROC   *fpYieldProc*

Specifies the callback procedure to be called when the given device is yielding. Specify a NULL value to disable any existing yield procedure.

DWORD   *dwYieldData*

Specifies the data sent to the yield procedure when it is called for the given device.

Return Value   Returns TRUE if successful. Returns FALSE for an invalid device ID.

Callback   int FAR PASCAL   **YieldProc**(*wDeviceID*, *dwData*)

YieldProc is a placeholder for the application-supplied function name. Export the actual name by including it in the EXPORTS statement in your module-definition file.

Parameters

WORD   *wDeviceID*
> Specifies the device ID of the MCI device.

DWORD   *dwData*
> Specifies the application-supplied yield data originally supplied in the *dwYieldData* parameter.

Return Value

Return zero to continue the operation. To cancel the operation, return a nonzero value.

Comments

This call overides any previous yield procedure for this device.

MessageBeep

Syntax   void   **MessageBeep**(*wAlert*)

This function plays a waveform sound corresponding to a given system alert level. The sound for each alert level is identified by an entry in the [sounds] section of WIN.INI.

Parameters   WORD   *wAlert*
> Specifies the alert level. Use one of the following values:

> MB_OK
>> Plays the sound identified by the "SystemDefault" entry in the [sounds] section of WIN.INI.

> MB_ICONASTERISK
>> Plays the sound identified by the "SystemAsterisk" entry in the [sounds] section of WIN.INI.

> MB_ICONEXCLAMATION
>> Plays the sound identified by the "SystemExclamation" entry in the [sounds] section of WIN.INI.

> MB_ICONHAND
>> Plays the sound identified by the "SystemHand" entry in the [sounds] section of WIN.INI.

> MB_ICONQUESTION
>> Plays the sound identified by the "SystemQuestion" entry in the [sounds] section of WIN.INI.

0

Plays the sound identified by the "SystemDefault" entry in the [sounds] section of WIN.INI.

-1

Produces a standard beep sound using the computer speaker.

Return Value   None

Comments   **MessageBeep** returns control to the caller after queuing the sound and plays the sound asynchronously.

If the specified alert sound can't be played, **MessageBeep** tries to play the system default sound. If the system default sound can't be played, it produces a standard beep sound using the computer speaker.

The user can disable the warning beep using the Sounds control-panel applet.

See Also   **sndPlaySound**

---

midiInAddBuffer

Syntax   WORD   **midiInAddBuffer**(*hMidiIn*, *lpMidiInHdr*, *wSize*)

This function sends an input buffer to a specified opened MIDI input device. When the buffer is filled, it is sent back to the application. Input buffers are used only for system exclusive messages.

Parameters   HMIDIIN   *hMidiIn*
Specifies a handle to the MIDI input device.

LPMIDIHDR   *lpMidiInHdr*
Specifies a far pointer to a **MIDIHDR** structure that identifies the buffer.

WORD   *wSize*
Specifies the size of the **MIDIHDR** structure.

Return Value   Returns zero if the function was successful. Otherwise, it returns an error number. Possible error returns are:

MMSYSERR_INVALHANDLE
Specified device handle is invalid.

MIDIERR_UNPREPARED
lpMidiInHdr hasn't been prepared.

Comments   The data buffer must be prepared with **midiInPrepareHeader** before it is passed to **midiInAddBuffer**. The **MIDIHDR** data structure and the data buffer pointed to by its

lpData field must be allocated with **GlobalAlloc** using the GMEM_MOVEABLE and GMEM_SHARE flags, and locked with **GlobalLock**.

See Also   **midiInPrepareHeader**

midiInClose

Syntax   WORD   **midiInClose**(*hMidiIn*)

This function closes the specified MIDI input device.

Parameters   HMIDIIN   *hMidiIn*

Specifies a handle to the MIDI input device. If the function is successful, the handle is no longer valid after this call.

Return Value   Returns zero if the function was successful. Otherwise, it returns an error number. Possible error returns are:

MMSYSERR_INVALHANDLE
Specified device handle is invalid.

MIDIERR_STILLPLAYING
There are still buffers in the queue.

Comments   If there are input buffers that have been sent with **midiInAddBuffer** and haven't been returned to the application, the close operation will fail. Call **midiInReset** to mark all pending buffers as being done.

See Also   **midiInOpen, midiInReset**

midiInGetDevCaps

Syntax   WORD   **midiInGetDevCaps**(*wDeviceID*, *lpCaps*, *wSize*)

This function queries a specified MIDI input device to determine its capabilities.

Parameters   WORD   *wDeviceID*
Identifies the MIDI input device.

LPMIDIINCAPS   *lpCaps*
Specifies a far pointer to a **MIDIINCAPS** data structure. This structure is filled with information about the capabilities of the device.

WORD   *wSize*
Specifies the size of the **MIDIINCAPS** structure.

Return Value   Returns zero if the function was successful. Otherwise, it returns an error number. Possible error returns are:

MMSYSERR_BADDEVICEID
>   Specified device ID is out of range.

MMSYSERR_NODRIVER
>   The driver was not installed.

Comments   Use **midiInGetNumDevs** to determine the number of MIDI input devices present in the system. The device ID specified by *wDeviceID* varies from zero to one less than the number of devices present. Only *wSize* bytes (or less) of information is copied to the location pointed to by *lpCaps*. If *wSize* is zero, nothing is copied, and the function returns zero.

See Also   **midiInGetNumDevs**

---

midiInGetErrorText

Syntax   WORD   **midiInGetErrorText**(*wError, lpText, wSize*)

This function retrieves a textual description of the error identified by the specified error number.

Parameters   WORD   *wError*
>   Specifies the error number.

LPSTR   *lpText*
>   Specifies a far pointer to the buffer to be filled with the textual error description.

WORD   *wSize*
>   Specifies the length of buffer pointed to by *lpText*.

Return Value   Returns zero if the function was successful. Otherwise, it returns an error number. Possible error returns are:

MMSYSERR_BADERRNUM
>   Specified error number is out of range.

Comments   If the textual error description is longer than the specified buffer, the description is truncated. The returned error string is always null-terminated. If *wSize* is zero, nothing is copied, and the function returns zero. All error descriptions are less than MAXERRORLENGTH characters long.

midiInGetID

Syntax

WORD **midiInGetID**(*hMidiIn*, *lpwDeviceID*)

This function gets the device ID for a MIDI input device.

Parameters

HMIDIIN *hMidiIn*

Specifies the handle to the MIDI input device.

LPWORD *lpwDeviceID*

Specifies a pointer to the WORD-sized memory location to be filled with the device ID.

Return Value

Returns zero if successful. Otherwise, returns an error number. Possible error returns are:

MMSYSERR_INVALHANDLE

The *hMidiIn* parameter specifies an invalid handle.

midiInGetNumDevs

Syntax

WORD **midiInGetNumDevs**()

This function retrieves the number of MIDI input devices in the system.

Parameters

None

Return Value

Returns the number of MIDI input devices present in the system.

See Also

midiInGetDevCaps

midiInOpen

Syntax

WORD **midiInOpen**(*lphMidiIn*, *wDeviceID*, *dwCallback*, *dwCallbackInstance*, *dwFlags*)

This function opens a specified MIDI input device.

Parameters

LPHMIDIIN *lphMidiIn*

Specifies a far pointer to an HMIDIIN handle. This location is filled with a handle identifying the opened MIDI input device. Use the handle to identify the device when calling other MIDI input functions.

WORD *wDeviceID*

Identifies the MIDI input device to be opened.

DWORD   *dwCallback*

Specifies the address of a fixed callback function or a handle to a window called with information about incoming MIDI messages.

DWORD   *dwCallbackInstance*

Specifies user instance data passed to the callback function. This parameter is not used with window callbacks.

DWORD   *dwFlags*

Specifies a callback flag for opening the device.

CALLBACK_WINDOW

If this flag is specified, *dwCallback* is assumed to be a window handle.

CALLBACK_FUNCTION

If this flag is specified, *dwCallback* is assumed to be a callback procedure address.

Return Value   Returns zero if the function was successful. Otherwise, it returns an error number. Possible error returns are:

MMSYSERR_BADDEVICEID

Specified device ID is out of range.

MMSYSERR_ALLOCATED

Specified resource is already allocated.

MMSYSERR_NOMEM

Unable to allocate or lock memory.

Comments   Use **midiInGetNumDevs** to determine the number of MIDI input devices present in the system. The device ID specified by *wDeviceID* varies from zero to one less than the number of devices present.

If a window is chosen to receive callback information, the following messages are sent to the window procedure function to indicate the progress of MIDI input:

- **MM_MIM_OPEN**
- **MM_MIM_CLOSE**
- **MM_MIM_DATA**
- **MM_MIM_LONGDATA**
- **MM_MIM_ERROR**
- **MM_MIM_LONGERROR**

If a function is chosen to receive callback information, the following messages are sent to the function to indicate the progress of MIDI input:

- **MIM_OPEN, MIM_CLOSE**

- **MIM_DATA**

- **MIM_LONGDATA**

- **MIM_ERROR**

- **MIM_LONGERROR**

The callback function must reside in a DLL. You do not have to use **MakeProcInstance** to get a procedure-instance address for the callback function.

Callback

void FAR PASCAL   **MidiInFunc**(*hMidiIn*, *wMsg*, *dwInstance*, *dwParam1*, *dwParam2*)

MidiInFunc is a placeholder for the application-supplied function name. The actual name must be exported by including it in an EXPORTS statement in the DLL's module definition file.

Parameters

HMIDIIN   *hMidiIn*
> Specifies a handle to the MIDI input device.

WORD   *wMsg*
> Specifies a MIDI input message.

DWORD   *dwInstance*
> Specifies the instance data supplied with **midiInOpen**.

DWORD   *dwParam1*
> Specifies a parameter for the message.

DWORD   *dwParam2*
> Specifies a parameter for the message.

Comments

Because the callback is accessed at interrupt time, it must reside in a DLL, and its code segment must be specified as FIXED in the module-definition file for the DLL. Any data that the callback accesses must be in a FIXED data segment as well. The callback may not make any system calls except for **PostMessage**, **timeGetSystemTime**, **timeGetTime**, **timeSetEvent**, **timeKillEvent**, **midiOutShortMsg**, **midiOutLongMsg**, and **OutputDebugStr**.

See Also

midiInClose

midiInPrepareHeader

Syntax   WORD   **midiInPrepareHeader**(*hMidiIn*, *lpMidiInHdr*, *wSize*)

This function prepares a buffer for MIDI input.

Parameters   HMIDIIN   *hMidiIn*
Specifies a handle to the MIDI input device.

LPMIDIHDR   *lpMidiInHdr*
Specifies a pointer to a **MIDIHDR** structure that identifies the buffer to be prepared.

WORD   *wSize*
Specifies the size of the **MIDIHDR** structure.

Return Value Returns zero if the function was successful. Otherwise, it returns an error number. Possible error returns are:

MMSYSERR_INVALHANDLE
Specified device handle is invalid.

MMSYSERR_NOMEM
Unable to allocate or lock memory.

Comments   The **MIDIHDR** data structure and the data block pointed to by its **lpData** field must be allocated with **GlobalAlloc** using the GMEM_MOVEABLE and GMEM_SHARE flags, and locked with **GlobalLock**. Preparing a header that has already been prepared has no effect, and the function returns zero.

See Also   **midiInUnprepareHeader**

---

midiInReset

Syntax   WORD   **midiInReset**(*hMidiIn*)

This function stops input on a given MIDI input device and marks all pending input buffers as done.

Parameters   HMIDIIN   *hMidiIn*
Specifies a handle to the MIDI input device.

Return Value Returns zero if the function was successful. Otherwise, it returns an error number. Possible error returns are:

MMSYSERR_INVALHANDLE
Specified device handle is invalid.

See Also   **midiInStart, midiInStop, midiInAddBuffer, midiInClose**

midiInStart

Syntax   WORD   **midiInStart**(*hMidiIn*)

This function starts MIDI input on the specified MIDI input device.

Parameters   HMIDIIN   *hMidiIn*
    Specifies a handle to the MIDI input device.

Return Value Returns zero if the function was successful. Otherwise, it returns an error number. Possible error returns are:

MMSYSERR_INVALHANDLE
    Specified device handle is invalid.

Comments   This function resets the timestamps to zero; timestamp values for subsequently received messages are relative to the time this function was called.

All messages other than system exclusive messages are sent directly to the client when received. System exclusive messages are placed in the buffers supplied by **midiInAddBuffer**; if there are no buffers in the queue, the data is thrown away without notification to the client, and input continues.

Buffers are returned to the client when full, when a complete system exclusive message has been received, or when **midiInReset** is called. The **dwBytesRecorded** field in the header will contain the actual length of data received.

Calling this function when input is already started has no effect, and the function returns zero.

See Also   **midiInStop, midiInReset**

midiInStop

Syntax   WORD   **midiInStop**(*hMidiIn*)

This function terminates MIDI input on the specified MIDI input device.

Parameters   HMIDIIN   *hMidiIn*
    Specifies a handle to the MIDI input device.

Return Value Returns zero if the function was successful. Otherwise, it returns an error number. Possible error returns are:

MMSYSERR_INVALHANDLE
    Specified device handle is invalid.

Comments   Current status (running status, parsing state, etc.) is maintained across calls to **midiInStop** and **midiInStart**. If there are any system exclusive message buffers in the queue, the current buffer is marked as done (the **dwBytesRecorded** field in the header will contain the actual length of data), but any empty buffers in the queue remain there. Calling this function when input is not started has no no effect, and the function returns zero.

See Also   **midiInStart**, **midiInReset**

midiInUnprepareHeader

Syntax   WORD   **midiInUnprepareHeader**(*hMidiIn*, *lpMidiInHdr*, *wSize*)

This function cleans up the preparation performed by **midiInPrepareHeader**. The **midiInUnprepareHeader** function must be called after the device driver fills a data buffer and returns it to the application. You must call this function before freeing the data buffer.

Parameters   HMIDIIN   *hMidiIn*
Specifies a handle to the MIDI input device.

LPMIDIHDR   *lpMidiInHdr*
Specifies a pointer to a **MIDIHDR** structure identifying the data buffer to be cleaned up.

WORD   *wSize*
Specifies the size of the **MIDIHDR** structure.

Return Value   Returns zero if the function was successful. Otherwise, it returns an error number. Possible error returns are:

MMSYSERR_INVALHANDLE
Specified device handle is invalid.

MIDIERR_STILLPLAYING
lpMidiInHdr is still in the queue.

Comments   This function is the complementary function to **midiInPrepareHeader**. You must call this function before freeing the data buffer with **GlobalFree**. After passing a buffer to the device driver with **midiInAddBuffer**, you must wait until the driver is finished with the buffer before calling **midiInUnprepareHeader**. Unpreparing a buffer that has not been prepared has no effect, and the function returns zero.

See Also   **midiInPrepareHeader**

midiOutCacheDrumPatches

Syntax

WORD   **midiOutCacheDrumPatches**(*hMidiOut*, *wPatch*, *lpKeyArray*, *wFlags*)

This function requests that an internal MIDI synthesizer device preload a specified set of key-based percussion patches. Some synthesizers are not capable of keeping all percussion patches loaded simultaneously. Caching patches ensures specified patches are available.

Parameters

HMIDIOUT   *hMidiOut*

Specifies a handle to the opened MIDI output device. This device should be an internal MIDI synthesizer.

WORD   *wPatch*

Specifies which drum patch number should be used. Currently, this parameter must be set to zero.

LPKEYARRAY   *lpKeyArray*

Specifies a pointer to a **KEYARRAY** array indicating the key numbers of the specified percussion patches to be cached or uncached.

WORD   *wFlags*

Specifies options for the cache operation. Only one of the following flags can be specified:

MIDI_CACHE_ALL

Cache all of the specified patches. If they can't all be cached, cache none, clear the **KEYARRAY** array, and return MMSYSERR_NOMEM.

MIDI_CACHE_BESTFIT

Cache all of the specified patches. If all patches can't be cached, cache as many patches as possible, change the **KEYARRAY** array to reflect which patches were cached, and return MMSYSERR_NOMEM.

MIDI_CACHE_QUERY

Change the **KEYARRAY** array to indicate which patches are currently cached.

MIDI_UNCACHE

Uncache the specified patches and clear the **KEYARRAY** array.

Return Value

Returns zero if the function was successful. Otherwise, it returns one of the following error codes:

MMSYSERR_INVALHANDLE

The specified device handle is invalid.

MMSYSERR_NOTSUPPORTED

The specified device does not support patch caching.

MMSYSERR_NOMEM

The device does not have enough memory to cache all of the requested patches.

Comments   The **KEYARRAY** data type is defined as:

typedef WORD KEYARRAY[128];

Each element of the array represents one of the 128 key-based percussion patches and has bits set for each of the 16 MIDI channels that use that particular patch. The least-significant bit represents physical channel 0; the most-significant bit represents physical channel 15. For example, if the patch on key number 60 is used by physical channels 9 and 15, element 60 would be set to 0x8200.

This function applies only to internal MIDI synthesizer devices. Not all internal synthesizers support patch caching. Use the MIDICAPS_CACHE flag to test the **dwSupport** field of the **MIDIOUTCAPS** structure filled by **midiOutGetDevCaps** to see if the device supports patch caching.

See Also   **midiOutCachePatches**

midiOutCachePatches

Syntax   WORD   **midiOutCachePatches**(*hMidiOut, wBank, lpPatchArray, wFlags*)

This function requests that an internal MIDI synthesizer device preload a specified set of patches. Some synthesizers are not capable of keeping all patches loaded simultaneously and must load data from disk when they receive MIDI program change messages. Caching patches ensures specified patches are immediately available.

Parameters   HMIDIOUT *hMidiOut*

Specifies a handle to the opened MIDI output device. This device must be an internal MIDI synthesizer.

WORD *wBank*

Specifies which bank of patches should be used. Currently, this parameter must be set to zero.

LPPATCHARRAY *lpPatchArray*

Specifies a pointer to a **PATCHARRAY** array indicating the patches to be cached or uncached.

WORD *wFlags*

Specifies options for the cache operation. Only one of the following flags can be specified:

MIDI_CACHE_ALL

Cache all of the specified patches. If they can't all be cached, cache none, clear the **PATCHARRAY** array, and return MMSYSERR_NOMEM.

MIDI_CACHE_BESTFIT

Cache all of the specified patches. If all patches can't be cached, cache as many patches as possible, change the **PATCHARRAY** array to reflect which patches were cached, and return MMSYSERR_NOMEM.

MIDI_CACHE_QUERY

Change the **PATCHARRAY** array to indicate which patches are currently cached.

MIDI_UNCACHE

Uncache the specified patches and clear the **PATCHARRAY** array.

Return Value Returns zero if the function was successful. Otherwise, it returns one of the following error codes:

MMSYSERR_INVALHANDLE

The specified device handle is invalid.

MMSYSERR_NOTSUPPORTED

The specified device does not support patch caching.

MMSYSERR_NOMEM

The device does not have enough memory to cache all of the requested patches.

Comments The **PATCHARRAY** data type is defined as:

typedef WORD PATCHARRAY[128];

Each element of the array represents one of the 128 patches and has bits set for each of the 16 MIDI channels that use that particular patch. The least-significant bit represents physical channel 0; the most-significant bit represents physical channel 15 (0x0F). For example, if patch 0 is used by physical channels 0 and 8, element 0 would be set to 0x0101.

This function only applies to internal MIDI synthesizer devices. Not all internal synthesizers support patch caching. Use the MIDICAPS_CACHE flag to test the **dwSupport** field of the **MIDIOUTCAPS** structure filled by **midiOutGetDevCaps** to see if the device supports patch caching.

See Also **midiOutCacheDrumPatches**

midiOutClose

Syntax	WORD **midiOutClose**(*hMidiOut*)

This function closes the specified MIDI output device.

Parameters   HMIDIOUT   *hMidiOut*
> Specifies a handle to the MIDI output device. If the function is successful, the handle is no longer valid after this call.

Return Value   Returns zero if the function was successful. Otherwise, it returns an error number. Possible error returns are:

MMSYSERR_INVALHANDLE
> Specified device handle is invalid.

MIDIERR_STILLPLAYING
> There are still buffers in the queue.

Comments   If there are output buffers that have been sent with **midiOutLongMsg** and haven't been returned to the application, the close operation will fail. Call **midiOutReset** to mark all pending buffers as being done.

See Also   **midiOutOpen**, **midiOutReset**

midiOutGetDevCaps

Syntax	WORD **midiOutGetDevCaps**(*wDeviceID*, *lpCaps*, *wSize*)

This function queries a specified MIDI output device to determine its capabilities.

Parameters   WORD   *wDeviceID*
> Identifies the MIDI output device.

LPMIDIOUTCAPS   *lpCaps*
> Specifies a far pointer to a **MIDIOUTCAPS** structure. This structure is filled with information about the capabilities of the device.

WORD   *wSize*
> Specifies the size of the **MIDIOUTCAPS** structure.

Return Value   Returns zero if the function was successful. Otherwise, it returns an error number. Possible error returns are:

MMSYSERR_BADDEVICEID
> Specified device ID is out of range.

MMSYSERR_NODRIVER

The driver was not installed.

Comments   Use **midiOutGetNumDevs** to determine the number of MIDI output devices present in the system. The device ID specified by *wDeviceID* varies from zero to one less than the number of devices present. Only *wSize* bytes (or less) of information is copied to the location pointed to by *lpCaps*. If *wSize* is zero, nothing is copied, and the function returns zero.

See Also   **midiOutGetNumDevs**

midiOutGetErrorText

Syntax   WORD   **midiOutGetErrorText**(*wError*, *lpText*, *wSize*)

This function retrieves a textual description of the error identified by the specified error number.

Parameters   WORD   *wError*

Specifies the error number.

LPSTR   *lpText*

Specifies a far pointer to a buffer to be filled with the textual error description.

WORD   *wSize*

Specifies the length of the buffer pointed to by *lpText*.

Return Value   Returns zero if the function was successful. Otherwise, it returns an error number. Possible error returns are:

MMSYSERR_BADERRNUM

Specified error number is out of range.

Comments   If the textual error description is longer than the specified buffer, the description is truncated. The returned error string is always null-terminated. If *wSize* is zero, nothing is copied, and the function returns MMSYSERR_NOERROR. All error descriptions are less than MAXERRORLENGTH characters long.

midiOutGetID

Syntax   WORD   **midiOutGetID**(*hMidiOut*, *lpwDeviceID*)

This function gets the device ID for a MIDI output device.

Parameters   HMIDIOUT   *hMidiOut*

Specifies the handle to the MIDI output device.

LPWORD   *lpwDeviceID*
   Specifies a pointer to the WORD-sized memory location to be filled with the device ID.

Return Value   Returns MMSYSERR_NOERROR if successful. Otherwise, returns an error number. Possible error returns are:

MMSYSERR_INVALHANDLE
   The *hMidiOut* parameter specifies an invalid handle.

midiOutGetNumDevs

Syntax   WORD   **midiOutGetNumDevs**()

This function retrieves the number of MIDI output devices present in the system.

Parameters   None

Return Value   Returns the number of MIDI output devices present in the system.

See Also   **midiOutGetDevCaps**

midiOutGetVolume

Syntax   WORD   **midiOutGetVolume**(*wDeviceID*, *lpdwVolume*)

This function returns the current volume setting of a MIDI output device.

Parameters   WORD   *wDeviceID*
   Identifies the MIDI output device.

LPDWORD   *lpdwVolume*
   Specifies a far pointer to a location to be filled with the current volume setting. The low-order word of this location contains the left channel volume setting, and the high-order word contains the right channel setting. A value of 0xFFFF represents full volume, and a value of 0x0000 is silence.

   If a device does not support both left and right volume control, the low-order word of the specified location contains the mono volume level.

   The full 16-bit setting(s) set with **midiOutSetVolume** is returned, regardless of whether the device supports the full 16 bits of volume level control.

Return Value   Returns zero if the function was successful. Otherwise, it returns an error number. Possible error returns are:

MMSYSERR_INVALHANDLE
   Specified device handle is invalid.

MMSYSERR_NOTSUPPORTED

Function isn't supported.

MMSYSERR_NODRIVER

The driver was not installed.

Comments   Not all devices support volume control. To determine whether the device supports volume control, use the MIDICAPS_VOLUME flag to test the **dwSupport** field of the **MIDIOUTCAPS** structure (filled by **midiOutGetDevCaps**).

To determine whether the device supports volume control on both the left and right channels, use the MIDICAPS_LRVOLUME flag to test the **dwSupport** field of the **MIDIOUTCAPS** structure (filled by **midiOutGetDevCaps**).

See Also   **midiOutSetVolume**

midiOutLongMsg

Syntax   WORD **midiOutLongMsg**(*hMidiOut, lpMidiOutHdr, wSize*)

This function sends a long MIDI message to the specified MIDI output device. Use this function to send system exclusive messages or to send a buffer filled with short messages.

Parameters   HMIDIOUT   *hMidiOut*

Specifies a handle to the MIDI output device.

LPMIDIHDR   *lpMidiOutHdr*

Specifies a far pointer to a **MIDIHDR** structure that identifies the MIDI data buffer.

WORD   *wSize*

Specifies the size of the **MIDIHDR** structure.

Return Value   Returns zero if the function was successful. Otherwise, it returns an error number. Possible error returns are:

MMSYSERR_INVALHANDLE

Specified device handle is invalid.

MIDIERR_UNPREPARED

lpMidiOutHdr hasn't been prepared.

MIDIERR_NOTREADY

The hardware is busy with other data.

Comments   The data buffer must be prepared with **midiOutPrepareHeader** before it is passed to **midiOutLongMsg**. The **MIDIHDR** data structure and the data buffer pointed to by its **lpData** field must be allocated with **GlobalAlloc** using the GMEM_MOVEABLE and

GMEM_SHARE flags, and locked with **GlobalLock**. This function may or may not return until the data block has been sent to the output device.

See Also   **midiOutShortMsg, midiOutPrepareHeader**

midiOutOpen

Syntax   WORD **midiOutOpen**(*lphMidiOut, wDeviceID, dwCallback, dwCallbackInstance, dwFlags*)

This function opens a specified MIDI output device for playback.

Parameters   LPHMIDIOUT *lphMidiOut*

Specifies a far pointer to an HMIDIOUT handle. This location is filled with a handle identifying the opened MIDI output device. Use the handle to identify the device when calling other MIDI output functions.

WORD *wDeviceID*

Identifies the MIDI output device that is to be opened.

DWORD *dwCallback*

Specifies the address of a fixed callback function or a handle to a window called during MIDI playback to process messages related to the progress of the playback. Specify NULL for this parameter if no callback is desired.

DWORD *dwCallbackInstance*

Specifies user instance data passed to the callback. This parameter is not used with window callbacks.

DWORD *dwFlags*

Specifies a callback flag for opening the device.

CALLBACK_WINDOW

If this flag is specified, *dwCallback* is assumed to be a window handle.

CALLBACK_FUNCTION

If this flag is specified, *dwCallback* is assumed to be a callback procedure address.

Return Value   Returns zero if the function was successful. Otherwise, it returns an error number. Possible error returns are as follows:

MMSYSERR_BADDEVICEID

Specified device ID is out of range.

MMSYSERR_ALLOCATED

Specified resource is already allocated.

MMSYSERR_NOMEM

Unable to allocate or lock memory.

MIDIERR_NOMAP

There is no current MIDI map. This occurs only when opening the mapper.

MIDIERR_NODEVICE

A port in the current MIDI map doesn't exist. This occurs only when opening the mapper.

Comments   Use **midiOutGetNumDevs** to determine the number of MIDI output devices present in the system. The device ID specified by *wDeviceID* varies from zero to one less than the number of devices present. You may also specify MIDIMAPPER as the device ID to open the MIDI mapper.

If a window is chosen to receive callback information, the following messages are sent to the window procedure function to indicate the progress of MIDI output: **MM_MOM_OPEN, MM_MOM_CLOSE, MM_MOM_DONE**.

If a function is chosen to receive callback information, the following messages are sent to the function to indicate the progress of MIDI output: **MOM_OPEN, MOM_CLOSE, MOM_DONE**. The callback function must reside in a DLL. You do not have to use **MakeProcInstance** to get a procedure-instance address for the callback function.

Callback   void FAR PASCAL   **MidiOutFunc**(*hMidiOut*, *wMsg*, *dwInstance*, *dwParam1*, *dwParam2*)

MidiOutFunc is a placeholder for the application-supplied function name. The actual name must be exported by including it in an EXPORTS statement in the DLL's module-definition file.

Parameters

HMIDIOUT   *hMidiOut*

Specifies a handle to the MIDI device associated with the callback.

WORD   *wMsg*

Specifies a MIDI output message.

DWORD   *dwInstance*

Specifies the instance data supplied with **midiOutOpen**.

DWORD   *dwParam1*

Specifies a parameter for the message.

DWORD   *dwParam2*

Specifies a parameter for the message.

Comments

Because the callback is accessed at interrupt time, it must reside in a DLL and its code segment must be specified as FIXED in the module-definition file for the DLL. Any data that the callback accesses must be in a FIXED data segment as well. The callback may not make any system calls except for **PostMessage, timeGetSystemTime, timeGetTime, timeSetEvent, timeKillEvent, midiOutShortMsg, midiOutLongMsg,** and **OutputDebugStr**.

See Also   **midiOutClose**

midiOutPrepareHeader

Syntax   WORD   **midiOutPrepareHeader**(*hMidiOut, lpMidiOutHdr, wSize*)

This function prepares a MIDI system exclusive data block for output.

Parameters   HMIDIOUT   *hMidiOut*
Specifies a handle to the MIDI output device.

LPMIDIHDR   *lpMidiOutHdr*
Specifies a far pointer to a **MIDIHDR** structure that identifies the data block to be prepared.

WORD   *wSize*
Specifies the size of the **MIDIHDR** structure.

Return Value   Returns zero if the function was successful. Otherwise, it returns an error number. Possible error returns are:

MMSYSERR_INVALHANDLE
Specified device handle is invalid.

MMSYSERR_NOMEM
Unable to allocate or lock memory.

Comments   The **MIDIHDR** data structure and the data block pointed to by its **lpData** field must be allocated with **GlobalAlloc** using the GMEM_MOVEABLE and GMEM_SHARE flags and locked with **GlobalLock**. Preparing a header that has already been prepared has no effect, and the function returns zero.

See Also   **midiOutUnprepareHeader**

midiOutReset

Syntax	WORD **midiOutReset**(*hMidiOut*)

This function turns off all notes on all MIDI channels for the specified MIDI output device.

Parameters

HMIDIOUT   *hMidiOut*
> Specifies a handle to the MIDI output device.

Return Value

Returns zero if the function was successful. Otherwise, it returns an error number. Possible error returns are:

MMSYSERR_INVALHANDLE
> Specified device handle is invalid.

Comments

If the specified MIDI output device is an output port, a note off message for each note of each channel is sent. In addition, a sustain (damper pedal) off controller message is sent for each channel.

See Also

midiOutLongMsg, **midiOutClose**

midiOutSetVolume

Syntax

WORD   **midiOutSetVolume**(*wDeviceID*, *dwVolume*)

This function sets the volume of a MIDI output device.

Parameters

WORD   *wDeviceID*
> Identifies the MIDI output device.

DWORD   *dwVolume*
> Specifies the new volume setting. The low-order word contains the left channel volume setting, and the high-order word contains the right channel setting. A value of 0xFFFF represents full volume, and a value of 0x0000 is silence.

> If a device does not support both left and right volume control, the low-order word of *dwVolume* specifies the volume level, and the high-order word is ignored.

Return Value

Returns zero if the function was successful. Otherwise, it returns an error number. Possible error returns are:

MMSYSERR_INVALHANDLE
> Specified device handle is invalid.

MMSYSERR_NOTSUPPORTED
> Function isn't supported.

MMSYSERR_NODRIVER

The driver was not installed.

Comments Not all devices support volume changes. To determine whether the device supports volume control, use the MIDICAPS_VOLUME flag to test the **dwSupport** field of the **MIDIOUTCAPS** structure (filled by **midiOutGetDevCaps**).

To determine whether the device supports volume control on both the left and right channels, use the MIDICAPS_LRVOLUME flag to test the **dwSupport** field of the **MIDIOUTCAPS** structure (filled by **midiOutGetDevCaps**).

Most devices do not support the full 16 bits of volume level control and will use only the high-order bits of the requested volume setting. For example, for a device that supports 4 bits of volume control, requested volume level values of 0x4000, 0x4fff, and 0x43be will all produce the same physical volume setting, 0x4000. The **midiOutGetVolume** function will return the full 16-bit setting set with **midiOutSetVolume**.

Volume settings are interpreted logarithmically. This means the perceived increase in volume is the same when increasing the volume level from 0x5000 to 0x6000 as it is from 0x4000 to 0x5000.

See Also **midiOutGetVolume**

midiOutShortMsg

Syntax WORD   **midiOutShortMsg**(*hMidiOut*, *dwMsg*)

This function sends a short MIDI message to the specified MIDI output device. Use this function to send any MIDI message except for system exclusive messages.

Parameters HMIDIOUT   *hMidiOut*

Specifies a handle to the MIDI output device.

DWORD   *dwMsg*

Specifies the MIDI message. The message is packed into a DWORD with the first byte of the message in the low order byte.

Return Value Returns zero if the function was successful. Otherwise, it returns an error number. Possible error returns are:

MMSYSERR_INVALHANDLE

Specified device handle is invalid.

MIDIERR_NOTREADY

The hardware is busy with other data.

Comments This function may not return until the message has been sent to the output device.

See Also **midiOutLongMsg**

midiOutUnprepareHeader

Syntax WORD **midiOutUnprepareHeader**(*hMidiOut*, *lpMidiOutHdr*, *wSize*)

This function cleans up the preparation performed by **midiOutPrepareHeader**. The **midiOutUnprepareHeader** function must be called after the device driver fills a data buffer and returns it to the application. You must call this function before freeing the data buffer.

Parameters HMIDIOUT *hMidiOut*
Specifies a handle to the MIDI output device.

LPMIDIHDR *lpMidiOutHdr*
Specifies a pointer to a **MIDIHDR** structure identifying the buffer to be cleaned up.

WORD *wSize*
Specifies the size of the **MIDIHDR** structure.

Return Value Returns zero if the function was successful. Otherwise, it returns an error number. Possible error returns are:

MMSYSERR_INVALHANDLE
Specified device handle is invalid.

MIDIERR_STILLPLAYING
lpMidiOutHdr is still in the queue.

Comments This function is the complementary function to **midiOutPrepareHeader**. You must call this function before freeing the data buffer with **GlobalFree**. After passing a buffer to the device driver with **midiOutLongMsg**, you must wait until the driver is finished with the buffer before calling **midiOutUnprepareHeader**.

Unpreparing a buffer that has not been prepared has no effect, and the function returns zero.

See Also **midiOutPrepareHeader**

mmioAdvance

Syntax WORD **mmioAdvance**(*hmmio*, *lpmmioinfo*, *wFlags*)

This function advances the I/O buffer of a file set up for direct I/O buffer access with **mmioGetInfo**. If the file is opened for reading, the I/O buffer is filled from the disk. If the file is opened for writing and the MMIO_DIRTY flag is set in the **dwFlags** field of the **MMIOINFO** structure, the buffer is written to disk. The **pchNext**, **pchEndRead**, and **pchEndWrite** fields of the **MMIOINFO** structure are updated to reflect the new state of the I/O buffer.

Parameters   HMMIO   *hmmio*

                      Specifies the file handle for a file opened with **mmioOpen**.

                  LPMMIOINFO   *lpmmioinfo*

                      Specifies a far pointer to the **MMIOINFO** structure obtained with **mmioGetInfo**.

                  WORD   *wFlags*

                      Specifies options for the operation. Contains exactly one of the following two flags:

                      MMIO_READ

                            The buffer is filled from the file.

                      MMIO_WRITE

                            The buffer is written to the file.

Return Value   The return value is zero if the operation is successful. Otherwise, the return value specifies an error code. The error code can be one of the following codes:

                  MMIOERR_CANNOTWRITE

                      The contents of the buffer could not be written to disk.

                  MMIOERR_CANNOTREAD

                      An error occurred while re-filling the buffer.

                  MMIOERR_UNBUFFERED

                      The specified file is not opened for buffered I/O.

                  MMIOERR_CANNOTEXPAND

                      The specified memory file cannot be expanded, probably because the **adwInfo[0]** field was set to zero in the initial call to **mmioOpen**.

                  MMIOERR_OUTOFMEMORY

                      There was not enough memory to expand a memory file for further writing.

Comments   If the specified file is opened for writing or for both reading and writing, the I/O buffer will be flushed to disk before the next buffer is read. If the I/O buffer cannot be written to disk because the disk is full, then **mmioAdvance** will return MMIOERR_CANNOTWRITE.

                  If the specified file is only open for writing, the MMIO_WRITE flag must be specified.

                  If you have written to the I/O buffer, you must set the MMIO_DIRTY flag in the **dwFlags** field of the **MMIOINFO** structure before calling **mmioAdvance**. Otherwise, the buffer will not be written to disk.

                  If the end of file is reached, **mmioAdvance** will still return success, even though no more data can be read. Thus, to check for the end of the file, it is necessary to see if the **pchNext** and **pchEndRead** fields of the **MMIOINFO** structure are equal after calling **mmioAdvance**.

See Also   **mmioGetInfo**, **MMIOINFO**

---

mmioAscend

Syntax   WORD **mmioAscend**(*hmmio*, *lpck*, *wFlags*)

This function ascends out of a chunk in a RIFF file descended into with **mmioDescend** or created with **mmioCreateChunk**.

Parameters   HMMIO *hmmio*
   Specifies the file handle of an open RIFF file.

   LPMMCKINFO *lpck*
   Specifies a far pointer to a caller-supplied **MMCKINFO** structure previously filled by **mmioDescend** or **mmioCreateChunk**.

   WORD *wFlags*
   Is not used and should be set to zero.

Return Value   The return value is zero if the function is successful. Otherwise, the return value specifies an error code. The error code can be one of the following codes:

   MMIOERR_CANNOTWRITE
   The contents of the buffer could not be written to disk.

   MMIOERR_CANNOTSEEK
   There was an error while seeking to the end of the chunk.

Comments   If the chunk was descended into using **mmioDescend**, then **mmioAscend** seeks to the location following the end of the chunk (past the extra pad byte, if any).

   If the chunk was created and descended into using **mmioCreateChunk**, or if the MMIO_DIRTY flag is set in the **dwFlags** field of the **MMCKINFO** structure referenced by *lpck*, then the current file position is assumed to be the end of the data portion of the chunk. If the chunk size is not the same as the value stored in the **cksize** field when **mmioCreateChunk** was called, then **mmioAscend** corrects the chunk size in the file before ascending from the chunk. If the chunk size is odd, **mmioAscend** writes a null pad byte at the end of the chunk. After ascending from the chunk, the current file position is the location following the end of the chunk (past the extra pad byte, if any).

See Also   **mmioDescend**, **mmioCreateChunk**, **MMCKINFO**

mmioClose

Syntax

WORD   **mmioClose**(*hmmio*, *wFlags*)

This function closes a file opened with **mmioOpen**.

Parameters

HMMIO   *hmmio*

    Specifies the file handle of the file to close.

WORD   *wFlags*

    Specifies options for the close operation.

    MMIO_FHOPEN

        If the file was opened by passing the DOS file handle of an already-opened file to **mmioOpen**, then using this flag tells **mmioClose** to close the MMIO file handle, but not the DOS file handle.

Return Value

The return value is zero if the function is successful. Otherwise, the return value is an error code, either from **mmioFlush** or from the I/O procedure. The error code can be one of the following codes:

MMIOERR_CANNOTWRITE

    The contents of the buffer could not be written to disk.

See Also

mmioOpen, mmioFlush

mmioCreateChunk

Syntax

WORD   **mmioCreateChunk**(*hmmio*, *lpck*, *wFlags*)

This function creates a chunk in a RIFF file opened with **mmioOpen**. The new chunk is created at the current file position. After the new chunk is created, the current file position is the beginning of the data portion of the new chunk.

Parameters

HMMIO   *hmmio*

    Specifies the file handle of an open RIFF file.

LPMMCKINFO   *lpck*

    Specifies a pointer to a caller-supplied **MMCKINFO** structure containing information about the chunk to be created. Set up the **MMCKINFO** structure as follows:

    • The **ckid** field specifies the chunk ID of the chunk. If *wFlags* includes MMIO_CREATERIFF or MMIO_CREATELIST, this field will be filled by **mmioCreateChunk**.

- The **cksize** field specifies the size of the data portion of the chunk, including the form type or list type (if any). If this value is not correct when **mmioAscend** is called to mark the end of the chunk, them **mmioAscend** will correct the chunk size.

- The **fccType** field specifies the form type or list type if the chunk is a "RIFF" or "LIST" chunk. If the chunk is not a "RIFF" or "LIST" chunk, this field need not be filled in.

- The **dwDataOffset** field need not be filled in. The **mmioCreateChunk** function will fill this field with the file offset of the data portion of the chunk.

- The **dwFlags** field need not be filled in. The **mmioCreateChunk** function will set the MMIO_DIRTY flag in **dwFlags**.

WORD   *wFlags*
> Specifies flags to optionally create either a "RIFF" chunk or a "LIST" chunk. Can contain one of the following flags:

> MMIO_CREATERIFF
>> Creates a "RIFF" chunk.

> MMIO_CREATELIST
>> Creates a "LIST" chunk.

Return Value The return value is zero if the function is successful. Otherwise, the return value specifies an error code. The error code can be one of the following codes:

MMIOERR_CANNOTWRITE
> Unable to write the chunk header.

MMIOERR_CANNOTSEEK
> Uanble to determine offset of data portion of the chunk.

Comments This function cannot insert a chunk into the middle of a file. If a chunk is created anywhere but the end of a file, **mmioCreateChunk** will overwrite existing information in the file.

mmioDescend

Syntax WORD   **mmioDescend**(*hmmio*, *lpck*, *lpckParent*, *wFlags*)

This function descends into a chunk of a RIFF file opened with **mmioOpen**. It can also search for a given chunk.

Parameters HMMIO   *hmmio*
> Specifies the file handle of an open RIFF file.

LPMMCKINFO *lpck*

Specifies a far pointer to a caller-supplied **MMCKINFO** structure that **mmioDescend** fills with the following information:

- The **ckid** field is the chunk ID of the chunk.

- The **cksize** field is the size of the data portion of the chunk. The data size includes the form type or list type (if any), but does not include the 8-byte chunk header or the pad byte at the end of the data (if any).

- The **fccType** field is the form type if **ckid** is "RIFF", or the list type if **ckid** is "LIST". Otherwise, it is NULL.

- The **dwDataOffset** field is the file offset of the beginning of the data portion of the chunk. If the chunk is a "RIFF" chunk or a "LIST" chunk, then **dwDataOffset** is the offset of the form type or list type.

- The **dwFlags** contains other information about the chunk. Currently, this information is not used and is set to zero.

If the MMIO_FINDCHUNK, MMIO_FINDRIFF, or MMIO_FINDLIST flag is specified for *wFlags*, then the **MMCKINFO** structure is also used to pass parameters to **mmioDescend**:

- The **ckid** field specifies the four-character code of the chunk ID, form type, or list type to search for.

LPMMCKINFO *lpckParent*

Specifies a far pointer to an optional caller-supplied **MMCKINFO** structure identifying the parent of the chunk being searched for. A parent of a chunk is the enclosing chunk—only "RIFF" and "LIST" chunks can be parents. If *lpckParent* is not NULL, then **mmioDescend** assumes the **MMCKINFO** structure it refers to was filled when **mmioDescend** was called to descend into the parent chunk, and **mmioDescend** will only search for a chunk within the parent chunk. Set *lpckParent* to NULL if no parent chunk is being specified.

WORD *wFlags*

Specifies search options. Contains up to one of the following flags. If no flags are specified, **mmioDescend** descends into the chunk beginning at the current file position.

MMIO_FINDCHUNK

Searches for a chunk with the specified chunk ID.

MMIO_FINDRIFF

Searches for a chunk with chunk ID "RIFF" and with the specified form type.

MMIO_FINDLIST

Searches for a chunk with chunk ID "LIST" and with the specified form type.

Return Value   The return value is zero if the function is successful. Otherwise, the return value specifies an error code. If the end of the file (or the end of the parent chunk, if given) is reached before the desired chunk is found, the return value is MMIOERR_CHUNKNOTFOUND.

Comments   A RIFF chunk consists of a four-byte chunk ID (type FOURCC), followed by a four-byte chunk size (type DWORD), followed by the data portion of the chunk, followed by a null pad byte if the size of the data portion is odd. If the chunk ID is "RIFF" or "LIST", the first four bytes of the data portion of the chunk are a form type or list type (type FOURCC).

If **mmioDescend** is used to search for a chunk, the file position should be at the beginning of a chunk before calling **mmioDescend**. The search begins at the current file position and continues to the end of the file. If a parent chunk is specified, the file position should be somewhere within the parent chunk before calling **mmioDescend**. In this case, the search begins at the current file position and continues to the end of the parent chunk.

If **mmioDescend** is unsuccessful in searching for a chunk, the current file position is undefined. If **mmioDescend** is successful, the current file position is changed. If the chunk is a "RIFF" or "LIST" chunk, the new file position will be just after the form type or list type (12 bytes from the beginning of the chunk). For other chunks, the new file position will be the start of the data portion of the chunk (8 bytes from the beginning of the chunk).

For efficient RIFF file I/O, use buffered I/O.

See Also   **mmioAscend, MMCKINFO**

mmioFlush

Syntax   WORD   **mmioFlush**(*hmmio, wFlags*)

This function writes the I/O buffer of a file to disk, if the I/O buffer has been written to.

Parameters   HMMIO   *hmmio*
Specifies the file handle of a file opened with **mmioOpen**.

WORD   *wFlags*
Is not used and should be set to zero.

Return Value   The return value is zero if the function is successful. Otherwise, the return value specifies an error code. The error code can be one of the following codes:

MMIOERR_CANNOTWRITE
The contents of the buffer could not be written to disk.

Comments   Closing a file with **mmioClose** will automatically flush its buffer.

If there is insufficient disk space to write the buffer, **mmioFlush** will fail, even if the preceding **mmioWrite** calls were successful.

mmioFOURCC

Syntax   FOURCC   **mmioFOURCC**(*ch0*, *ch1*, *ch2*, *ch3*)

This macro converts four characters to to a four-character code.

Parameters   CHAR   *ch0*
The first character of the four-character code.

CHAR   *ch1*
The second character of the four-character code.

CHAR   *ch2*
The third character of the four-character code.

CHAR   *ch3*
The fourth character of the four-character code.

Return Value   The return value is the four-character code created from the given characters.

Comments   This macro does not check to see if the four character code follows any conventions regarding which characters to include in a four-character code.

See Also   **mmioStringToFOURCC**

mmioGetInfo

Syntax   WORD   **mmioGetInfo**(*hmmio*, *lpmmioinfo*, *wFlags*)

This function retrieves information about a file opened with **mmioOpen**. This information allows the caller to directly access the I/O buffer, if the file is opened for buffered I/O.

Parameters   HMMIO   *hmmio*
Specifies the file handle of the file.

LPMMIOINFO   *lpmmioinfo*
Specifies a far pointer to a caller-allocated **MMIOINFO** structure that **mmioGetInfo** fills with information about the file. See the **MMIOINFO** structure and the **mmioOpen** function for information about the fields in this structure.

WORD   *wFlags*
Is not used and should be set to zero.

Return Value   The return value is zero if the function is successful.

Comments   To directly access the I/O buffer of a file opened for buffered I/O, use the following fields of the **MMIOINFO** structure filled by **mmioGetInfo**:

- The **pchNext** field points to the next byte in the buffer that can be read or written. When you read or write, increment **pchNext** by the number of bytes read or written.

- The **pchEndRead** field points to one byte past the last valid byte in the buffer that can be read.

- The **pchEndWrite** field points to one byte past the last location in the buffer that can be written.

Once you read or write to the buffer and modify **pchNext**, do not call any MMIO function except **mmioAdvance** until you call **mmioSetInfo**. Call **mmioSetInfo** when you are finished directly accessing the buffer.

When you reach the end of the buffer specified by **pchEndRead** or **pchEndWrite**, call **mmioAdvance** to fill the buffer from the disk, or write the buffer to the disk. The **mmioAdvance** function will update the **pchNext**, **pchEndRead**, and **pchEndWrite** fields in the **MMIOINFO** structure for the file.

Before calling **mmioAdvance** or **mmioSetInfo** to flush a buffer to disk, set the MMIO_DIRTY flag in the **dwFlags** field of the **MMIOINFO** structure for the file. Otherwise, the buffer will not get written to disk.

Do not decrement **pchNext** or modify any fields in the **MMIOINFO** structure other than **pchNext** and **dwFlags**. Do not set any flags in **dwFlags** except MMIO_DIRTY.

See Also   mmioSetInfo, MMIOINFO

mmioInstallIOProc

Syntax   LPMMIOPROC   **mmioInstallIOProc**(*fccIOProc*, *pIOProc*, *dwFlags*)

This function installs or removes a custom I/O procedure. It will also locate an installed I/O procedure, given its corresponding four-character code.

Parameters   FOURCC   *fccIOProc*

Specifies a four-character code identifying the I/O procedure to install, remove, or locate. All characters in this four-character code should be uppercase characters.

LPMMIOPROC   *pIOProc*

Specifies the address of the I/O procedure to install. To remove or locate an I/O procedure, set this parameter to NULL.

DWORD   *dwFlags*

Specifies one of the following flags indicating whether the I/O procedure is being installed, removed, or located:

MMIO_INSTALLPROC

Installs the specified I/O procedure.

MMIO_REMOVEPROC

Removes the specified I/O procedure.

MMIO_FINDPROC

Searches for the specified I/O procedure.

Return Value   The return value is the address of the I/O procedure installed, removed, or located. If there is an error, the return value is NULL.

Comments   If the I/O procedure resides in the application, use **MakeProcInstance** to get a procedure-instance address and specify this address for *pIOProc*. You don't need to get a procedure-instance address if the I/O procedure resides in a DLL.

Callback   LONG FAR PASCAL   **IOProc**(*lpmmioinfo*, *wMsg*, *lParam1*, *lParam2*)

IOProc is a placeholder for the application-supplied function name. The actual name must be exported by including it in a EXPORTS statement in the application's module-definitions file.

Parameters

LPSTR   *lpmmioinfo*

Specifies a far pointer to an **MMIOINFO** structure containing information about the open file. The I/O procedure must maintain the **lDiskOffset** field in this structure to indicate the file offset to the next read or write location. The I/O procedure can use the **adwInfo[]** field to store state information. The I/O procedure should not modify any other fields of the **MMIOINFO** structure.

WORD   *wMsg*

Specifies a message indicating the requested I/O operation. Messages that can be received include **MMIOM_OPEN**, **MMIOM_CLOSE**, **MMIOM_READ**, **MMIOM_WRITE**, and **MMIOM_SEEK**.

LONG   *lParam1*

Specifies a parameter for the message.

LONG   *lParam2*

Specifies a parameter for the message.

Return Value

The return value depends on the message specified by *wMsg*. If the I/O procedure does not recognize a message, it should return zero.

Comments

The four-character code specified by the **fccIOProc** field in the **MMIOINFO** structure associated with a file identifies a filename extension for a custom storage system. When an application calls **mmioOpen** with a filename like "foo.xyz!bar", the I/O procedure associated with the four-character code "XYZ " is called to open the "bar" element of the file "foo.xyz".

The **mmioInstallIOProc** function maintains a separate list of installed I/O procedures for each Windows application. Therefore, different applications can use the same I/O procedure identifier for different I/O procedures without conflict.

To share an I/O procedure among applications, the I/O procedure must reside in a DLL called by each application using it. Each application using the shared I/O procedure must call **mmioInstallIOProc** to install the procedure (or call the DLL to install the procedure on behalf of the application). Each application must call **mmioInstallIOProc** to remove the I/O procedure before terminating.

If an application calls **mmioInstallIOProc** more than once to register the same I/O procedure, then it must call **mmioInstallIOProc** to remove the procedure once for each time it installed the procedure.

mmioInstallIOProc will not prevent an application from installing two different I/O procedures with the same identifier, or installing an I/O procedure with one of the predefined identifiers ("DOS ", "MEM ", or "BND "). The most recently installed procedure takes precedence, and the most recently installed procedure is the first one to get removed.

See Also   **mmioOpen**

mmioOpen

Syntax   HMMIO   **mmioOpen**(*szFilename*, *lpmmioinfo*, *dwOpenFlags*)

This function opens a file for unbuffered or buffered I/O. The file can be a DOS file, a memory file, or an element of a custom storage system.

Parameters   LPSTR   *szFilename*

Specifies a far pointer to a string containing the filename of the file to open. If no I/O procedure is specified to open the file, then the filename determines how the file is opened, as follows:

- If the filename does not contain "+", then it is assumed to be the name of a DOS file.
- If the filename is of the form "foo.ext+bar", then the extension "EXT " is assumed to identify an installed I/O procedure which is called to perform I/O on the file (see **mmioInstallIOProc**).
- If the filename is NULL and no I/O procedure is given, then **adwInfo[0]** is assumed to be the DOS file handle of a currently open file.

The filename should not be longer than 128 bytes, including the terminating NULL.

When opening a memory file, set *szFilename* to NULL.

LPMMIOINFO   *lpmmioinfo*

> Specifies a far pointer to an **MMIOINFO** structure containing extra parameters used by **mmioOpen**. Unless you are opening a memory file, specifying the size of a buffer for buffered I/O, or specifying an uninstalled I/O procedure to open a file, this parameter should be NULL.
>
> If *lpmmioinfo* is not NULL, all unused fields of the **MMIOINFO** structure it references must be set to zero, including the reserved fields.

DWORD   *dwOpenFlags*

> Specifies option flags for the open operation. The MMIO_READ, MMIO_WRITE, and MMIO_READWRITE flags are mutually exclusive—only one should be specified. The MMIO_COMPAT, MMIO_EXCLUSIVE, MMIO_DENYWRITE, MMIO_DENYREAD, and MMIO_DENYNONE flags are DOS file-sharing flags, and can only be used after the DOS command SHARE has been executed.

> MMIO_READ
>
>> Opens the file for reading only. This is the default, if MMIO_WRITE and MMIO_READWRITE are not specified.

> MMIO_WRITE
>
>> Opens the file for writing. You should not read from a file opened in this mode.

> MMIO_READWRITE
>
>> Opens the file for both reading and writing.

> MMIO_CREATE
>
>> Creates a new file. If the file already exists, it is truncated to zero length. For memory files, MMIO_CREATE indicates the end of the file is initially at the start of the buffer.

> MMIO_DELETE
>
>> Deletes a file. If this flag is specified, *szFilename* should not be NULL. The return value will be TRUE (cast to HMMIO) if the file was deleted successfully, FALSE otherwise. Do not call **mmioClose** for a file that has been deleted. If this flag is specified, all other flags are ignored.

> MMIO_ALLOCBUF
>
>> Opens a file for buffered I/O. To allocate a buffer larger or smaller than the default buffer size (8K), set the **cchBuffer** field of the **MMIOINFO** structure to the desired buffer size. If **cchBuffer** is zero, then the default buffer size is used. If you are providing your own I/O buffer, then the MMIO_ALLOCBUF flag should not be used.

MMIO_COMPAT

Opens the file with compatibility mode, allowing any process on a given machine to open the file any number of times. **mmioOpen** fails if the file has been opened with any of the other sharing modes.

MMIO_EXCLUSIVE

Opens the file with exclusive mode, denying other processes both read and write access to the file. **mmioOpen** fails if the file has been opened in any other mode for read or write access, even by the current process.

MMIO_DENYWRITE

Opens the file and denies other processes write access to the file. **mmioOpen** fails if the file has been opened in compatibility or for write access by any other process.

MMIO_DENYREAD

Opens the file and denies other processes read access to the file. **mmioOpen** fails if the file has been opened in compatibility mode or for read access by any other process.

MMIO_DENYNONE

Opens the file without denying other processes read or write access to the file. **mmioOpen** fails if the file has been opened in compatibility mode by any other process.

Return Value   The return value is a handle to the opened file. This handle is not a DOS file handle—do not use it with any file I/O functions other than MMIO functions.

If the file cannot be opened, the return value is NULL. If *lpmmioinfo* is not NULL, then its **wError** field will contain extended error information returned by the I/O procedure.

Comments   If *lpmmioinfo* references an **MMIOINFO** structure, set up the fields as described below. All unused fields must be set to zero, including reserved fields.

- To request that a file be opened with an installed I/O procedure, set the **fccIOProc** field to the four-character code of the I/O procedure, and set the **pIOProc** field to NULL.

- To request that a file be opened with an uninstalled I/O procedure, set the **pIOProc** field to point to the I/O procedure, and set **fccIOProc** to NULL.

- To request that **mmioOpen** determine which I/O procedure to use to open the file based on the filename contained in *szFilename*, set both **fccIOProc** and **pIOProc** to NULL. This is the default behavior if no **MMIOINFO** structure is specified.

- To open a memory file using an internally allocated and managed buffer, set the **pchBuffer** field to NULL, **fccIOProc** to FOURCC_MEM, **cchBuffer** to the initial size of the buffer, and **adwInfo[0]** to the incremental expansion size of the buffer. This memory file will automatically be expanded in increments of **adwInfo[0]** bytes when necessary. Specify the MMIO_CREATE flag for the *dwOpenFlags* parameter to initially set the end of the file to be the beginning of the buffer.

■ To open a memory file using a caller-supplied buffer, set the **pchBuffer** field to point to the memory buffer, **fccIOProc** to FOURCC_MEM, **cchBuffer** to the size of the buffer, and **adwInfo[0]** to the incremental expansion size of the buffer. The expansion size in **adwInfo[0]** should only be non-zero if **pchBuffer** is a pointer obtained by calling **GlobalAlloc** and **GlobalLock**, since **GlobalReAlloc** will be called to expand the buffer. In particular, if **pchBuffer** points to a local or global array, a block of memory in the local heap, or a block of memory allocated by **GlobalDosAlloc**, **adwInfo[0]** must be zero.

Specify the MMIO_CREATE flag for the *dwOpenFlags* parameter to initially set the end of the file to be the beginning of the buffer; otherwise, the entire block of memory will be considered readable.

■ To use a currently open DOS file handle with MMIO, set the **fccIOProc** field to FOURCC_DOS, **pchBuffer** to NULL, and **adwInfo[0]** to the DOS file handle. Note that offsets within the file will be relative to the beginning of the file, and will not depend on the DOS file position at the time **mmioOpen** is called; the initial MMIO offset will be the same as the DOS offset when **mmioOpen** is called. Later, to close the MMIO file handle without closing the DOS file handle, pass the MMIO_FHOPEN flag to **mmioClose**.

You must call **mmioClose** to close a file opened with **mmioOpen**. Open files are not automatically closed when an application exits.

See Also   **mmioClose**

mmioRead

Syntax   LONG   **mmioRead**(*hmmio, pch, cch*)

This function reads a specified number of bytes from a file opened with **mmioOpen**.

Parameters   HMMIO   *hmmio*
Specifies the file handle of the file to be read.

HPSTR   *pch*
Specifies a huge pointer to a buffer to contain the data read from the file.

LONG   *cch*
Specifies the number of bytes to read from the file.

Return Value   The return value is the number of bytes actually read. If the end of the file has been reached and no more bytes can be read, the return value is zero. If there is an error reading from the file, the return value is -1.

See Also   **mmioWrite**

mmioSeek

Syntax

LONG   **mmioSeek**(*hmmio*, *lOffset*, *iOrigin*)

This function changes the current file position in a file opened with **mmioOpen**. The current file position is the location in the file where data is read or written.

Parameters

HMMIO   *hmmio*
  Specifies the file handle of the file to seek in.

LONG   *lOffset*
  Specifies an offset to change the file position.

int   *iOrigin*
  Specifies how the offset specified by *lOffset* is interpreted. Contains one of the following flags:

  SEEK_SET
    Seeks to *lOffset* bytes from the beginning of the file.

  SEEK_CUR
    Seeks to *lOffset* bytes from the current file position.

  SEEK_END
    Seeks to *lOffset* bytes from the end of the file.

Return Value

The return value is the new file position in bytes, relative to the beginning of the file. If there is an error, the return value is -1.

Comments

Seeking to an invalid location in the file, such as past the end of the file, may not cause **mmioSeek** to return an error, but may cause subsequent I/O operations on the file to fail.

To locate the end of a file, call **mmioSeek** with *lOffset* set to zero and *iOrigin* set to SEEK_END.

mmioSendMessage

Syntax

LONG   **mmioSendMessage**(*hmmio*, *wMsg*, *lParam1*, *lParam2*)

This function sends a message to the I/O procedure associated with the specified file.

Parameters

HMMIO   *hmmio*
  Specifies the file handle for a file opened with **mmioOpen**.

WORD   *wMsg*
  Specifies the message to send to the I/O procedure.

LONG *lParam1*
>   Specifies a parameter for the message.

LONG *lParam2*
>   Specifies a parameter for the message.

Return Value   The return value depends on the message. If the I/O procedure does not recognize the message, the return value is zero.

Comments   Use this function to send custom user-defined messages. Do not use it to send the **MMIOM_OPEN, MMIOM_CLOSE, MMIOM_READ, MMIOM_WRITE, MMIOM_WRITEFLUSH,** or **MMIOM_SEEK** messages. Define custom messages to be greater than or equal to the MMIOM_USER constant.

See Also   **mmioInstallIOProc**

mmioSetBuffer

Syntax   WORD **mmioSetBuffer**(*hmmio, pchBuffer, cchBuffer, wFlags*)

This function enables or disables buffered I/O, or changes the buffer or buffer size for a file opened with **mmioOpen**.

Parameters   HMMIO *hmmio*
>   Specifies the file handle of the file.

LPSTR *pchBuffer*
>   Specifies a far pointer to a caller-supplied buffer to use for buffered I/O. If NULL, **mmioSetBuffer** allocates an internal buffer for buffered I/O.

LONG *cchBuffer*
>   Specifies the size of the caller-supplied buffer, or the size of the buffer for **mmioSetBuffer** to allocate.

WORD *wFlags*
>   Is not used and should be set to zero.

Return Value   The return value is zero if the function is successful. Otherwise, the return value specifies an error code. If an error occurs, the file handle remains valid. The error code can be one of the following codes:

MMIOERR_CANNOTWRITE
>   The contents of the old buffer could not be written to disk, so the operation was aborted.

MMIOERR_OUTOFMEMORY
>   The new buffer could not be allocated, probably due to a lack of available memory.

Comments   To enable buffering using an internal buffer, set *pchBuffer* to NULL and *cchBuffer* to the desired buffer size.

To supply your own buffer, set *pchBuffer* to point to the buffer, and set *cchBuffer* to the size of the buffer.

To disable buffered I/O, set *pchBuffer* to NULL and *cchBuffer* to zero.

If buffered I/O is already enabled using an internal buffer, you can reallocate the buffer to a different size by setting *pchBuffer* to NULL and *cchBuffer* to the new buffer size. The contents of the buffer may be changed after resizing.

mmioSetInfo

Syntax   WORD   **mmioSetInfo**(*hmmio*, *lpmmioinfo*, *wFlags*)

This function updates the information retrieved by **mmioGetInfo** about a file opened with **mmioOpen**. Use this function to terminate direct buffer access of a file opened for buffered I/O.

Parameters   HMMIO   *hmmio*
Specifies the file handle of the file.

LPMMIOINFO   *lpmmioinfo*
Specifies a far pointer to an **MMIOINFO** structure filled with information with **mmioGetInfo**.

WORD   *wFlags*
Is not used and should be set to zero.

Return Value   The return value is zero if the function is successful.

Comments   If you have written to the file I/O buffer, set the MMIO_DIRTY flag in the **dwFlags** field of the **MMIOINFO** structure before calling **mmioSetInfo** to terminate direct buffer access. Otherwise, the buffer will not get flushed to disk.

See Also   **mmioGetInfo, MMIOINFO**

mmioStringToFOURCC

Syntax   FOURCC   **mmioStringToFOURCC**(*sz*, *wFlags*)

This function converts a null-terminated string to a four-character code.

Parameters   LPSTR   *sz*
Specifies a far pointer to a null-terminated string to a four-character code.

WORD *wFlags*
>   Specifies options for the conversion:

>   MMIO_TOUPPER
> >   Converts all characters to uppercase.

Return Value   The return value is the four character code created from the given string.

Comments   This function does not check to see if the string *sz* follows conventions regarding legal characters to use in a four-character code. The string is simply copied to a four-character code and padded to the right with blanks or truncated to four characters as required.

See Also   **mmioFOURCC**

---

mmioWrite

Syntax   LONG **mmioWrite**(*hmmio*, *pch*, *cch*)

>   This function writes a specified number of bytes to a file opened with **mmioOpen**.

Parameters   HMMIO *hmmio*
>   Specifies the file handle of the file.

>   HPSTR *pch*
>   Specifies a huge pointer to the buffer to be written to the file.

>   LONG *cch*
>   Specifies the number of bytes to write to the file.

Return Value   The return value is the number of bytes actually written. If there is an error writing to the file, the return value is -1.

Comments   The current file position is incremented by the number of bytes written.

See Also   **mmioRead**

---

mmpAnimate

Syntax   int **mmpAnimate**(*idMovie*)

>   This function prompts the Movie Player to advance to the next segment in the animation. The action taken by the Movie Player depends on the current state of the animation. The **mmpAnimate** return values describe the action taken and report the animation status.

Parameters   MMPID *idMovie*
>   Identifies the movie ID of the Movie Player instance.

Return Value   Returns zero if unsuccessful or a status code if successful. Negative status codes indicate the Movie Player is waiting for a Windows message; when calling **mmpAnimate** from the message loop, you should call **WaitMessage** if **mmpAnimate** returns a negative value. The following return values report the current state of the animation:

MMP_ANIM_DRAW

The Movie Player drew a subframe on this call. If the movie frame contains complex transitions involving subframes, the MMP_ANIM_DRAW value is returned multiple times until the last drawing step is completed for the given frame (at which point the function returns MMP_ANIM_DRAWN).

If the movie frame contains a simple transition such as a straight copy, the transition requires only one **mmpAnimate** call and the function never returns MMP_ANIM_DRAW for the current frame.

MMP_ANIM_DRAWN

The Movie Player finished drawing the frame on this call. This value is returned once per frame.

MMP_TEMPO_WAIT

The Movie Player is waiting for the frame's display period (defined by its tempo setting) to expire. This value is also returned when the Movie Player is waiting for a cast sound to finish playing. This value can be returned multiple times per frame.

MMP_ANIM_SCRIPT_PROCESSED

The Movie Player processed the frame script text on this call. This value is returned once for each frame that contains script-channel text.

MMP_FRAME_DONE

The Movie Player has completed all processing for the current frame and will begin processing the next frame. This flag is returned once for each frame and is always the last value returned for the frame. If you want to stop the animation on a certain frame number, call **mmpStopAnimating** after receiving this return flag for the given frame.

MMP_MOUSE_WAIT

The Movie Player is waiting for the stage window to receive a mouse-button message. This return value occurs on movie frames that specify a wait-for-mouse tempo value. This value can be returned multiple times per frame.

MMP_DEVICE_WAIT

The Movie Player is waiting for an MCI device to finish playing. This return value occurs on movie frames that specify an mciWait script-channel command. This value can be returned multiple times per frame.

MMP_ANIM_STOPPED

The animation is stopped. Possible reasons are **mmpStartAnimating** has not been called, **mmpStopAnimating** was called, or the movie reached the last frame.

Comments	To notify the Movie Player that animation is to begin, you must call **mmpStartAnimating** once before calling this function.
See Also	**mmpStartAnimating, mmpStopAnimating, mmpAnimStatus, mmpAnimStopped**

mmpAnimStatus

Syntax	int **mmpAnimStatus**(*idMovie*)
	This function reports the animation status. It does not initiate any animation action.
Parameters	MMPID *idMovie*
	Identifies the movie ID of the Movie Player instance.
Return Value	Returns one of the following values indicating the current status of the animation:

- MMP_ANIM_DRAW
- MMP_FRAME_DONE
- MMP_DEVICE_WAIT, MMP_TEMPO_WAIT, MMP_MOUSE_WAIT
- MMP_ANIM_STOPPED

Refer to the **mmpAnimate** information for a description of these return values.

See Also	**mmpAnimate, mmpAnimStopped**

mmpAnimStopped

Syntax	BOOL **mmpAnimStopped**(*idMovie*)
	This function determines whether the movie is stopped.
Parameters	MMPID *idMovie*
	Identifies the movie ID of the Movie Player instance.
Return Value	Returns TRUE if the movie is stopped. Returns FALSE if the movie is running.

mmpClose

Syntax	BOOL **mmpClose**(*idMovie*, *wOptions*)
	This function shuts down an instance of the Movie Player.
Parameters	MMPID *idMovie*
	Identifies the movie ID of the Movie Player instance.

WORD *wOptions*
: Not used.

Return Value
: Returns TRUE if successful, otherwise returns FALSE.

Comments
: This function stops the animation, clears the playback window, unloads the movie file, frees memory associated with the Movie Player instance, and closes the Movie Player instance.

A return value of FALSE indicates a Movie Player error; the movie ID is no longer valid. To get an error value, immediately call **mmpError** with a NULL movie ID.

See Also
: **mmpOpen**, **mmpError**

mmpError

Syntax
: int **mmpError**(*idMovie*, *lpszErrorString*, *wLen*)

This function returns the status of a Movie Player instance and optionally fills a character buffer with a descriptive error message. The error code reflects the status of the movie following the previous Movie Player API call.

Parameters
: MMPID *idMovie*
: Identifies the movie ID of the Movie Player instance. Pass a NULL value to this parameter to retrieve error information about the last Movie Player API call for all instances.

LPSTR *lpszErrorString*
: Pointer to an error message buffer. If this pointer is not NULL, the buffer is filled with a descriptive error message. If you pass a NULL pointer, no error message string is copied.

WORD *wLen*
: Specifies the length of the buffer referenced by the *lpszErrorString* parameter. The maximum message length is specified by the constant MMP_MAXERRORLENGTH.

Return Value
: Returns one of the following codes, which identify the last error that occurred:

MMPERR_NO_ERROR
: Indicates no error occurred.

MMPERR_FATAL_ERROR
: Indicates that a fatal error occurred.

MMPERR_STAGE_ERROR
: Indicates an error occurred while creating the stage window.

MMPERR_FILE_VER

Indicates the movie file version is incompatible with the Movie Player.

MMPERR_FILE_TYPE

Indicates the file is not a RIFF RMMP movie file.

MMPERR_OPEN_ERROR

Indicates a DOS error occurred while trying to open the file.

MMPERR_READ_ERROR

Indicates a DOS error occurred while trying to read from the file.

MMPERR_EOF_ERROR

Indicates the Movie Player encountered an unexpected end-of-file.

MMPERR_REC_HEADER

Indicates an error in the file record header.

MMPERR_CAST_ERROR

Indicates an error occurred while trying to read a cast member.

MMPERR_CAST_MAP_ERROR

Indicates a cast-list mapping mismatch.

MMPERR_MEM_ALLOC

Indicates insufficient memory to complete the operation.

MMERR_BAD_PARM

Indicates a bad or missing parameter passed to the Movie Player function.

MMPERR_BAD_ID

Indicates an incorrect movie ID was used when calling a Movie Player function from a frame-hook function.

Comments   After receiving an error return value from a Movie Player function, you should call **mmpError** to retrieve a specific error code and optional error text string.

---

mmpFileLoaded

Syntax   BOOL   **mmpFileLoaded**(*idMovie*)

This function determines whether a movie file has been loaded into the Movie Player instance.

Parameters   MMPID   *idMovie*

Identifies the movie ID of the Movie Player instance.

Return Value   Returns TRUE if a file is loaded, otherwise returns FALSE.

See Also   **mmpLoadFile**

mmpFreeFile

Syntax   BOOL   **mmpFreeFile**(*idMovie*, *wOptions*)

This function frees memory associated with a movie file previously loaded by
mmpLoadFile.

Parameters   MMPID   *idMovie*
Identifies the movie ID of the Movie Player instance.

WORD   *wOptions*
Can contain the following flag:

MMP_ERASE_FRAME
Clear the stage window.

Return Value   Returns TRUE if successful, otherwise returns FALSE.

Comments   If the movie is currently running, the animation is stopped and the file is unloaded.

See Also   **mmpLoadFile**, **mmpFileLoaded**

mmpGetCurFrame

Syntax   int   **mmpGetCurFrame**(*idMovie*)

This function returns the number of the frame displayed in the stage window.

Parameters   MMPID   *idMovie*
Identifies the movie ID of the Movie Player instance.

Return Value   Returns the current frame index. Returns zero if an error occurs.

Comments   Frame numbering starts at 1.

See Also   **mmpGoToFrame**

mmpGetFileInfo

Syntax   BOOL   **mmpGetFileInfo**(*lpszFileName*, *lpInfo*)

This function returns information about a movie file on disk.

Parameters   LPSTR   *lpszFileName*
Specifies the name or file handle of an RMMP-format movie file.

To specify a movie filename, pass a far pointer to a character buffer containing the DOS filename of the movie file.

To specify a file handle, set the high-order word to zero and set the low-order word to the file handle of an open file. If you specify a file handle, the file pointer must point to the beginning of the RMMP chunk (at the first byte of the "RIFF" chunk ID).

LPMMPMOVIEINFO   *lpInfo*
Points to an MMPMOVIEINFO structure to be filled with information about the specified movie file.

Return Value   Returns TRUE if successful, otherwise returns FALSE.

Comments   The **dwInitialFramesPerSecond** field of the MMPMOVIEINFO structure is set to zero.

See Also   **mmpGetInfo, mmpGetMovieInfo**

mmpGetFrameHook

Syntax   FARPROC   **mmpGetFrameHook**(*idMovie*)

This function returns a pointer to the most recently attached callback function for the Movie Player instance.

Parameters   MMPID   *idMovie*
Identifies the movie ID of the Movie Player instance.

Return Value   Returns a FARPROC pointer to the most recently attached callback function. Returns NULL if no function is attached.

See Also   **mmpSetFrameHook, MMP_PROCESS_FRAME, MMP_PROCESS_SCRIPT**

mmpGetInfo

Syntax   BOOL   **mmpGetInfo**(*idMovie*, *nIndex*, *lpData*, *wLen*)

This function returns internal movie data stored for the Movie Player instance. Since **mmpGetInfo** allows access to data structures used by the movie, improperly using the returned information can cause a general protection fault or crash the Movie Player. Do not call **mmpGetInfo** or change the returned data while the movie is animating.

Parameters

MMPID   *idMovie*

Identifies the movie ID of the Movie Player instance.

int   *nIndex*

Specifies the type of data to be returned in the memory location pointed to by the *lpData* parameter. Use one of the following constants:

MMPINFO_LABELLIST

Return a handle to the label-list array. Function places a handle to the array of **MMPLABEL** records in the memory location pointed to by *lpData*.

MMPINFO_LABELTEXT

Return a handle to the label-text block. Function places a handle to the label-text block in the memory location pointed to by *lpData*.

MMPINFO_LABELCOUNT

Return the count of label entries. Function places a WORD-sized count value in the memory location pointed to by *lpData*.

MMPINFO_ACTIONLIST

Return a handle to the action-list array. The action list contains the script-channel commands for the movie. Function places a handle to the array of **MMPACTION** records in the memory location pointed to by *lpData*.

MMPINFO_ACTIONTEXT

Return a handle to the action-text block. Function places a handle to the action-text block in the memory location pointed to by *lpData*.

MMPINFO_ACTIONCOUNT

Return the count of action entries. Function places a WORD-sized count value in the memory location pointed to by *lpData*.

LPVOID   *lpData*

Specifies a far pointer to the memory area to receive the Movie Player instance data. The memory area pointed to by this parameter must be large enough to receive the requested data item.

WORD   *wLen*

Specifies the length of the memory location pointed to by the *lpData* parameter.

Return Value   Returns TRUE if successful; otherwise, returns FALSE.

Comments   All handles returned by this function reference global memory objects.

For both the label and action-entry data, the three data items (label-list or action-list array, text block, and count value) are dependent on each other. When changing the label or action entry information, change all relevant data items as a single operation before yielding control. Use the **mmpSetInfo** command to change the memory handles or count values for the label list and action-text list.

See Also   **mmpGetMovieInfo, mmpGetPaletteHandle, mmpSetInfo, MMPLABEL, MMPACTION**

---

mmpGetMovieInfo

Syntax   BOOL   **mmpGetMovieInfo**(*idMovie*, *lpInfo*)

This function returns information about a movie file in memory.

Parameters   MMPID   *idMovie*
Identifies the movie ID of the Movie Player instance.

LPMMPMOVIEINFO   *lpInfo*
Points to an MMPMOVIEINFO structure to be filled with information about the specified movie file.

Return Value Returns TRUE if successful, otherwise returns FALSE.

Comments   This function fills out an MMPMOVIEINFO structure for the movie loaded into the specified Movie Player instance.

See Also   **mmpGetInfo, mmpGetFileInfo, mmpGetPaletteHandle**

---

mmpGetMute

Syntax   BOOL   **mmpGetMute**(*idMovie*)

This function returns TRUE if the Movie Player instance is set to disable sound playback.

Parameters   MMPID   *idMovie*
Identifies the movie ID of the Movie Player instance.

Return Value Returns TRUE if sound playback is disabled, otherwise returns FALSE.

Comments   The mute setting affects only the playback of embedded sound cast members. It does not affect **mci** or **mciWait** script-channel commands, including those used to play streamed audio resources.

See Also   **mmpSetMute**

mmpGetPaletteHandle

Syntax   HPALETTE   **mmpGetPaletteHandle**(*idMovie*)

This function returns a handle to the logical palette for the current frame.

Parameters   MMPID   *idMovie*
Identifies the movie ID of the Movie Player instance.

Return Value   Returns a handle to a logical palette if successful, otherwise returns NULL.

See Also   **mmpGetFileInfo, mmpGetInfo, mmpGetMovieInfo**

mmpGetRepeat

Syntax   BOOL   **mmpGetRepeat**(*idMovie*)

This function determines whether the Movie Player instance is set to repeat the movie.

Parameters   MMPID   *idMovie*
Identifies the movie ID of the Movie Player instance.

Return Value   Returns TRUE if repeat is on. Returns FALSE if repeat is off.

Comments   If the repeat flag is set to TRUE, the Movie Player automatically rewinds and continues play after the last frame is shown.

See Also   **mmpSetRepeat**

mmpGetStage

Syntax   BOOL   **mmpGetStage**(*idMovie, lphWndStage, lprectStage, wOptions*)

This function returns information about the stage window for a given Movie Player instance.

Parameters   MMPID   *idMovie*
Identifies the movie ID of the Movie Player instance.

LPHWND   *lphWndStage*
Points to an HWND variable to be set to the handle of the stage window associated with the movie ID.

LPRECT   *lprectStage*
Points to a **RECT** structure to be set to the offset and extents of the playback area within the stage-window client area.

LPWORD   *wOptions*

Points to a WORD variable to be set to the stage options in effect for the Movie Player instance. For information on the stage options, refer to the description of the **mmpSetStage** function.

Return Value   Returns TRUE if successful, otherwise returns FALSE.

See Also   **mmpSetStage, mmpOpen**

---

mmpGetTempo

Syntax   short   **mmpGetTempo**(*idMovie*)

This function returns the movie tempo in frames per second.

Parameters   MMPID   *idMovie*

Identifies the movie ID of the Movie Player instance.

Return Value   Returns the movie tempo in frames per second.

Comments   The returned tempo value remains correct until the movie changes the frames-per-second rate in the tempo channel.

See Also   **mmpSetTempo**

---

mmpGoToFrame

Syntax   BOOL   **mmpGoToFrame**(*idMovie, sNewFrame, wOptions*)

This function jumps to a specified frame in the movie.

Parameters   MMPID   *idMovie*

Identifies the movie ID of the Movie Player instance.

short   *sNewFrame*

Identifies the number of the frame to jump to. Frames are numbered starting at 1. This parameter can take a frame number you specify or either of the following flags:

MMP_FRAME_FIRST

Jump to the first frame of the movie.

MMP_FRAME_LAST

Jump to the last frame of the movie.

WORD   *wOptions*

Specifies the following flags:

MMP_DRAW_FRAME

Draw the frame to the stage window.

Return Value   Returns TRUE if successful. Returns FALSE if an invalid frame number is passed to *sNewFrame*.

See Also   **mmpGetCurFrame**

mmpLoadFile

Syntax   BOOL   **mmpLoadFile**(*idMovie, lpszFileName, wOptions*)

This function loads a movie file for playback and establishes playback options for the movie.

Parameters   MMPID   *idMovie*

Identifies the movie ID of the Movie Player instance.

LPSTR   *lpszFileName*

Specifies the name or file handle of an RMMP-format movie file.

To specify a movie filename, pass a far pointer to a character buffer containing the DOS filename of the movie file.

To specify a file handle, set the high-order word to zero and set the low-order word to the file handle of an open file. If you specify a file handle, the file pointer must point to the beginning of the RMMP chunk (at the first byte of the "RIFF" chunk ID).

WORD   *wOptions*

Specifies playback and load options. Use any combination of the following flags:

MMP_DRAW_FRAME

Draw the first frame to the stage window. By default, the Movie Player does not display the first frame.

MMP_ERASE_FRAME

Erase the stage window before loading the movie file.

MMP_LOAD_REFERENCED

Load only those cast members that are referenced in the score. Using this flag can reduce memory requirements for movie files containing unused cast members. Default setting is to load all cast members contained in the movie file.

MMP_LOAD_NOBUFFER

Create no off-screen buffer for imaging movie frames. Use this flag in low-memory situations. Default setting is to create the off-screen buffer. Some movies require the use of the off-screen buffer.

MMP_LOAD_NOSTATIC

Reduce the system colors to black and white, leaving up to 254 colors for Movie Player use. When the stage window is the active window in the system, the Windows color scheme switches to black and white. Default setting is to reserve the 20 system colors, leaving up to 236 colors for Movie Player use.

Return Value   Returns TRUE if operation successful, otherwise returns FALSE.

Comments   If the Movie Player is playing a movie file when this function is called, it stops animation and frees the currently loaded file before attempting to load the new movie file.

System color scheme changes caused by calling **mmpLoadFile** with the MMP_LOAD_NOSTATIC flag are canceled when the movie file is unloaded, when the stage window is inactive, and when the stage window is closed.

See Also   **mmpFreeFile, mmpFileLoaded**

mmpOpen

Syntax   MMPID   **mmpOpen**(*hWndStage*, *wOptions*)

This function initializes a Movie Player instance.

Parameters   HWND   *hWndStage*

Specifies a handle to the window to be used as the stage window. If *hWndStage* is NULL, you must supply a stage window handle (using **mmpSetStage**) before starting the animation.

WORD   *wOptions*
Not used.

Return Value   Returns a Movie Player instance identifier (movie ID) if successful. If the Movie Player fails to start an instance, the function returns NULL.

Comments   Each instance of the Movie Player is identified by the unique movie ID returned from the call to **mmpOpen**. Most Movie Player APIs require the movie ID returned by this function.

The Movie Player supports up to eight instances system-wide. A single application can play multiple movies simultaneously by opening multiple Movie Player instances and saving the movie ID for each instance.

If **mmpOpen** fails, you can call **mmpError** with a NULL value for the movie ID to retrieve the error that occurred.

See Also   **mmpClose, mmpError, mmpSetStage**

mmpSetDC

Syntax   BOOL   **mmpSetDC**(*idMovie*, *hDC*)

This function sets a device context for a Movie Player instance, allowing the Movie Player to direct frame updates to a private or class device context.

Parameters   MMPID   *idMovie*

Identifies the movie ID of the Movie Player instance.

HDC   *hDC*

Identifies the handle to a device context to which the Movie Player instance will draw movie frames. To cancel the use of the alternate device context, pass a NULL value to this parameter.

Return Value   Returns TRUE if successful, otherwise returns FALSE.

Comments   By default, the Movie Player obtains a handle to a device context with most operations. To improve performance, you can use the **mmpSetDC** function to specify a private or class device context to use when displaying movie frames. Be sure to register the playback window with the CS_CLASSDC or CS_OWNDC style flags.

mmpSetFrameHook

Syntax   BOOL   **mmpSetFrameHook**(*idMovie*, *lpFrameHook*)

This function hooks a callback function into the movie playback. The callback function is called after each frame update and before script-channel commands are processed.

Parameters   MMPID   *idMovie*

Identifies the movie ID of the Movie Player instance.

LPMMPFRAMEHOOK   *lpFrameHook*

Specifies the procedure-instance address of the callback function. To remove your callback function, pass the original callback-function address (obtained using **mmpGetFrameHook**) to this parameter.

Return Value   Returns TRUE if successful, otherwise returns FALSE.

Comments   The attached function is called after screen updates for each frame and subframe are concluded.

Callback   BOOL FAR PASCAL   **FrameHook**(*idMovie*, *wMsg*, *wParam*, *lParam*)

FrameHook is a placeholder for the application-supplied function name. Export the actual name by including it in the EXPORTS statement in your module-definition file.

Parameters

MMPID   *idMovie*

Identifies the movie ID of the Movie Player instance.

WORD   *wMsg*

Specifies a message indicating the reason for calling the frame-hook function. This message is either **MMP_HOOK_FRAME** or **MMP_HOOK_SCRIPT**.

WORD   *wParam*

Specifies the frame index.

LONG   *lParam*

Specifies a parameter for the message.

Return Value

The return value depends on the message specified by *wMsg*.

Comments

Any Movie Player functions called from the callback function must be directed to the current Movie Player instance. Do not close the movie file or the Movie Player instance from the frame-hook function; you can use **PostMessage** to notify a window function to close a movie file or Movie Player instance.

You should call any existing callback function at the end of your callback function. In this way, you can chain the frame-hook functions. Before hooking your callback function, use **mmpGetFrameHook** to obtain the address of the current callback function. If this value is not NULL, call the existing function at the end of your callback function.

To unhook your callback function, call **mmpSetFrameHook** and pass the original callback-function value (which may be NULL if no function was attached) to the *lpFrameHook* parameter.

See Also   **mmpGetFrameHook, MMP_HOOK_FRAME, MMP_HOOK_SCRIPT**

mmpSetInfo

Syntax   BOOL   **mmpSetInfo**(*idMovie, nIndex, lpData, wLen*)

Sets new values for internal movie data of the Movie Player instance. Since this function directly sets variables used by the movie, setting improper values can cause a general protection fault or crash the Movie Player. Do not call this function while the movie is animating.

Parameters   MMPID   *idMovie*

Identifies the movie ID of the Movie Player instance.

int   *nIndex*

Specifies the type of data to provide to the Movie Player instance. Use one of the following constants:

MMPINFO_LABELLIST

Sets the handle to the label-list array. The *lpData* parameter must point to a handle that references a global memory block containing an array of **MMPLABEL** records. The label-list information must be compatible with the MMP label-text block. See the documentation on the **MMPLABEL** structure for information on the label-list format.

MMPINFO_LABELTEXT

Set the handle to the label text block. The *lpData* parameter must point to a handle that references a global memory block containing a block of label text. The label text must be compatible with the MMP label-list information.

MMPINFO_LABELCOUNT

Set the count of label entries. The *lpData* parameter must point to a WORD-sized count value.

MMPINFO_ACTIONLIST

Set the handle to the action-list array. The action list contains the script-channel commands for the movie. The *lpData* parameter must point to a handle that references a global memory block containing an array of **MMPACTION** records. The action-list information must be compatible with the MMP action-text block. See the documentation on the **MMPACTION** structure for information on the action-list format.

MMPINFO_ACTIONTEXT

Set the handle to the action-text block. The *lpData* parameter must point to a handle that references a global memory block containing a block of action text. The action text must be compatible with the MMP action-list information.

MMPINFO_ACTIONCOUNT

Set the count of action entries. The *lpData* parameter must point to a WORD-sized count value.

LPVOID   *lpData*

Specifies a far pointer to the data to supply to the Movie Player instance. The memory area pointed to by this parameter must be the correct size for the data item identified by the *nIndex* value.

WORD   *wLen*

Specifies the length of the memory location pointed to by the *lpData* parameter.

Return Value   Returns TRUE if successful; otherwise, returns FALSE.

Comments	For both the label and action-entry data, the three data items (label-list or action-list array, text block, and count value) are dependent on each other. When changing the label or action entry information, change all relevant data items as a single operation before yielding control.
See Also	**mmpGetInfo**

mmpSetMute

Syntax	BOOL **mmpSetMute**(*idMovie, bMuteOn*)
	This function disables or enables any sound playback produced by the Movie Player instance. This setting is associated with the Movie Player instance, not with the movie; loading a new movie into the Movie Player instance does not change the mute setting.
Parameters	MMPID *idMovie*
	Identifies the movie ID of the Movie Player instance.
	WORD *bMuteOn*
	Identifies whether to mute the sound. Set this to TRUE to turn off sound playback, or set it to FALSE to resume sound playback.
Return Value	Returns TRUE if successful, otherwise returns FALSE.
Comments	The mute setting affects the playback of sound cast members. The mute setting does not affect **mci** or **mciWait** script-channel commands, including those used to play streamed audio resources.
See Also	**mmpGetMute**

mmpSetRepeat

Syntax	BOOL **mmpSetRepeat**(*idMovie, bRepeat*)
	This function tells the Movie Player instance whether to continuously repeat the movie.
Parameters	MMPID *idMovie*
	Identifies the movie ID of the Movie Player instance.
	WORD *bRepeat*
	Indicates whether to automatically repeat the movie after the last frame. Set this to TRUE to repeat the movie or FALSE to turn off the automatic repeat.
Return Value	Returns TRUE if successful, otherwise returns FALSE.
Comments	If the repeat flag is set to TRUE, the Movie Player automatically rewinds and continues play after the last frame is shown.

See Also   mmpGetRepeat

mmpSetStage

Syntax   BOOL   **mmpSetStage**(*idMovie*, *hWndStage*, *lprectStage*, *wOptions*)

This function provides the playback window, or stage window, for the Movie Player instance. It also specifies the position and size of the playback region within the window. It brings the stage window to the foreground and optionally updates the current frame.

Parameters   MMPID   *idMovie*

Identifies the movie ID of the Movie Player instance.

HWND   *hWndStage*

Identifies the handle to the window to associate with the Movie Player instance.

LPRECT   *lprectStage*

Points to a **RECT** structure specifying the origin and extents of the playback area within the stage window.

The **top** and **left** fields of the **RECT** contain the offset of the playback area within the stage-window client area, and the **right** and **bottom** fields contain the extents.

If the movie as authored is larger than the specified extents, the playback area is clipped. If this parameter is NULL, the authored size of the movie is used.

WORD   *wOptions*

Specifies the following flags:

MMP_DRAW_FRAME

Draw the current frame to the stage window.

MMP_STAGE_OFFSET

Use the **RECT** structure pointed to by the *lprectStage* parameter to position and size the playback area.

MMP_STAGE_CENTER

Center the playback area in the window client area.

MMP_STAGE_BORDER

Draw a border around the playback area. Use the MMP_STAGE_CENTER or MMP_STAGE_OFFSET flags to provide room for the left and top borders.

The border consists of a shadow placed under the movie and over a backdrop of the Windows desktop color. The border is visible whenever the stage window is larger than the authored movie size; otherwise, portions of the border and movie are clipped by Windows.

MMP_STAGE_FIXED

> Fix the size and position of the movie playback area. When the window is resized, or when a new movie is loaded, the playback area remains fixed at either the size of the client area at the time **mmpSetStage** was called or, if the MMP_STAGE_OFFSET flag was specified, the offset and extents specified by the **RECT** values.

Return Value Returns TRUE if operation successful, otherwise returns FALSE.

Comments You can use any pop-up or overlapped window for the stage window.

The Movie Player must have a movie file loaded when you call this API; otherwise, the function fails and reports error code MMPERR_STAGE_ERROR.

See Also **mmpGetStage, mmpOpen**

---

mmpSetTempo

Syntax BOOL   **mmpSetTempo**(*idMovie*, *nTempo*)

This function changes the tempo value for the Movie Player instance.

Parameters MMPID   *idMovie*
Identifies the movie ID of the Movie Player instance.

int   *nTempo*
Specifies one of the following tempo values:

1 to 60

> Specifies a new tempo rate of *nTempo* frames per second. The frames-per-second setting continues to the first change-tempo command encountered in the tempo channel.

-1 through -120

> Specifies a delay value of -*nTempo* seconds for the current frame. The Movie Player waits -*nTempo* seconds before advancing to the next frame.

MMTEMPO_MOUSEWAIT

> Specifies to wait at the current frame. The Movie Player pauses the animation until the stage window receives a mouse click or keystroke.

Return Value Returns TRUE if successful, otherwise returns FALSE.

Comments If the tempo is locked, the **mmpSetTempo** command has no effect.

See Also **mmpGetTempo**

mmpStartAnimating

Syntax   BOOL   **mmpStartAnimating**(*idMovie*, *wOptions*)

This function notifies the Movie Player instance that animation is to begin. Actual frame advance is handled by the **mmpAnimate** function.

Parameters   MMPID   *idMovie*
Identifies the movie ID of the Movie Player instance.

WORD   *wOptions*
Specifies the following flags:

MMP_DRAW_FRAME
Draw the current frame to the stage window.

Return Value   Returns TRUE if successful. Returns FALSE if the animation is already running.

See Also   **mmpAnimate, mmpStopAnimating, mmpAnimStopped, mmpAnimStatus**

mmpStopAnimating

Syntax   BOOL   **mmpStopAnimating**(*idMovie*, *wOptions*)

This function notifies the Movie Player that animation is to stop.

Parameters   MMPID   *idMovie*
Identifies the movie ID of the Movie Player instance.

WORD   *wOptions*
Specifies the following flags:

MMP_DRAW_FRAME
Draw the next frame in the stage window.

Return Value   Returns TRUE if successful. Returns FALSE if the animation is not running.

See Also   **mmpStartAnimating, mmpAnimStopped, mmpAnimStatus**

mmpUpdate

Syntax   BOOL **mmpUpdate**(*idMovie*, *hDC*, *lprectArea*)

This function draws the current frame into the given display context. It is normally used to update an invalid rectangle on the stage window.

Parameters   MMPID *idMovie*
Identifies the movie ID of the Movie Player instance.

HDC *hDC*
Identifies the handle to the device context.

LPRECT *lprectArea*
Points to a **RECT** data structure that contains the rectangle to be updated.

Return Value   Returns TRUE if successful, otherwise returns FALSE.

mmsystemGetVersion

Syntax   WORD **mmsystemGetVersion**()

This function returns the current version number of the Multimedia extensions system software.

Parameters   None

Return Value   The return value specifies the major and minor version numbers of the Multimedia extensions. The high-order byte specifies the major version number. The low-order byte specifies the minor version number.

OutputDebugStr

Syntax   void **OutputDebugStr**(*lpOutputString*)

This function sends a debugging message directly to the COM1 port or to a secondary monochrome display adapter. Because it bypasses DOS, it can be called by low-level callback functions and other code at interrupt time.

Parameters   LPSTR *lpOutputString*
Specifies a far pointer to a null-terminated string.

Comments   This function is available only in the debugging version of the Multimedia extensions. The DebugOutput keyname in the [mmsystem] section of SYSTEM.INI controls where the debugging information is sent. If DebugOutput is 0, all debug output is disabled. If DebugOutput is 1, debug output is sent to the COM1 port. If DebugOutput is 2, debug output is sent to a secondary monochrome display adapter.

To print the contents of a register, use the pound sign (#) followed by one of the following register designations: "ax", "bx", "cx", "dx", "si", "di", "bp", "sp", "al", "bl", "cl", "dl". For example, to print the stack pointer and accumulator registers, pass the following string to **OutputDebugStr**:

```
"SP=#sp\r\nAX=#ax\r\n"
```

sndPlaySound

Syntax   BOOL   **sndPlaySound**(*lpszSoundName*, *wFlags*)

This function plays a waveform sound specified by a filename or by an entry in the [sounds] section of WIN.INI. If the sound can't be found, it plays the default sound specified by the SystemDefault entry in the [sounds] section of WIN.INI. If there is no SystemDefault entry or if the default sound can't be found, the function makes no sound and returns FALSE.

Parameters   LPSTR   *lpszSoundName*

Specifies the name of the sound to play. The function searches the [sounds] section of WIN.INI for an entry with this name and plays the associated waveform file. If no entry by this name exists, then it assumes the name is the name of a waveform file. If this parameter is NULL, any currently playing sound is stopped.

WORD   *wFlags*

Specifies options for playing the sound using one or more of the following flags:

SND_SYNC

The sound is played synchronously and the function does not return until the sound ends.

SND_ASYNC

The sound is played asynchronously and the function returns immediately after beginning the sound. To terminate an asynchronously-played sound, call **sndPlaySound** with *lpszSoundName* set to NULL.

SND_NODEFAULT

If the sound can't be found, the function returns silently without playing the default sound.

SND_MEMORY

The parameter specified by *lpszSoundName* points to an in-memory image of a waveform sound.

SND_LOOP

The sound will continue to play repeatedly until **sndPlaySound** is called again with the *lpszSoundName* parameter set to NULL. You must also specify the SND_ASYNC flag to loop sounds.

SND_NOSTOP

> If a sound is currently playing, the function will immediately return FALSE without playing the requested sound.

Return Value   Returns TRUE if the sound is played, otherwise returns FALSE.

Comments   The sound must fit in available physical memory and be playable by an installed waveform audio device driver. The directories searched for sound files are, in order: the current directory; the Windows directory; the Windows system directory; the directories listed in the PATH environment variable; the list of directories mapped in a network. See the Windows **OpenFile** function for more information about the directory search order.

If you specify the SND_MEMORY flag, *lpszSoundName* must point to an in-memory image of a waveform sound. If the sound is stored as a resource, use **LoadResource** and **LockResource** to load and lock the resource and get a pointer to it. If the sound is not a resource, you must use **GlobalAlloc** with the GMEM_MOVEABLE and GMEM_SHARE flags set and then **GlobalLock** to allocate and lock memory for the sound.

See Also   **MessageBeep**

---

timeBeginPeriod

Syntax   WORD   **timeBeginPeriod**(*wPeriod*)

This function sets the minimum (lowest number of milliseconds) timer resolution that an application or driver is going to use. Call this function immediately before starting to use timer-event services, and call **timeEndPeriod** immediately after finishing with the timer-event services.

Parameters   WORD   *wPeriod*
> Specifies the minimum timer-event resolution that the application or driver will use.

Return Value   Returns zero if successful. Returns TIMERR_NOCANDO if the specified *wPeriod* resolution value is out of range.

Comments   For each call to **timeBeginPeriod**, you must call **timeEndPeriod** with a matching *wPeriod* value. An application or driver can make multiple calls to **timeBeginPeriod**, as long as each **timeBeginPeriod** call is matched with a **timeEndPeriod** call.

See Also   **timeEndPeriod, timeSetEvent**

---

timeEndPeriod

Syntax   WORD   **timeEndPeriod**(*wPeriod*)

This function clears a previously set minimum (lowest number of milliseconds) timer resolution that an application or driver is going to use. Call this function immediately after using timer event services.

Parameters   WORD   *wPeriod*

Specifies the minimum timer-event resolution value specified in the previous call to **timeBeginPeriod**.

Return Value   Returns zero if successful. Returns TIMERR_NOCANDO if the specified *wPeriod* resolution value is out of range.

Comments   For each call to **timeBeginPeriod**, you must call **timeEndPeriod** with a matching *wPeriod* value. An application or driver can make multiple calls to **timeBeginPeriod**, as long as each **timeBeginPeriod** call is matched with a **timeEndPeriod** call.

See Also   **timeBeginPeriod**, **timeSetEvent**

timeGetDevCaps

Syntax   WORD   **timeGetDevCaps**(*lpTimeCaps*, *wSize*)

This function queries the timer device to determine its capabilities.

Parameters   LPTIMECAPS   *lpTimeCaps*

Specifies a far pointer to a **TIMECAPS** structure. This structure is filled with information about the capabilities of the timer device.

WORD   *wSize*

Specifies the size of the **TIMECAPS** structure.

Return Value   Returns zero if successful. Returns TIMERR_NOCANDO if it fails to return the timer device capabilities.

timeGetSystemTime

Syntax   WORD   **timeGetSystemTime**(*lpTime*, *wSize*)

This function retrieves the system time in milliseconds. The system time is the time elapsed since Windows was started.

Parameters   LPMMTIME   *lpTime*

Specifies a far pointer to an **MMTIME** data structure.

WORD   *wSize*

Specifies the size of the **MMTIME** structure.

Return Value   Returns zero. The system time is returned in the **ms** field of the **MMTIME** structure.

Comments   The time is always returned in milliseconds.

See Also   **timeGetTime**

timeGetTime

Syntax	DWORD **timeGetTime**()
	This function retrieves the system time in milliseconds. The system time is the time elapsed since Windows was started.
Parameters	None
Return Value	The return value is the system time in milliseconds.
Comments	The only difference between this function and the **timeGetSystemTime** function is **timeGetSystemTime** uses the standard multimedia time structure **MMTIME** to return the system time. The **timeGetTime** function has less overhead than **timeGetSystemTime**.
See Also	**timeGetSystemTime**

timeKillEvent

Syntax	WORD **timeKillEvent**(*wID*)
	This functions destroys a specified timer callback event.
Parameters	WORD *wID*
	Identifies the event to be destroyed.
Return Value	Returns zero if successful. Returns TIMERR_NOCANDO if the specified timer event does not exist.
Comments	The timer event ID specified by *wID* must be an ID returned by **timeSetEvent**.
See Also	**timeSetEvent**

timeSetEvent

Syntax	WORD **timeSetEvent**(*wDelay, wResolution, lpFunction, dwUser, wFlags*)
	This function sets up a timed callback event. The event can be a one-time event or a periodic event. Once activated, the event calls the specified callback function.
Parameters	WORD *wDelay*
	Specifies the event period in milliseconds. If the delay is less than the minimum period supported by the timer, or greater than the maximum period supported by the timer, the function returns an error.

WORD   *wResolution*

Specifies the accuracy of the delay in milliseconds. The resolution of the timer event increases with smaller *wResolution* values. To reduce system overhead, use the maximum *wResolution* value appropriate for your application.

LPTIMECALLBACK   *lpFunction*

Specifies the procedure address of a callback function that is called once upon expiration of a one-shot event or periodically upon expiration of periodic events.

DWORD   *dwUser*

Contains user-supplied callback data.

WORD   *wFlags*

Specifies the type of timer event, using one of the following flags:

TIME_ONESHOT

Event occurs once, after *wPeriod* milliseconds.

TIME_PERIODIC

Event occurs every *wPeriod* milliseconds.

Return Value   Returns an ID code that identifies the timer event. Returns NULL if the timer event was not created. The ID code is also passed to the callback function.

Comments   Using this function to generate a high-frequency periodic-delay event (with a period less than 10 milliseconds) can consume a significant portion of the system CPU bandwidth. Any call to **timeSetEvent** for a periodic-delay timer must be paired with a call to **timeKillEvent**.

The callback function must reside in a DLL. You don't have to use **MakeProcInstance** to get a procedure-instance address for the callback function.

Callback   void FAR PASCAL   **TimeFunc**(*wID*, *wMsg*, *dwUser*, *dw1*, *dw2*)

TimeFunc is a placeholder for the application-supplied function name. The actual name must be exported by including it in the EXPORTS statement of the module-definition file for the DLL.

Parameters

WORD   *wID*

The ID of the timer event. This is the ID returned by **timeSetEvent**.

WORD   *wMsg*

Not used.

DWORD   *dwUser*

User instance data supplied to the *dwUser* parameter of **timeSetEvent**.

DWORD *dw1*
> Not used.

DWORD *dw2*
> Not used.

Comments

Because the callback is accessed at interrupt time, it must reside in a DLL, and its code segment must be specified as FIXED in the module-definition file for the DLL. Any data that the callback accesses must be in a FIXED data segment as well. The callback may not make any system calls except for **PostMessage**, **timeGetSystemTime**, **timeGetTime**, **timeSetEvent**, **timeKillEvent**, **midiOutShortMsg**, **midiOutLongMsg**, and **OutputDebugStr**.

See Also   **timeKillEvent, timeBeginPeriod, timeEndPeriod**

waveInAddBuffer

Syntax   WORD   **waveInAddBuffer**(*hWaveIn*, *lpWaveInHdr*, *wSize*)

This function sends an input buffer to a waveform input device. When the buffer is filled, it is sent back to the application.

Parameters   HWAVEIN   *hWaveIn*
> Specifies a handle to the waveform input device.

LPWAVEHDR   *lpWaveInHdr*
> Specifies a far pointer to a **WAVEHDR** structure that identifies the buffer.

WORD   *wSize*
> Specifies the size of the **WAVEHDR** structure.

Return Value   Returns zero if the function was successful. Otherwise, it returns an error number. Possible error returns are:

MMSYSERR_INVALHANDLE
> Specified device handle is invalid.

WAVERR_UNPREPARED
> *lpWaveInHdr* hasn't been prepared.

Comments   The data buffer must be prepared with **waveInPrepareHeader** before it is passed to **waveInAddBuffer**. The **WAVEHDR** data structure and the data buffer pointed to by its **lpData** field must be allocated with **GlobalAlloc** using the GMEM_MOVEABLE and GMEM_SHARE flags, and locked with **GlobalLock**.

See Also   **waveInPrepareHeader**

waveInClose

Syntax

WORD **waveInClose**(*hWaveIn*)

This function closes the specified waveform input device.

Parameters

HWAVEIN *hWaveIn*

Specifies a handle to the waveform input device. If the function is successful, the handle is no longer valid after this call.

Return Value

Returns zero if the function was successful. Otherwise, it returns an error number. Possible error returns are:

MMSYSERR_INVALHANDLE

Specified device handle is invalid.

WAVERR_STILLPLAYING

There are still buffers in the queue.

Comments

If there are input buffers that have been sent with **waveInAddBuffer**, and haven't been returned to the application, the close operation will fail. Call **waveInReset** to mark all pending buffers as done.

See Also

waveInOpen, waveInReset

waveInGetDevCaps

Syntax

WORD **waveInGetDevCaps**(*wDeviceID*, *lpCaps*, *wSize*)

This function queries a specified waveform input device to determine its capabilities.

Parameters

WORD *wDeviceID*

Identifies the waveform input device.

LPWAVEINCAPS *lpCaps*

Specifies a far pointer to a **WAVEINCAPS** structure. This structure is filled with information about the capabilities of the device.

WORD *wSize*

Specifies the size of the **WAVEINCAPS** structure.

Return Value

Returns zero if the function was successful. Otherwise, it returns an error number. Possible error returns are:

MMSYSERR_BADDEVICEID

Specified device ID is out of range.

MMSYSERR_NODRIVER

The driver was not installed.

Comments   Use **waveInGetNumDevs** to determine the number of waveform input devices present in the system. The device ID specified by *wDeviceID* varies from zero to one less than the number of devices present. Only *wSize* bytes (or less) of information is copied to the location pointed to by *lpCaps*. If *wSize* is zero, nothing is copied, and the function returns zero.

See Also   **waveInGetNumDevs**

---

waveInGetErrorText

Syntax   WORD   **waveInGetErrorText**(*wError*, *lpText*, *wSize*)

This function retrieves a textual description of the error identified by the specified error number.

Parameters   WORD   *wError*

Specifies the error number.

LPSTR   *lpText*

Specifies a far pointer to the buffer to be filled with the textual error description.

WORD   *wSize*

Specifies the size of the buffer pointed to by *lpText*.

Return Value   Returns zero if the function was successful. Otherwise, it returns an error number. Possible error returns are:

MMSYSERR_BADERRNUM

Specified error number is out of range.

Comments   If the textual error description is longer than the buffer, the description is truncated. The returned string is always null-terminated. If *wSize* is zero, nothing is copied, and the function returns zero. All error descriptions are less than MAXERRORLENGTH characters long.

---

waveInGetID

Syntax   WORD   **waveInGetID**(*hWaveIn*, *lpwDeviceID*)

This function gets the device ID for a waveform input device.

Parameters   HWAVEIN   *hWaveIn*

Specifies the handle to the waveform input device.

LPWORD *lpwDeviceID*
> Specifies a pointer to the WORD-sized memory location to fill with the device ID.

Return Value
Returns zero if successful. Otherwise, it returns an error number. Possible error returns are:

MMSYSERR_INVALHANDLE
> The *hWaveIn* parameter specifies an invalid handle.

waveInGetNumDevs

Syntax
WORD **waveInGetNumDevs**()

This function returns the number of waveform input devices.

Parameters
None

Return Value
Returns the number of waveform input devices present in the system.

See Also
waveInGetDevCaps

waveInGetPosition

Syntax
WORD **waveInGetPosition**(*hWaveIn, lpInfo, wSize*)

This function retrieves the current input position of the specified waveform input device.

Parameters
HWAVEIN *hWaveIn*
> Specifies a handle to the waveform input device.

LPMMTIME *lpInfo*
> Specifies a far pointer to an **MMTIME** structure.

WORD *wSize*
> Specifies the size of the **MMTIME** structure.

Return Value
Returns zero if the function was successful. Possible error returns are:

MMSYSERR_INVALHANDLE
> Specified device handle is invalid.

Comments
Before calling **waveInGetPosition**, set the **wType** field of the **MMTIME** structure to indicate the time format that you desire. After calling **waveInGetPosition**, be sure to check the **wType** field to determine if the desired time format is supported. If the desired format is not supported, **wType** will specify an alternative format.

The position is set to zero when the device is opened or reset.

waveInOpen

Syntax   WORD   **waveInOpen**(*lphWaveIn*, *wDeviceID*, *lpFormat*, *dwCallback*, *dwCallbackInstance*, *dwFlags*)

This function opens a specified waveform input device for recording.

Parameters   LPHWAVEIN   *lphWaveIn*

Specifies a far pointer to a HWAVEIN handle. This location is filled with a handle identifying the opened waveform input device. Use this handle to identify the device when calling other waveform input functions. This parameter may be NULL if the WAVE_FORMAT_QUERY flag is specified for *dwFlags*.

WORD   *wDeviceID*

Identifies the waveform input device to open. Use a valid device ID or the following flag:

WAVE_MAPPER

If this flag is specified, the function selects a waveform input device capable of recording in the given format.

LPWAVEFORMAT   *lpFormat*

Specifies a pointer to a **WAVEFORMAT** data structure that identifies the desired format for recording waveform data.

DWORD   *dwCallback*

Specifies the address of a callback function or a handle to a window called during waveform recording to process messages related to the progress of recording.

DWORD   *dwCallbackInstance*

Specifies user instance data passed to the callback. This parameter is not used with window callbacks.

DWORD   *dwFlags*

Specifies flags for opening the device.

WAVE_FORMAT_QUERY

If this flag is specified, the device will be queried to determine if it supports the given format but will not actually be opened.

CALLBACK_WINDOW

If this flag is specified, *dwCallback* is assumed to be a window handle.

CALLBACK_FUNCTION

If this flag is specified, *dwCallback* is assumed to be a callback procedure address.

Return Value   Returns zero if the function was successful. Otherwise, it returns an error number. Possible error returns are:

MMSYSERR_NODRIVER
>   The driver was not installed.

MMSYSERR_BADDEVICEID
>   Specified device ID is out of range.

MMSYSERR_ALLOCATED
>   Specified resource is already allocated.

MMSYSERR_NOMEM
>   Unable to allocate or lock memory.

WAVERR_BADFORMAT
>   Attempted to open with an unsupported wave format.

Comments   Use **waveInGetNumDevs** to determine the number of waveform input devices present in the system. The device ID specified by *wDeviceID* varies from zero to one less than the number of devices present.

If a window is chosen to receive callback information, the following messages are sent to the window procedure function to indicate the progress of waveform input: **MM_WIM_OPEN, MM_WIM_CLOSE, MM_WIM_DATA**

If a function is chosen to receive callback information, the following messages are sent to the function to indicate the progress of waveform input: **WIM_OPEN, WIM_CLOSE, WIM_DATA**. The callback function must reside in a DLL. You do not have to use **MakeProcInstance** to get a procedure-instance address for the callback function.

Callback   void FAR PASCAL   **WaveInFunc**(*hWaveIn*, *wMsg*, *dwInstance*, *dwParam1*, *dwParam2*)

WaveInFunc is a placeholder for the application-supplied function name. The actual name must be exported by including it in an EXPORTS statement in the DLL's module-definition file.

Parameters

HWAVEIN   *hWaveIn*
>   Specifies a handle to the waveform device associated with the callback.

WORD   *wMsg*
>   Specifies a waveform input device.

DWORD   *dwInstance*
>   Specifies the user instance data specified with **waveInOpen**.

DWORD *dwParam1*

Specifies a parameter for the message.

DWORD *dwParam2*

Specifies a parameter for the message.

Comments

Because the callback is accessed at interrupt time, it must reside in a DLL and its code segment must be specified as FIXED in the module-definition file for the DLL. Any data that the callback accesses must be in a FIXED data segment as well. The callback may not make any system calls except for **PostMessage, timeGetSystemTime, timeGetTime, timeSetEvent, timeKillEvent, midiOutShortMsg, midiOutLongMsg**, and **OutputDebugStr**.

See Also   **waveInClose**

waveInPrepareHeader

Syntax   WORD **waveInPrepareHeader**(*hWaveIn*, *lpWaveInHdr*, *wSize*)

This function prepares a buffer for waveform input.

Parameters   HWAVEIN *hWaveIn*

Specifies a handle to the waveform input device.

LPWAVEHDR *lpWaveInHdr*

Specifies a pointer to a **WAVEHDR** structure that identifies the buffer to be prepared.

WORD *wSize*

Specifies the size of the **WAVEHDR** structure.

Return Value   Returns zero if the function was successful. Otherwise, it returns an error number. Possible error returns are:

MMSYSERR_INVALHANDLE

Specified device handle is invalid.

MMSYSERR_NOMEM

Unable to allocate or lock memory.

Comments   The **WAVEHDR** data structure and the data block pointed to by its **lpData** field must be allocated with **GlobalAlloc** using the GMEM_MOVEABLE and GMEM_SHARE flags, and locked with **GlobalLock**. Preparing a header that has already been prepared will have no effect, and the function will return zero.

See Also   **waveInUnprepareHeader**

waveInReset

Syntax
WORD   **waveInReset**(*hWaveIn*)

This function stops input on a given waveform input device and resets the current position to 0. All pending buffers are marked as done and returned to the application.

Parameters
HWAVEIN   *hWaveIn*
Specifies a handle to the waveform input device.

Return Value
Returns zero if the function was successful. Otherwise, it returns an error number. Possible error returns are:

MMSYSERR_INVALHANDLE
Specified device handle is invalid.

See Also
waveInStart, waveInStop, waveInAddBuffer, waveInClose

waveInStart

Syntax
WORD   **waveInStart**(*hWaveIn*)

This function starts input on the specified waveform input device.

Parameters
HWAVEIN   *hWaveIn*
Specifies a handle to the waveform input device.

Return Value
Returns zero if the function was successful. Otherwise, it returns an error number. Possible error returns are:

MMSYSERR_INVALHANDLE
Specified device handle is invalid.

Comments
Buffers are returned to the client when full or when **waveInReset** is called (the **dwBytesRecorded** field in the header will contain the actual length of data). If there are no buffers in the queue, the data is thrown away without notification to the client, and input continues.

Calling this function when input is already started has no effect, and the function returns zero.

See Also
waveInStop, waveInReset

waveInStop

Syntax   WORD   **waveInStop**(*hWaveIn*)

This function stops waveform input.

Parameters   HWAVEIN   *hWaveIn*
Specifies a handle to the waveform input device.

Return Value   Returns zero if the function was successful. Otherwise, it returns an error number. Possible error returns are:

MMSYSERR_INVALHANDLE
Specified device handle is invalid.

Comments   If there are any buffers in the queue, the current buffer will be marked as done (the **dwBytesRecorded** field in the header will contain the actual length of data), but any empty buffers in the queue will remain there. Calling this function when input is not started has no effect, and the function returns zero.

See Also   **waveInStart**, **waveInReset**

waveInUnprepareHeader

Syntax   WORD   **waveInUnprepareHeader**(*hWaveIn*, *lpWaveInHdr*, *wSize*)

This function cleans up the preparation performed by **waveInPrepareHeader**. The function must be called after the device driver fills a data buffer and returns it to the application. You must call this function before freeing the data buffer.

Parameters   HWAVEIN   *hWaveIn*
Specifies a handle to the waveform input device.

LPWAVEHDR   *lpWaveInHdr*
Specifies a pointer to a **WAVEHDR** structure identifying the data buffer to be cleaned up.

WORD   *wSize*
Specifies the size of the **WAVEHDR** structure.

Return Value   Returns zero if the function was successful. Otherwise, it returns an error number. Possible error returns are:

MMSYSERR_INVALHANDLE
Specified device handle is invalid.

WAVERR_STILLPLAYING
lpWaveInHdr is still in the queue.

Comments This function is the complementary function to **waveInPrepareHeader**. You must call this function before freeing the data buffer with **GlobalFree**. After passing a buffer to the device driver with **waveInAddBuffer**, you must wait until the driver is finished with the buffer before calling **waveInUnprepareHeader**. Unpreparing a buffer that has not been prepared has no effect, and the function returns zero.

See Also **waveInPrepareHeader**

waveOutBreakLoop

Syntax WORD **waveOutBreakLoop**(*hWaveOut*)

This function breaks a loop on a given waveform output device and allows playback to continue with the next block in the driver list.

Parameters HWAVEOUT *hWaveOut*
Specifies a handle to the waveform output device.

Return Value Returns zero if the function was successful. Otherwise, it returns an error number. Possible error returns are:

MMSYSERR_INVALHANDLE
Specified device handle is invalid.

Comments Waveform looping is controlled by the **dwLoops** and **dwFlags** fields in the **WAVEHDR** structures passed to the device with **waveOutWrite**. Use the WHDR_BEGINLOOP and WHDR_ENDLOOP flags in the **dwFlags** field to specify the beginning and ending data blocks for looping.

To loop on a single block, specify both flags for the same block. To specify the number of loops, use the **dwLoops** field in the **WAVEHDR** structure for the first block in the loop.

The blocks making up the loop are played to the end before the loop is terminated.

Calling this function when the nothing is playing or looping has no effect, and the function returns zero.

See Also **waveOutWrite, waveOutPause, waveOutRestart**

waveOutClose

Syntax	WORD **waveOutClose**(*hWaveOut*)

This function closes the specified waveform output device.

Parameters   HWAVEOUT   *hWaveOut*
> Specifies a handle to the waveform output device. If the function is successful, the handle is no longer valid after this call.

Return Value   Returns zero if the function was successful. Otherwise, it returns an error number. Possible error returns are:

MMSYSERR_INVALHANDLE
> Specified device handle is invalid.

WAVERR_STILLPLAYING
> There are still buffers in the queue.

Comments   If the device is still playing a waveform, the close operation will fail. Use **waveOutReset** to terminate waveform playback before calling **waveOutClose**.

See Also   **waveOutOpen**, **waveOutReset**

waveOutGetDevCaps

Syntax	WORD **waveOutGetDevCaps**(*wDeviceID*, *lpCaps*, *wSize*)

This function queries a specified waveform device to determine its capabilities.

Parameters   WORD   *wDeviceID*
> Identifies the waveform output device.

LPWAVEOUTCAPS   *lpCaps*
> Specifies a far pointer to a **WAVEOUTCAPS** structure. This structure is filled with information about the capabilities of the device.

WORD   *wSize*
> Specifies the size of the **WAVEOUTCAPS** structure.

Return Value   Returns zero if the function was successful. Otherwise, it returns an error number. Possible error returns are:

MMSYSERR_BADDEVICEID
> Specified device ID is out of range.

MMSYSERR_NODRIVER
   The driver was not installed.

Comments   Use **waveOutGetNumDevs** to determine the number of waveform output devices present in the system. The device ID specified by *wDeviceID* varies from zero to one less than the number of devices present. Only *wSize* bytes (or less) of information is copied to the location pointed to by *lpCaps*. If *wSize* is zero, nothing is copied, and the function returns zero.

See Also   **waveOutGetNumDevs**

waveOutGetErrorText

Syntax   WORD   **waveOutGetErrorText**(*wError, lpText, wSize*)

This function retrieves a textual description of the error identified by the specified error number.

Parameters   WORD   *wError*
   Specifies the error number.

   LPSTR   *lpText*
   Specifies a far pointer to a buffer to be filled with the textual error description.

   WORD   *wSize*
   Specifies the length of the buffer pointed to by *lpText*.

Return Value   Returns zero if the function was successful. Otherwise, it returns an error number. Possible error returns are:

MMSYSERR_BADERRNUM
   Specified error number is out of range.

Comments   If the textual error description is longer than the specified buffer, the description is truncated. The returned error string is always null-terminated. If *wSize* is zero, nothing is copied, and the function returns zero. All error descriptions are less than MAXERRORLENGTH characters long.

waveOutGetID

Syntax   WORD   **waveOutGetID**(*hWaveOut, lpwDeviceID*)

This function gets the device ID for a waveform output device.

Parameters   HWAVEOUT   *hWaveOut*
   Specifies the handle to the waveform output device.

LPWORD *lpwDeviceID*
> Specifies a pointer to the WORD-sized memory location to be filled with the device ID.

Return Value   Returns zero if successful. Otherwise, it returns an error number. Possible error returns are:

MMSYSERR_INVALHANDLE
> The *hWaveOut* parameter specifies an invalid handle.

waveOutGetNumDevs

Syntax   WORD **waveOutGetNumDevs**()

This function retrieves the number of waveform output devices present in the system.

Parameters   None

Return Value   Returns the number of waveform output devices present in the system.

See Also   **waveOutGetDevCaps**

waveOutGetPitch

Syntax   WORD **waveOutGetPitch**(*hWaveOut, lpdwPitch*)

This function queries the the current pitch setting of a waveform output device.

Parameters   HWAVEOUT *hWaveOut*
> Specifies a handle to the waveform output device.

LPDWORD *lpdwPitch*
> Specifies a far pointer to a location to be filled with the current pitch multiplier setting. The pitch multiplier indicates the current change in pitch from the original authored setting. The pitch multiplier must be a positive value.

> The pitch multiplier is specified as a fixed-point value. The high-order word of the DWORD location contains the signed integer part of the number, and the low-order word contains the fractional part. The fraction is expressed as a WORD in which a value of 0x8000 represents one half, and 0x4000 represents one quarter. For example, the value 0x00010000 specifies a multiplier of 1.0 (no pitch change), and a value of 0x000F8000 specifies a multiplier of 15.5.

Return Value   Returns zero if the function was successful. Otherwise, it returns an error number. Possible error returns are:

MMSYSERR_INVALHANDLE
> Specified device handle is invalid.

MMSYSERR_NOTSUPPORTED
Function isn't supported.

Comments   Changing the pitch does not change the playback rate, sample rate, or playback time. Not all devices support pitch changes. To determine whether the device supports pitch control, use the WAVECAPS_PITCH flag to test the **dwSupport** field of the **WAVEOUTCAPS** structure (filled by **waveOutGetDevCaps**).

See Also   **waveOutSetPitch, waveOutGetPlaybackRate, waveOutSetPlaybackRate**

waveOutGetPlaybackRate

Syntax   WORD   **waveOutGetPlaybackRate**(*hWaveOut*, *lpdwRate*)

This function queries the current playback rate setting of a waveform output device.

Parameters   HWAVEOUT   *hWaveOut*
Specifies a handle to the waveform output device.

LPDWORD   *lpdwRate*
Specifies a far pointer to a location to be filled with the current playback rate. The playback rate setting is a multiplier indicating the current change in playback rate from the original authored setting. The playback rate multiplier must be a positive value.

The rate is specified as a fixed-point value. The high-order word of the DWORD location contains the signed integer part of the number, and the low-order word contains the fractional part. The fraction is expressed as a WORD in which a value of 0x8000 represents one half, and 0x4000 represents one quarter. For example, the value 0x00010000 specifies a multiplier of 1.0 (no playback rate change), and a value of 0x000F8000 specifies a multiplier of 15.5.

Return Value   Returns zero if the function was successful. Otherwise, it returns an error number. Possible error returns are:

MMSYSERR_INVALHANDLE
Specified device handle is invalid.

MMSYSERR_NOTSUPPORTED
Function isn't supported.

Comments   Changing the playback rate does not change the sample rate but does change the playback time.

Not all devices support playback rate changes. To determine whether a device supports playback rate changes, use the WAVECAPS_PLAYBACKRATE flag to test the **dwSupport** field of the **WAVEOUTCAPS** structure (filled by **waveOutGetDevCaps**).

See Also   **waveOutSetPlaybackRate, waveOutSetPitch, waveOutGetPitch**

waveOutGetPosition

Syntax
WORD **waveOutGetPosition**(*hWaveOut*, *lpInfo*, *wSize*)

This function retrieves the current playback position of the specified waveform output device.

Parameters
HWAVEOUT *hWaveOut*
Specifies a handle to the waveform output device.

LPMMTIME *lpInfo*
Specifies a far pointer to an **MMTIME** structure.

WORD *wSize*
Specifies the size of the **MMTIME** structure.

Return Value
Returns zero if the function was successful. Otherwise, it returns an error number. Possible error returns are:

MMSYSERR_INVALHANDLE
Specified device handle is invalid.

Comments
Before calling **waveOutGetPosition**, set the **wType** field of the MMTIME structure to indicate the time format that you desire. After calling **waveOutGetPosition**, check the **wType** field to determine if the desired time format is supported. If the desired format is not supported, **wType** will specify an alternative format.

The position is set to zero when the device is opened or reset.

waveOutGetVolume

Syntax
WORD **waveOutGetVolume**(*wDeviceID*, *lpdwVolume*)

This function queries the current volume setting of a waveform output device.

Parameters
WORD *wDeviceID*
Identifies the waveform output device.

LPDWORD *lpdwVolume*
Specifies a far pointer to a location to be filled with the current volume setting. The low-order word of this location contains the left channel volume setting, and the high-order word contains the right channel setting. A value of 0xFFFF represents full volume, and a value of 0x0000 is silence.

If a device does not support both left and right volume control, the low-order word of the specified location contains the mono volume level.

The full 16-bit setting(s) set with **waveOutSetVolume** is returned, regardless of whether the device supports the full 16 bits of volume-level control.

Return Value   Returns zero if the function was successful. Otherwise, it returns an error number. Possible error returns are:

MMSYSERR_INVALHANDLE
    Specified device handle is invalid.

MMSYSERR_NOTSUPPORTED
    Function isn't supported.

MMSYSERR_NODRIVER
    The driver was not installed.

Comments   Not all devices support volume changes. To determine whether the device supports volume control, use the WAVECAPS_VOLUME flag to test the **dwSupport** field of the **WAVEOUTCAPS** structure (filled by **waveOutGetDevCaps**).

To determine whether the device supports volume control on both the left and right channels, use the WAVECAPS_VOLUME flag to test the **dwSupport** field of the **WAVEOUTCAPS** structure (filled by **waveOutGetDevCaps**).

See Also   **waveOutSetVolume**

---

waveOutOpen

Syntax   WORD   **waveOutOpen**(*lphWaveOut*, *wDeviceID*, *lpFormat*, *dwCallback*, *dwCallbackInstance*, *dwFlags*)

This function opens a specified waveform output device for playback.

Parameters   LPHWAVEOUT   *lphWaveOut*

Specifies a far pointer to an HWAVEOUT handle. This location is filled with a handle identifying the opened waveform output device. Use the handle to identify the device when calling other waveform output functions. This parameter may be NULL if the WAVE_FORMAT_QUERY flag is specified for *dwFlags*.

WORD   *wDeviceID*

Identifies the waveform output device to open. Use a valid device ID or the following flag:

WAVE_MAPPER

If this flag is specified, the function selects a waveform output device capable of playing the given format.

LPWAVEFORMAT   *lpFormat*

Specifies a pointer to a **WAVEFORMAT** structure that identifies the format of the waveform data to be sent to the waveform output device.

DWORD *dwCallback*

Specifies the address of a callback function or a handle to a window called during waveform playback to process messages related to the progress of the playback. Specify NULL for this parameter if no callback is desired.

DWORD *dwCallbackInstance*

Specifies user instance data passed to the callback. This parameter is not used with window callbacks.

DWORD *dwFlags*

Specifies flags for opening the device.

WAVE_FORMAT_QUERY

If this flag is specified, the device is be queried to determine if it supports the given format but is not actually opened.

CALLBACK_WINDOW

If this flag is specified, *dwCallback* is assumed to be a window handle.

CALLBACK_FUNCTION

If this flag is specified, *dwCallback* is assumed to be a callback procedure address.

Return Value Returns zero if the function was successful. Otherwise, it returns an error number. Possible error returns are:

MMSYSERR_BADDEVICEID

Specified device ID is out of range.

MMSYSERR_ALLOCATED

Specified resource is already allocated.

MMSYSERR_NOMEM

Unable to allocate or lock memory.

WAVERR_BADFORMAT

Attempted to open with an unsupported wave format.

Comments Use **waveOutGetNumDevs** to determine the number of waveform output devices present in the system. The device ID specified by *wDeviceID* varies from zero to one less than the number of devices present.

The **WAVEFORMAT** structure pointed to by *lpFormat* may be extended to include type-specific information for certain data formats. For example, for PCM data, an extra WORD is added to specify the number of bits per sample. Use the **PCMWAVEFORMAT** structure in this case.

If a window is chosen to receive callback information, the following messages are sent to the window procedure function to indicate the progress of waveform output: **MM_WOM_OPEN**, **MM_WOM_CLOSE**, **MM_WOM_DONE**

If a function is chosen to receive callback information, the following messages are sent to the function to indicate the progress of waveform output: **WOM_OPEN**, **WOM_CLOSE**, **WOM_DONE**. The callback function must reside in a DLL. You do not have to use **MakeProcInstance** to get a procedure-instance address for the callback function.

Callback

void FAR PASCAL   **WaveOutFunc**(*hWaveOut*, *wMsg*, *dwInstance*, *dwParam1*, *dwParam2*)

WaveOutFunc is a placeholder for the application-supplied function name. The actual name must be exported by including it in an EXPORTS statement in the DLL's module-definition file.

Parameters

HWAVEOUT   *hWaveOut*
> Specifies a handle to the waveform device associated with the callback.

WORD   *wMsg*
> Specifies a waveform output message.

DWORD   *dwInstance*
> Specifies the user instance data specified with **waveOutOpen**.

DWORD   *dwParam1*
> Specifies a parameter for the message.

DWORD   *dwParam2*
> Specifies a parameter for the message.

Comments

Because the callback is accessed at interrupt time, it must reside in a DLL and its code segment must be specified as FIXED in the module-definition file for the DLL. Any data that the callback accesses must be in a FIXED data segment as well. The callback may not make any system calls except for **PostMessage**, **timeGetSystemTime**, **timeGetTime**, **timeSetEvent**, **timeKillEvent**, **midiOutShortMsg**, **midiOutLongMsg**, and **OutputDebugStr**.

See Also   **waveOutClose**

waveOutPause

Syntax	WORD **waveOutPause**(*hWaveOut*)

This function pauses playback on a specified waveform output device. The current playback position is saved. Use **waveOutRestart** to resume playback from the current playback position.

Parameters

HWAVEOUT   *hWaveOut*
> Specifies a handle to the waveform output device.

Return Value

Returns zero if the function was successful. Otherwise, it returns an error number. Possible error returns are:

MMSYSERR_INVALHANDLE
> Specified device handle is invalid.

Comments

Calling this function when the output is already paused has no effect, and the function returns zero.

See Also

waveOutRestart, waveOutBreakLoop

waveOutPrepareHeader

Syntax	WORD **waveOutPrepareHeader**(*hWaveOut*, *lpWaveOutHdr*, *wSize*)

This function prepares a waveform data block for playback.

Parameters

HWAVEOUT   *hWaveOut*
> Specifies a handle to the waveform output device.

LPWAVEHDR   *lpWaveOutHdr*
> Specifies a pointer to a **WAVEHDR** structure that identifies the data block to be prepared.

WORD   *wSize*
> Specifies the size of the **WAVEHDR** structure.

Return Value

Returns zero if the function was successful. Otherwise, it returns an error number. Possible error returns are:

MMSYSERR_INVALHANDLE
> Specified device handle is invalid.

MMSYSERR_NOMEM
> Unable to allocate or lock memory.

Comments   The **WAVEHDR** data structure and the data block pointed to by its **lpData** field must be allocated with **GlobalAlloc** using the GMEM_MOVEABLE and GMEM_SHARE flags, and locked with **GlobalLock**. Preparing a header that has already been prepared has no effect, and the function returns zero.

See Also   **waveOutUnprepareHeader**

waveOutReset

Syntax   WORD   **waveOutReset**(*hWaveOut*)

This function stops playback on a given waveform output device and resets the current position to 0. All pending playback buffers are marked as done and returned to the application.

Parameters   HWAVEOUT   *hWaveOut*
  Specifies a handle to the waveform output device.

Return Value   Returns zero if the function was successful. Otherwise, it returns an error number. Possible error returns are:

MMSYSERR_INVALHANDLE
  Specified device handle is invalid.

See Also   **waveOutWrite, waveOutClose**

waveOutRestart

Syntax   WORD   **waveOutRestart**(*hWaveOut*)

This function restarts a paused waveform output device.

Parameters   HWAVEOUT   *hWaveOut*
  Specifies a handle to the waveform output device.

Return Value   Returns zero if the function was successful. Otherwise, it returns an error number. Possible error returns are:

MMSYSERR_INVALHANDLE
  Specified device handle is invalid.

Comments   Calling this function when the output is not paused has no effect, and the function returns zero.

See Also   **waveOutPause, waveOutBreakLoop**

waveOutSetPitch

Syntax

WORD **waveOutSetPitch**(*hWaveOut*, *dwPitch*)

This function sets the pitch of a waveform output device.

Parameters

HWAVEOUT *hWaveOut*

Specifies a handle to the waveform output device.

DWORD *dwPitch*

Specifies the new pitch multiplier setting. The pitch multiplier setting indicates the current change in pitch from the original authored setting. The pitch multiplier must be a positive value.

The pitch multiplier is specified as a fixed-point value. The high-order word location contains the signed integer part of the number, and the low-order word contains the fractional part. The fraction is expressed as a WORD in which a value of 0x8000 represents one half, and 0x4000 represents one quarter. For example, the value 0x00010000 specifies a multiplier of 1.0 (no pitch change), and a value of 0x000F8000 specifies a multiplier of 15.5.

Return Value

Returns zero if the function was successful. Otherwise, it returns an error number. Possible error returns are:

MMSYSERR_INVALHANDLE

Specified device handle is invalid.

MMSYSERR_NOTSUPPORTED

Function isn't supported.

Comments

Changing the pitch does not change the playback rate or the sample rate. The playback time is also unchanged. Not all devices support pitch changes. To determine whether the device supports pitch control, use the WAVECAPS_PITCH flag to test the **dwSupport** field of the **WAVEOUTCAPS** structure (filled by **waveOutGetDevCaps**).

See Also

waveOutGetPitch, **waveOutSetPlaybackRate**, **waveOutGetPlaybackRate**

waveOutSetPlaybackRate

Syntax

WORD   **waveOutSetPlaybackRate**(*hWaveOut*, *dwRate*)

This function sets the playback rate of a waveform output device.

Parameters

HWAVEOUT   *hWaveOut*
Specifies a handle to the waveform output device.

DWORD   *dwRate*
Specifies the new playback rate setting. The playback rate setting is a multiplier indicating the current change in playback rate from the original authored setting. The playback rate multiplier must be a positive value.

The rate is specified as a fixed-point value. The high-order word contains the signed integer part of the number, and the low-order word contains the fractional part. The fraction is expressed as a WORD in which a value of 0x8000 represents one half, and 0x4000 represents one quarter. For example, the value 0x00010000 specifies a multiplier of 1.0 (no playback rate change), and a value of 0x000F8000 specifies a multiplier of 15.5.

Return Value

Returns zero if the function was successful. Otherwise, it returns an error number. Possible error returns are:

MMSYSERR_INVALHANDLE
Specified device handle is invalid.

MMSYSERR_NOTSUPPORTED
Function isn't supported.

Comments

Changing the playback rate does not change the sample rate but does change the playback time.

Not all devices support playback rate changes. To determine whether a device supports playback rate changes, use the WAVECAPS_PLAYBACKRATE flag to test the **dwSupport** field of the **WAVEOUTCAPS** structure (filled by **waveOutGetDevCaps**).

See Also

waveOutGetPlaybackRate, **waveOutSetPitch**, **waveOutGetPitch**

waveOutSetVolume

Syntax WORD **waveOutSetVolume**(*wDeviceID*, *dwVolume*)

This function sets the volume of a waveform output device.

Parameters WORD *wDeviceID*
Identifies the waveform output device.

DWORD *dwVolume*
Specifies the new volume setting. The low-order word contains the left channel volume setting, and the high-order word contains the right channel setting. A value of 0xFFFF represents full volume, and a value of 0x0000 is silence.

If a device does not support both left and right volume control, the low-order word of *dwVolume* specifies the volume level, and the high-order word is ignored.

Return Value Returns zero if the function was successful. Otherwise, it returns an error number. Possible error returns are:

MMSYSERR_INVALHANDLE
Specified device handle is invalid.

MMSYSERR_NOTSUPPORTED
Function isn't supported.

MMSYSERR_NODRIVER
The driver was not installed.

Comments Not all devices support volume changes. To determine whether the device supports volume control, use the WAVECAPS_VOLUME flag to test the **dwSupport** field of the **WAVEOUTCAPS** structure (filled by **waveOutGetDevCaps**).

To determine whether the device supports volume control on both the left and right channels, use the WAVECAPS_LRVOLUME flag flag to test the **dwSupport** field of the **WAVEOUTCAPS** structure (filled by **waveOutGetDevCaps**).

Most devices don't support the full 16 bits of volume level control and will not use the high-order bits of the requested volume setting. For example, for a device that supports 4 bits of volume control, requested volume level values of 0x4000, 0x4fff, and 0x43be all produce the same physical volume setting, 0x4000. The **waveOutGetVolume** function returns the full 16-bit setting set with **waveOutSetVolume**.

Volume settings are interpreted logarithmically. This means the perceived increase in volume is the same when increasing the volume level from 0x5000 to 0x6000 as it is from 0x4000 to 0x5000.

See Also **waveOutGetVolume**

waveOutUnprepareHeader

Syntax

WORD   **waveOutUnprepareHeader**(*hWaveOut*, *lpWaveOutHdr*, *wSize*)

This function cleans up the preparation performed by **waveOutPrepareHeader**. The function must be called after the device driver is finished with a data block. You must call this function before freeing the data buffer.

Parameters

HWAVEOUT   *hWaveOut*
Specifies a handle to the waveform output device.

LPWAVEHDR   *lpWaveOutHdr*
Specifies a pointer to a **WAVEHDR** structure identifying the data block to be cleaned up.

WORD   *wSize*
Specifies the size of the **WAVEHDR** structure.

Return Value

Returns zero if the function was successful. Otherwise, it returns an error number. Possible error returns are:

MMSYSERR_INVALHANDLE
Specified device handle is invalid.

WAVERR_STILLPLAYING
lpWaveOutHdr is still in the queue.

Comments

This function is the complementary function to **waveOutPrepareHeader**. You must call this function before freeing the data buffer with **GlobalFree**. After passing a buffer to the device driver with **waveOutWrite**, you must wait until the driver is finished with the buffer before calling **waveOutUnprepareHeader**.

Unpreparing a buffer that has not been prepared has no effect, and the function returns zero.

See Also

waveOutPrepareHeader

waveOutWrite

Syntax   WORD   **waveOutWrite**(*hWaveOut*, *lpWaveOutHdr*, *wSize*)

This function sends a data block to the specified waveform output device.

Parameters   HWAVEOUT   *hWaveOut*
Specifies a handle to the waveform output device.

LPWAVEHDR   *lpWaveOutHdr*
Specifies a far pointer to a **WAVEHDR** structure containing information about
the data block.

WORD   *wSize*
Specifies the size of the **WAVEHDR** structure.

Return Value   Returns zero if the function was successful. Otherwise, it returns an error number. Possible
error returns are:

MMSYSERR_INVALHANDLE
Specified device handle is invalid.

WAVERR_UNPREPARED
lpWaveOutHdr hasn't been prepared.

Comments   The data buffer must be prepared with **waveOutPrepareHeader** before it is passed to
waveOutWrite. The **WAVEHDR** data structure and the data buffer pointed to by its
lpData field must be allocated with **GlobalAlloc** using the GMEM_MOVEABLE and
GMEM_SHARE flags, and locked with **GlobalLock**. Unless the device is paused by
calling **waveOutPause**, playback begins when the first data block is sent to the device.

See Also   **waveOutPrepareHeader, waveOutPause, waveOutReset, waveOutRestart**

C h a p t e r   4
Message Overview

This chapter gives an overview of the messages in the Multimedia extensions to Windows. The messages are organized into the following categories, some of which contain smaller groups of related messages:

- Audio Messages

- Media Control Interface Messages

- Joystick Messages

- File I/O Messages

- Movie Player Messages

- Screen Saver Messages

For detailed information on any of the messages listed in this chapter, see Chapter 5, "Message Directory." Chapter 5 is an alphabetical listing of the messages in the Multimedia extensions to Windows.

About Multimedia Extensions Messages

The messages in the Multimedia extensions fall into two broad categories:

- Messages sent to windows. These are processed by window functions and are similar to the messages defined in the WINDOWS.H header file. The Multimedia extensions messages that are sent to windows all have an MM_ prefix.

- Messages specific to a callback function or message-based API. Thesc include Media Control Interface command messages, which an application sends to communicate with MCI, as well as messages sent to callback functions.

All the Multimedia extensions messages have a related set of parameters. This chapter describes each message in detail.

Audio Messages

Audio messages are sent by low-level audio device drivers to an application so that the application can manage audio playback and recording. An application may choose to have audio messages sent either to a window, or to a low-level callback function. There is a set of messages for windows and a parallel set of messages for low-level callback functions. The Multimedia extensions provide the following groups of audio messages:

- Waveform Output Messages
- Waveform Input Messages
- MIDI Output Messages
- MIDI Input Messages

Waveform Output Messages

Waveform output messages are sent by audio device drivers to an application to inform the application about the status of waveform output operations. By specifying flags with the **waveOutOpen** function, applications may choose to have messages sent either to a window or to a low-level callback function. Use these messages to manage waveform playback:

MM_WOM_CLOSE

Sent to a window when a waveform output device is closed.

MM_WOM_DONE

Sent to a window when a data block has been played and is being returned to the application.

MM_WOM_OPEN

Sent to a window when a waveform output device is opened.

WOM_CLOSE

Sent to a low-level callback function when a waveform output device is closed.

WOM_DONE

Sent to a low-level callback function when a data block has been played and is being returned to the application.

WOM_OPEN

Sent to a low-level callback function when a waveform output device is opened.

Waveform Input Messages

Waveform input messages are sent by audio device drivers to an application to inform the application about the status of waveform input operations. By specifying flags with the **waveInOpen** function, applications may choose to have messages sent either to a window or to a low-level callback function. Use these messages to manage waveform audio recording:

MM_WIM_CLOSE

Sent to a window when a waveform input device is closed.

MM_WIM_DATA

Sent to a window when an input data buffer is full and is being returned to the application.

MM_WIM_OPEN

Sent to a window when a waveform input device is opened.

WIM_CLOSE

Sent to a low-level callback function when a waveform input device is closed.

WIM_DATA

Sent to a low-level callback function when an input data buffer is full and is being returned to the application.

WIM_OPEN

Sent to a low-level callback function when a waveform input device is opened.

MIDI Output Messages

MIDI output messages are sent by audio device drivers to an application to inform the application about the status of MIDI output operations. By specifying flags with the **midiOutOpen** function, applications may choose to have messages sent either to a window or to a low-level callback function. Use these messages to manage MIDI output:

MM_MOM_CLOSE

Sent to a window when a MIDI output device is closed.

MM_MOM_DONE

Sent to a window when a MIDI system exclusive data block has been played and is being returned to the application.

MM_MOM_OPEN

Sent to a window when a MIDI output device is opened.

MOM_CLOSE

Sent to a low-level callback function when a MIDI output device is closed.

MOM_DONE

Sent to a low-level callback function when a MIDI system exclusive data block has been played and is being returned to the application.

MOM_OPEN

Sent to a low-level callback function when a MIDI output device is opened.

MIDI Input Messages

MIDI input messages are sent by audio device drivers to an application to inform the application about the status of MIDI input operations. By specifying flags with the **midiInOpen** function, applications may choose to have messages sent either to a window or to a low-level callback function. Use these messages to manage MIDI input:

MM_MIM_CLOSE

Sent to a window when a MIDI input device is closed.

MM_MIM_DATA

Sent to a window when a MIDI message is received by the device.

MM_MIM_ERROR

Sent to a window when an invalid MIDI message is received by the device.

MM_MIM_LONGERROR

Sent to a window when an invalid MIDI system exclusive message is received by the device.

MM_MIM_LONGDATA

Sent to a window when a MIDI system exclusive data buffer is filled and is being returned to the application.

MM_MIM_OPEN

Sent to a low-level callback function when a MIDI input device is opened.

MIM_OPEN

Sent to a window when a MIDI input device is opened.

MIM_CLOSE

Sent to a low-level callback function when a MIDI input device is closed.

MIM_DATA

Sent to a low-level callback function when a MIDI message is received by the device. The parameters to this message include a timestamp specifying the time that the MIDI message was received.

MIM_ERROR

Sent to a low-level callback function when an invalid MIDI message is received by the device.

MIM_LONGERROR

Sent to a low-level callback function when an invalid MIDI system exclusive message is received by the device.

MIM_LONGDATA

Sent to a low-level callback function when a MIDI system exclusive message is received by the device. The parameters to this message include a timestamp specifying the time that the MIDI message was received.

Media Control Interface Messages

Media Control Interface (MCI) messages control MCI devices and obtain information about device configuration and capabilities. Applications use the **mciSendCommand** function to send MCI command messages to MCI devices. MCI has the following groups of command messages:

- System Command Messages
- Required Command Messages
- Basic Command Messages
- Extended Command Messages

MCI also uses a window notification message to inform your application when an MCI command completes. If you want MCI notification, your application must specify a window to handle the notification message.

System Command Messages

System command messages are interpreted directly by MCI. These messages do not rely on the ability of a device to respond to them.

MCI_BREAK

Sent by an application to set a break key for a specified device.

MCI_SOUND

Sent by an application to play sounds identified by entries in the [sounds] section of WIN.INI.

MCI_SYSINFO

Sent by an application to obtain system-related information about a device.

Required Command Messages

Required command messages are supported by all MCI devices. These messages open, close, and obtain information about devices.

MCI_CLOSE

Sent by an application to request that the specified device be closed.

MCI_GETDEVCAPS

Sent by an application to obtain information about device capabilities.

MCI_INFO

Sent by an application to obtain information about a device.

MCI_OPEN

Sent by an application to open a device and get an MCI device identifier for use with other commands.

MCI_STATUS

Sent by an application to obtain status information about a device.

Basic Command Messages

Basic command messages are recognized by all MCI devices. Every device recognizes these commands, but some devices may not support certain commands. If a device does not support a basic command, it returns MCIERR_UNSUPPORTED_FUNCTION.

MCI_LOAD

Sent by an application to load a file.

MCI_PAUSE

Sent by an application to pause a device.

MCI_PLAY

Sent by an application to start a device playing.

MCI_RECORD

Sent by an application to start recording with a device.

MCI_RESUME

Sent by an application to resume playback or recording after a pause.

MCI_SAVE

Sent by an application to save the current file.

MCI_SEEK

Sent by an application to change locations within a media element.

MCI_SET

Sent by an application to set parameters for a device.

MCI_STOP

Sent by an application to stop a device from playing or recording.

Extended Command Messages

Extended command messages apply to particular device types such as animation devices. Device types with extended commands have capabilities that are not present in most types of MCI devices. MCI has the following types of extended commands:

- Extended Commands for Working with MCI Element Files

- Extended Commands for Device Operation and Positioning

- Extended Command for Windowed Video Devices

Extended Commands for Working with MCI Element Files

MCI devices that let you edit MCI data can have extended commands for manipulating data. The following commands apply to devices that support editing:

MCI_COPY

Sent by an application to copy data from the MCI element to the Clipboard.

MCI_CUT

Sent by an application to move data from the MCI element to the Clipboard.

MCI_DELETE

Sent by an application to remove data from the MCI element.

MCI_PASTE

Sent by an application to paste data from the Clipboard to the MCI element.

Extended Commands for Device Operation and Positioning

MCI devices can have operating capabilities that apply only to a device type or that apply to a device with unique features. The following commands apply to devices that have specialized operating capabilities:

MCI_CUE

Sent by an application to cue a device for playback or recording.

MCI_ESCAPE

Sent by an application to send a string command to a device handler.

MCI_RESUME

Sent by an application to continue playback or recording previously paused.

MCI_SPIN

Sent by an application to start or stop spinning a rotating media device such as a laserdisc.

MCI_STEP

Sent by an application to step a device one or more frames.

Extended Command for Windowed Video Devices

Video devices that display data in a window on the computer display can have MCI commands for controlling the video display and window. These devices include animation movie players and video overlay devices. The following commands apply to windowed video devices:

MCI_FREEZE

Sent by an application to stop capture.

MCI_PUT

Sent by an application to define a source or destination clipping rectangle.

MCI_REALIZE

Sent by an application to tell a graphic device to realize its palette.

MCI_UNFREEZE

Sent by an application to restore capture.

MCI_UPDATE

Sent by an application to tell a graphic device to update or paint the current frame.

MCI_WHERE

Sent by an application to determine the extent of a clipping rectangle.

MCI_WINDOW

Sent by an application to specify a window and the characteristics of the window for a graphic device to use for its display.

Window Notification Messages

Window notification messages are sent by MCI to a window function when an application wants to be notified of the completion of a command. Specify the window function in the data structure sent with **mciSendCommand**.

MM_MCINOTIFY

Notifies the window function of the command status. The *wParam* parameter of this message contains the status of the command.

Joystick Messages

Joystick messages are sent to an application to notify the application that a joystick has moved or that one of its buttons has been pressed or released. Use these messages to get input from a joystick:

MM_JOY1BUTTONDOWN

Sent to a window that has captured joystick 1 when a button has been pressed.

MM_JOY1BUTTONUP

Sent to a window that has captured joystick 1 when a button has been released.

MM_JOY1MOVE

Sent to a window that has captured joystick 1 when the joystick position has changed.

MM_JOY1ZMOVE

Sent to a window that has captured joystick 1 when the joystick z-axis position has changed.

MM_JOY2BUTTONDOWN

Sent to a window that has captured joystick 2 when a button has been pressed.

MM_JOY2BUTTONUP

Sent to a window that has captured joystick 2 when a button has been released.

MM_JOY2MOVE

Sent to a window that has captured joystick 2 when the joystick position has changed.

MM_JOY2ZMOVE

Sent to a window that has captured joystick 2 when the joystick z-axis position has changed.

File I/O Messages

File I/O messages are sent to custom I/O procedures to request I/O operations on a file. I/O procedures must respond to all of the following messages:

MMIOM_CLOSE

Sent to an I/O procedure to request that a file be closed.

MMIOM_OPEN

Sent to an I/O procedure to request that a file be opened.

MMIOM_READ

Sent to an I/O procedure to request that data be read from a file.

MMIOM_SEEK

Sent to an I/O procedure to request that the current position for reading and writing be changed.

MMIOM_WRITE

Sent to an I/O procedure to request that data be written to a file.

MMIOM_WRITEFLUSH

Sent to an I/O procedure to request that an I/O buffer be flushed to disk.

Movie Player Messages

Movie Player messages are sent to a frame callback function to notify the application that a movie frame has been advanced and to send script-channel text to an application. Use these messages to get frame-advance information:

MMP_HOOK_FRAME

Sent to a frame callback function after the Movie Player completes screen updates for the frame or subframe.

MMP_HOOK_SCRIPT

Sent to a frame callback function before the Movie Player processes the script-channel text for the frame.

Screen Saver Messages

A screen saver message is sent when the screen saver is about to be invoked. Use this message to prevent the screen saver from blanking the screen:

WM_SYSCOMMAND

Sent to an application when the screen saver is preparing to blank the screen.

Chapter 5

Message Directory

This chapter contains an alphabetical list of the messages in the Multimedia extensions to Windows. For information about standard Windows messages, see the *Microsoft Windows Software Development Kit Reference—Volume 1*.

For each message, this chapter lists the following items:

- The purpose of the message

- A description of the message parameters

- A description of return values

- Optional comments on using the message

- Optional cross references to other messages, functions, and data structures

Extensions to MCI Command Messages

MCI command messages can have extensions for specific types of MCI devices. The extensions include additional flags for parameters and are identified by one of the following headings in the "Parameters" section of the entry for the message:

Heading	Description
Animation Extensions	Extensions for animation devices
CD Audio Extensions	Extensions for compact disc audio devices
Sequencer Extensions	Extensions for MIDI sequencer devices
Videodisc Extensions	Extensions for videodisc player devices
Video Overlay Extensions	Extensions for video overlay devices
Wave Audio Extensions	Extensions for waveform audio devices

Message Prefixes

Groups of related messages in the Multimedia extensions are identified by a prefix in the message names. The following table summarizes groups of related messages and the prefixes for each group:

Message Prefix	Description
MCI	Media Control Interface command messages
MIM	MIDI input callback messages
MMIOM	Custom I/O procedure messages
MM_JOY	Joystick window messages
MM_MCI	Media Control Interface window messages
MM_MIM	MIDI input window messages
MM_MOM	MIDI output window messages
MM_WIM	Waveform input window messages
MM_WOM	Waveform output window messages
MOM	MIDI output callback messages
WIM	Waveform input callback messages
WOM	Waveform output callback messages

Message Descriptions

This section lists messages in the Multimedia extensions to Windows. The messages are presented in alphabetical order.

MCI_BREAK

This MCI command message sets a break key for an MCI device. MCI supports this message directly rather than passing it to the device.

Parameters   DWORD   *dwFlags*

The following flags apply to all devices:

MCI_NOTIFY

Specifies that MCI should post the MM_MCINOTIFY message when this command completes. The window to receive this message is specified in the **dwCallback** field of the data structure identified by *lpBreak*.

MCI_WAIT

> Specifies that the break operation should finish before MCI returns control to the application.

MCI_BREAK_KEY

> Indicates the **nVirtKey** field of the data structure identified by *lpBreak* specifies the virtual key code used for the break key. By default, MCI assigns CTRL+BREAK as the break key. This flag is required if MCI_BREAK_OFF is not specified.

MCI_BREAK_HWND

> Indicates the **hwndBreak** field of the data structure identified by *lpBreak* contains a window handle which must be the current window in order to enable break detection for that MCI device. This is usually the application's main window. If omitted, MCI does not check the window handle of the current window.

MCI_BREAK_OFF

> Used to disable any existing break key for the indicated device

LPMCI_BREAK_PARMS   *lpBreak*

> Specifies a far pointer to the **MCI_BREAK_PARMS** data structure.

Return Value   Returns zero if successful. Otherwise, it returns an MCI error code.

Comments   You might have to press the break key multiple times to interrupt a wait operation. Pressing the break key after a device wait is broken can send the break to an application. If an application has an action defined for the virtural key code, then it can inadvertently respond to the break. For example, an application using VK_CANCEL for an accelerator key can respond to the default CTRL+BREAK key if it is pressed after a wait is canceled.

MCI_CLOSE

This MCI command message realeases access to a device or device element. All devices respond to this message.

Parameters   DWORD   *dwFlags*

> The following flags apply to all devices:

MCI_NOTIFY

> Specifies that MCI should post the **MM_MCINOTIFY** message when this command completes. The window to receive this message is specified in the **dwCallback** field of the data structure identified by *lpDefault*.

MCI_WAIT

> Specifies that the close operation should finish before MCI returns control to the application.

LPMCI_GENERIC_PARMS *lpDefault*

> Specifies a far pointer to the **MCI_GENERIC_PARMS** data structure. (Devices with extended command sets might replace this data structure with a device-specific data structure.)

Return Value   Returns zero if successful. Otherwise, it returns an MCI error code.

Comments   Exiting an application without closing any MCI devices it has opened can leave the device opened and unaccessible. Your application should explicitly close each device or device element when it is finished with it. MCI unloads the device when all instances of the device or all device elements are closed.

See Also   **MCI_OPEN**

MCI_COPY

This MCI command message copies data to the Clipboard. Support of this message by a device is optional. The parameters and flags for this message vary according to the selected device.

Parameters   DWORD   *dwFlags*

> The following flags apply to all devices supporting **MCI_COPY**:

> MCI_NOTIFY

>> Specifies that MCI should post the **MM_MCINOTIFY** message when this command completes. The window to receive this message is specified in the **dwCallback** field of the data structure identified by *lpCopy*.

> MCI_WAIT

>> Specifies that the copy should finish before MCI returns control to the application.

LPMCI_GENERIC_PARMS   *lpCopy*

> Specifies a far pointer to an **MCI_GENERIC_PARMS** data structure. (Devices with extended command sets might replace this data structure with a device-specific data structure.)

Return Value   Returns zero if successful. Otherwise, it returns an MCI error code.

Comments   This command is not used by the device drivers supplied with the Multimedia Extensions 1.0.

See Also   **MCI_CUT, MCI_DELETE, MCI_PASTE**

MCI_CUE

This MCI command message cues a device so that playback or recording begins with minimum delay. Support of this message by a device is optional. The parameters and flags for this message vary according to the selected device.

Parameters

DWORD   *dwFlags*

The following flags apply to all devices supporting **MCI_CUE**:

MCI_NOTIFY

Specifies that MCI should post the **MM_MCINOTIFY** message when this command completes. The window to receive this message is specified in the **dwCallback** field of the data structure identified by *lpDefault*.

MCI_WAIT

Specifies that the cue operation should finish before MCI returns control to the application.

LPMCI_GENERIC_PARMS   *lpDefault*

Specifies a far pointer to the **MCI_GENERIC_PARMS** data structure. (Devices with extended command sets might replace this data structure with a device-specific data structure.)

Waveform Audio Extensions

DWORD   *dwFlags*

The following additional flags apply to wave audio devices:

MCI_WAVE_INPUT

Specifies that a wave input device should be cued.

MCI_WAVE_OUTPUT

Specifies that a wave output device should be cued. This is the default flag if a flag is not specified.

LPMCI_GENERIC_PARMS *lpDefault*

Specifies a far pointer to the **MCI_GENERIC_PARMS** data structure.

Return Value   Returns zero if successful. Otherwise, it returns an MCI error code.

See Also   **MCI_SEEK, MCI_PLAY, MCI_RECORD**

MCI_CUT

This MCI command message removes data from the MCI element and copies it to the Clipboard. Support of this message by a device is optional. The parameters and flags for this message vary according to the selected device.

Parameters　　DWORD   *dwFlags*

The following flags apply to all devices supporting **MCI_CUT**:

MCI_NOTIFY

Specifies that MCI should post the **MM_MCINOTIFY** message when this command completes. The window to receive this message is specified in the **dwCallback** field of the data structure identified by *lpCut*.

MCI_WAIT

Specifies that the cut operation should finish before MCI returns control to the application.

LPMCI_GENERIC_PARMS   *lpCut*

Specifies a far pointer to an **MCI_GENERIC_PARMS** data structure. (Devices with extended command sets might replace this data structure with a device-specific data structure.)

Return Value　　Returns zero if successful. Otherwise, it returns an MCI error code.

Comments　　This command is not used by the device drivers supplied with the Multimedia Extensions 1.0.

See Also　　**MCI_COPY, MCI_DELETE, MCI_PASTE**

MCI_DELETE

This MCI command message removes data from the MCI element. Support of this message by a device is optional. The parameters and flags for this message vary according to the selected device.

Parameters　　DWORD   *dwFlags*

The following flags apply to all devices supporting **MCI_DELETE**:

MCI_NOTIFY

Specifies that MCI should post the **MM_MCINOTIFY** message when this command completes. The window to receive this message is specified in the **dwCallback** field of the data structure identified by *lpDelete*.

MCI_WAIT

Specifies that the delete operation should finish before MCI returns control to the application.

LPMCI_GENERIC_PARMS *lpCut*

> Specifies a far pointer to an **MCI_GENERIC_PARMS** data structure. (Devices with extended command sets might replace this data structure with a device-specific data structure.)

Wave Audio Extensions

DWORD *dwFlags*

> The following extensions apply to wave audio devices:

MCI_FROM

> Specifies that a beginning position is included in the **dwFrom** field of the data structure identified by *lpDelete*. The units assigned to the position values is specified with the MCI_SET_TIME_FORMAT flag of the **MCI_SET** command.

MCI_TO

> Specifies that an ending position is included in the **dwTo** field of the data structure identified by *lpDelete*. The units assigned to the position values is specified with the MCI_SET_TIME_FORMAT flag of the **MCI_SET** command.

LPMCI_WAVE_DELETE_PARMS *lpDelete*

> Specifies a far pointer to an **MCI_WAVE_DELETE_PARMS** data structure. (Devices with extended command sets might replace this data structure with a device-specific data structure.)

Return Value   Returns zero if successful. Otherwise, it returns an MCI error code.

Comments   The waveform audio device uses this command.

See Also   **MCI_COPY, MCI_DELETE, MCI_PASTE**

MCI_FREEZE (VIDEO OVERLAY)

This MCI command message freezes motion on the display. This command is part of the video overlay command set. The parameters and flags for this message vary according to the selected device.

Parameters   DWORD *dwFlags*

> The following flags apply to all devices supporting **MCI_FREEZE**:

MCI_NOTIFY

> Specifies that MCI should post the **MM_MCINOTIFY** message when this command completes. The window to receive this message is specified in the **dwCallback** field of the data structure identified by *lpFreeze*.

           MCI_WAIT

               Specifies that the freeze operation should finish before MCI returns control to the application.

           MCI_OVLY_RECT

               Specifies that the **rc** field of the data structure identified by *lpFreeze* contains a valid rectangle. If this flag is not specified, the device driver will freeze the entire frame.

           LPMCI_OVLY_RECT_PARMS   *lpFreeze*

               Specifies a far pointer to a **MCI_OVLY_RECT_PARMS** data structure. (Devices with additional parameters might replace this data structure with a device-specific data structure.)

Return Value   Returns zero if successful. Otherwise, it returns an MCI error code.

See Also   **MCI_UNFREEZE**

MCI_GETDEVCAPS

           This MCI command message is used to obtain static information about a device. All devices must respond to this message. The parameters and flags available for this message depend on the selected device. Information is returned in the **dwReturn** field of the data structure identified by *lpCapsParms*.

Parameters   DWORD   *dwFlags*

               The following standard and command-specific flags apply to all devices:

           MCI_NOTIFY

               Specifies that MCI should post the **MM_MCINOTIFY** message when this command completes. The window to receive this message is specified in the **dwCallback** field of the data structure identified by *lpCapsParms*.

           MCI_WAIT

               Specifies that the query operation should finish before MCI returns control to the application.

           MCI_GETDEVCAPS_ITEM

               Specifies that the **dwItem** field of the data structure identified by *lpCapsParms* contains a constant specifying which device capability to obtain. The following constants define which capability to return in the **dwReturn** field of the data structure:

           MCI_GETDEVCAPS_CAN_EJECT

               The **dwReturn** field is set to TRUE if the device can eject the media; otherwise, it is set to FALSE.

MCI_GETDEVCAPS_CAN_PLAY

> The **dwReturn** field is set to TRUE if the device can play the media; otherwise, it is set to FALSE.
>
> If a device specifies TRUE, it implies the device supports **MCI_PAUSE** and **MCI_STOP** as well as **MCI_PLAY**.

MCI_GETDEVCAPS_CAN_RECORD

> The **dwReturn** field is set to TRUE if the device supports recording; otherwise, it is set to FALSE.
>
> If a device specifies TRUE, it implies the device supports **MCI_PAUSE** and **MCI_STOP** as well as **MCI_RECORD**.

MCI_GETDEVCAPS_CAN_SAVE

> The **dwReturn** field is set to TRUE if the device can save a file; otherwise, it is set to FALSE.

MCI_GETDEVCAPS_COMPOUND_DEVICE

> The **dwReturn** field is set to TRUE if the device uses device elements; otherwise, it is set to FALSE.

MCI_GETDEVCAPS_DEVICE_TYPE

> The **dwReturn** field is set to one of the following values indicating the device type:

- MCI_DEVTYPE_ANIMATION
- MCI_DEVTYPE_CD_AUDIO
- MCI_DEVTYPE_DAT
- MCI_DEVTYPE_DIGITAL_VIDEO
- MCI_DEVTYPE_OTHER
- MCI_DEVTYPE_OVERLAY
- MCI_DEVTYPE_SCANNER
- MCI_DEVTYPE_SEQUENCER
- MCI_DEVTYPE_VIDEODISC
- MCI_DEVTYPE_VIDEOTAPE
- MCI_DEVTYPE_WAVEFORM_AUDIO

MCI_GETDEVCAPS_HAS_AUDIO

> The **dwReturn** field is set to TRUE if the device has audio output; otherwise, it is set to FALSE.

MCI_GETDEVCAPS_HAS_VIDEO

The **dwReturn** field is set to TRUE if the device has video output; otherwise, it is set to FALSE.

For example, the field is set to TRUE for devices that support the animation or videodisc command set.

MCI_GETDEVCAPS_USES_FILES

The **dwReturn** field is set to TRUE if the device requires a filename as its element name; otherwise, it is set to FALSE.

Only compound devices use files.

LPMCI_GETDEVCAPS_PARMS   *lpCapsParms*

Specifies a far pointer to the **MCI_GETDEVCAPS_PARMS** data structure. (Devices with extended command sets might replace this data structure with a device-specific data structure.)

Animation Extensions

DWORD   *dwFlags*

The following extensions apply to animation devices:

MCI_GETDEVCAPS_ITEM

Specifies that the **dwItem** field of the data structure identified by *lpCapsParms* contains a constant specifying which device capability to obtain. The following additional device-capability constants are defined for animation devices and specify which value to return in the **dwReturn** field of the data structure:

MCI_ANIM_GETDEVCAPS_CAN_REVERSE

The **dwReturn** field is set to TRUE if the device can play in reverse; otherwise, it is set to FALSE.

MCI_ANIM_GETDEVCAPS_CAN_STRETCH

The **dwReturn** field is set to TRUE if the device can stretch the image to fill the frame; otherwise, it is set to FALSE.

MCIMMP returns FALSE.

MCI_ANIM_GETDEVCAPS_FAST_RATE

The **dwReturn** field is set to the standard fast play rate in frames per second.

MCIMMP returns MCIERR_UNSUPPORTED_FUNCTION.

MCI_ANIM_GETDEVCAPS_MAX_WINDOWS

The **dwReturn** field is set to the maximum number of windows that the device can handle simultaneously.

MCI_ANIM_GETDEVCAPS_NORMAL_RATE

The **dwReturn** field is set to the normal rate of play in frames per second.

MCIMMP returns MCIERR_UNSUPPORTED_FUNCTION.

MCI_ANIM_GETDEVCAPS_PALETTES

The **dwReturn** field is set to TRUE if the device can return a palette handle; otherwise, it is set to FALSE.

MCIMMP returns TRUE.

MCI_ANIM_GETDEVCAPS_SLOW_RATE

The **dwReturn** field is set to the standard slow play rate in frames per second.

MCIMMP returns MCIERR_UNSUPPORTED_FUNCTION.

LPMCI_GETDEVCAPS_PARMS   *lpCapsParms*

Specifies a far pointer to the **MCI_GETDEVCAPS_PARMS** data structure.

Videodisc Extensions

DWORD   *dwFlags*

The following extensions apply to videodisc devices:

MCI_GETDEVCAPS_ITEM

Specifies that the **dwItem** field of the data structure identified by *lpCapsParms* contains a constant specifying which device capability to obtain. The following additional device-capability constants are defined for videodisc devices and specify which value to return in the **dwReturn** field of the data structure:

MCI_VD_GETDEVCAPS_CAN_REVERSE

The **dwReturn** field is set to TRUE if the videodisc player can play in reverse; otherwise, it is set to FALSE.

Some players can play CLV discs in reverse as well as CAV discs.

MCI_VD_GETDEVCAPS_FAST_RATE

The **dwReturn** field is set to the standard fast play rate in frames per second.

MCI_VD_GETDEVCAPS_NORMAL_RATE

The **dwReturn** field is set to the normal play rate in frames per second.

MCI_VD_GETDEVCAPS_SLOW_RATE

The **dwReturn** field is set to the standard slow play rate in frames per second.

MCI_VD_GETDEVCAPS_CLV

Indicates the information requested applies to CLV format discs. By default, the capabilities apply to the current disc.

MCI_VD_GETDEVCAPS_CAV

Indicates the information requested applies to CAV format discs. By default, the capabilities apply to the current disc.

LPMCI_GETDEVCAPS_PARMS   *lpCapsParms*

Specifies a far pointer to the **MCI_GETDEVCAPS_PARMS** data structure.

Video Overlay Extensions

DWORD   *dwFlags*

The following extensions apply to video overlay devices:

MCI_GETDEVCAPS_ITEM

Specifies that the **dwItem** field of the data structure identified by *lpCapsParms* contains a constant specifying which device capability to obtain. The following additional device-capability constants are defined for video overlay devices and specify which value to return in the **dwReturn** field of the data structure:

MCI_OVLY_GETDEVCAPS_CAN_FREEZE

The **dwReturn** field is set to TRUE if the device can freeze the image; otherwise, it is set to FALSE.

MCI_OVLY_GETDEVCAPS_CAN_STRETCH

The **dwReturn** field is set to TRUE if the device can stretch the image to fill the frame; otherwise, it is set to FALSE.

MCI_OVLY_GETDEVCAPS_MAX_WINDOWS

The **dwReturn** field is set to the maximum number of windows that the device can handle simultaneously.

LPMCI_GETDEVCAPS_PARMS   *lpCapsParms*

Specifies a far pointer to the **MCI_GETDEVCAPS_PARMS** data structure.

Waveform Audio Extensions

DWORD   *dwFlags*

The following extended flag applies to waveform audio devices:

MCI_GETDEVCAPS_ITEM

Specifies that the **dwItem** field of the data structure identified by *lpCapsParms* contains a constant specifying which device capability to obtain. The following additional device-capability constants are defined for waveform audio devices and specify which value to return in the **dwReturn** field of the data structure:

MCI_WAVE_GETDEVCAPS_INPUT

The **dwReturn** field is set to the total number of waveform input (recording) devices.

MCI_WAVE_GETDEVCAPS_OUTPUT

The **dwReturn** field is set to the total number of waveform output (playback) devices.

LPMCI_GETDEVCAPS_PARMS   *lpCapsParms*

Specifies a far pointer to the **MCI_GETDEVCAPS_PARMS** data structure.

Return Value   Returns zero if successful. Otherwise, it returns an MCI error code.

MCI_INFO

This MCI command message obtains string information from a device. All devices respond to this message. The parameters and flags available for this message depend on the selected device. Information is returned in the **lpstrReturn** field of the data structure identified by *lpInfo*. The **dwReturnSize** field specifies the buffer length for the return data.

Parameters   DWORD   *dwFlags*

The following standard and command-specific flags apply to all devices:

MCI_NOTIFY

Specifies that MCI should post the **MM_MCINOTIFY** message when this command completes. The window to receive this message is specified in the **dwCallback** field of the data structure identified by *lpInfo*.

MCI_WAIT

Specifies that the query operation should finish before MCI returns control to the application.

MCI_INFO_PRODUCT

Obtains a description of the hardware associated with a device. Devices should supply a description that identifies both the driver and the hardware used.

LPMCI_INFO_PARMS   *lpInfo*

Specifies a far pointer to the **MCI_INFO_PARMS** data structure. (Devices with extended command sets might replace this data structure with a device-specific data structure.)

Animation Extensions

DWORD   *dwFlags*

The following additional flags apply to animation devices:

MCI_INFO_FILE
>   Obtains the filename of the current file. This flag is only supported by devices that return TRUE to the MCI_GETDEVCAPS_USES_FILES query.

MCI_ANIM_INFO_TEXT
>   Obtains the window caption.

LPMCI_INFO_PARMS   *lpInfo*
>   Specifies a far pointer to the **MCI_INFO_PARMS** data structure.

Video Overlay Extensions

DWORD   *dwFlags*
>   The following additional flags apply to video overlay devices:

MCI_INFO_FILE
>   Obtains the filename of the current file. This flag is only supported by devices that return TRUE to the MCI_GETDEVCAPS_USES_FILES query.

MCI_OVLY_INFO_TEXT
>   Obtains the caption of the window associated with the overlay device.

LPMCI_INFO_PARMS   *lpInfo*
>   Specifies a far pointer to the **MCI_INFO_PARMS** data structure.

Waveform Audio Extensions

DWORD   *dwFlags*
>   The following additional flags apply to waveform audio devices:

MCI_INFO_FILE
>   Obtains the filename of the current file. This flag is supported by devices that return TRUE to the MCI_GETDEVCAPS_USES_FILES query.

MCI_WAVE_INPUT
>   Obtains the product name of the current input.

MCI_WAVE_OUTPUT
>   Obtains the product name of the current output.

LPMCI_INFO_PARMS   *lpInfo*
>   Specifies a far pointer to the **MCI_INFO_PARMS** data structure.

Return Value   Returns zero if successful. Otherwise, it returns an MCI error code.

MCI_LOAD

This MCI command message loads a file. Support of this message by a device is optional. The parameters and flags for this message vary according to the selected device.

Parameters   DWORD   *dwFlags*

The following flags apply to all devices supporting **MCI_LOAD**:

MCI_NOTIFY

Specifies that MCI should post the **MM_MCINOTIFY** message when this command completes. The window to receive this message is specified in the **dwCallback** field of the data structure identified by *lpLoad*.

MCI_WAIT

Specifies that the load operation should finish before MCI returns control to the application.

MCI_LOAD_FILE

Indicates the **lpfilename** field of the data structure identified by *lpLoad* contains a pointer to a buffer containing the file name.

LPMCI_LOAD_PARMS   *lpLoad*

Specifies a far pointer to the **MCI_LOAD_PARMS** data structure. (Devices with additional parameters might replace this data structure with a device-specific data structure.)

Video Overlay Extensions

DWORD   *dwFlags*

The following additional flags apply to video overlay devices supporting **MCI_LOAD**:

MCI_OVLY_RECT

Specifies that the **rc** field of the data structure identified by *lpLoad* contains a valid display rectangle that identifies the area of the video buffer to update.

LPMCI_OVLY_LOAD_PARMS   *lpLoad*

Specifies a far pointer to a **MCI_OVLY_LOAD_PARMS** data structure.

Return Value   Returns zero if successful. Otherwise, it returns an MCI error code.

Comments   This command applies to video overlay devices.

See Also   **MCI_SAVE**

MCI_OPEN

This MCI command message initializes a device or device element. All devices respond to this message. The parameters and flags available for this message depend on the selected device.

Parameters   DWORD   *dwFlags*

The following flags apply to all devices:

MCI_NOTIFY

Specifies that MCI should post the **MM_MCINOTIFY** message when this command completes. The window to receive this message is specified in the **dwCallback** field of the data structure identified by *lpOpen*.

MCI_WAIT

Specifies that the open operation should finish before MCI returns control to the application.

MCI_OPEN_ALIAS

Specifies that an alias is included in the **lpstrAlias** field of the data structure identified by *lpOpen*.

MCI_OPEN_SHAREABLE

Specifies that the device or device element should be opened as shareable.

MCI_OPEN_TYPE

Specifies that a device type name or constant is included in the **lpstrDeviceType** field of the data structure identified by *lpOpen*.

MCI_OPEN_TYPE_ID

Specifies that the low-order word of the **lpstrDeviceType** field of the associated data structure contains a standard MCI device type ID and the high-order word optionally contains the ordinal index for the device. Use this flag with the MCI_OPEN_TYPE flag.

LPMCI_OPEN_PARMS   *lpOpen*

Specifies a far pointer to the **MCI_OPEN_PARMS** data structure. (Devices with extended command sets might replace this data structure with a device-specific data structure.)

Flags for Compound Devices

DWORD   *dwFlags*

The following additional flags apply to compound devices:

MCI_OPEN_ELEMENT

>   Specifies that an element name is included in the **lpstrElementName** field of
>   the data structure identified by *lpOpen*.

MCI_OPEN_ELEMENT_ID

>   Specifies that the **lpstrElementName** field of the data structure identified by
>   *lpOpen* is interpreted as a DWORD and has meaning internal to the device. Use
>   this flag with the MCI_OPEN_ELEMENT flag.

LPMCI_OPEN_PARMS   *lpOpen*

>   Specifies a far pointer to the **MCI_OPEN_PARMS** data structure. (Devices with
>   additional parameters might replace this data structure with a device-specific data
>   structure.)

Animation Extensions

DWORD   *dwFlags*

>   The following flags apply to animation devices:

MCI_ANIM_OPEN_NOSTATIC

>   Specifies that the device should reduce the number of static (system) colors in
>   the palette to two.

MCI_ANIM_OPEN_PARENT

>   Indicates the parent window handle is specified in the **hWndParent** field of the
>   data structure identified by *lpOpen*. The parent window handle is required for
>   some window styles.

MCI_ANIM_OPEN_WS

>   Indicates a window style is specified in the **dwStyle** field of the data structure
>   identified by *lpOpen*. The **dwStyle** value specifies the style of the window that
>   the driver will create and display if the application does not provide one.
>   The style parameter takes an integer which defines the window style. These
>   constants are the same as the ones in WINDOWS.H (such as WS_CHILD,
>   WS_OVERLAPPEDWINDOW, or WS_POPUP).

LPMCI_ANIM_OPEN_PARMS   *lpOpen*

>   Specifies a far pointer to the **MCI_ANIM_OPEN_PARMS** data structure.

Video Overlay Extensions

DWORD   *dwFlags*

>   The following flags apply to video overlay devices:

MCI_OVLY_OPEN_PARENT

>   Indicates the parent window handle is specified in the **hWndParent** field
>   of the data structure identified by *lpOpen*.

MCI_OVLY_OPEN_WS

Indicates a window style is specified in the **dwStyle** field of the data structure identified by *lpOpen*. The **dwStyle** value specifies the style of the window that the driver will create and display if the application does not provide one. The style parameter takes an integer that defines the window style. These constants are the same as those in WINDOWS.H (for example, WS_CHILD, WS_OVERLAPPEDWINDOW, or WS_POPUP).

LPMCI_OVLY_OPEN_PARMS   *lpOpen*

Specifies a far pointer to the **MCI_OVLY_OPEN_PARMS** data structure.

Waveform Audio Extensions

DWORD   *dwFlags*

The following flags apply to waveform audio devices:

MCI_WAVE_OPEN_BUFFER

Indicates a buffer length is specified in the **dwBuffer** field of the data structure identified by *lpOpen*.

LPMCI_WAVE_OPEN_PARMS   *lpOpen*

Specifies a far pointer to the **MCI_WAVE_OPEN_PARMS** data structure. (Devices with extended command sets might replace this data structure with a device-specific data structure.)

Return Value   Returns zero if the open is successful. If an error occurs, it returns the following values:

MCIERR_CANNOT_LOAD_DRIVER

Error loading media device driver.

MCIERR_DEVICE_OPEN

The device name is in use by this task. Use a unique alias.

MCIERR_DUPLICATE_ALIAS

The specified alias is an open device in this task.

MCIERR_EXTENSION_NOT_FOUND

Cannot deduce a device type from the given extension.

MCIERR_FILENAME_REQUIRED

A valid filename is required.

MCIERR_MISSING_PARAMETER

Required parameter is missing.

MCIERR_MUST_USE_SHAREABLE

The device is already open; use the shareable flag with each open.

MCIERR_NO_ELEMENT_ALLOWED

An element name cannot be used with this device.

Comments   If MCI_OPEN_SHAREABLE is not specified when a device or device element is initially opened, then all subsequent **MCI_OPEN** messages to the device or device element will fail. If the device or device element is already open, and this flag is not specified, the call will fail even if the first open command specified MCI_OPEN_SHAREABLE. Files for the MCIMMP, MCISEQ, and MCIWAVE devices are nonshareable.

Case is ignored in the device name, but there must not be any leading or trailing blanks.

To use automatic type selection (via the [mci extensions] section of the WIN.INI file), assign the file name (including file extension) to the **lpstrElementName** field, assign a NULL pointer to the **lpstrDeviceType** field, and set the MCI_OPEN_ELEMENT flag.

See Also   **MCI_CLOSE**

MCI_PASTE

This MCI command message pastes data from the Clipboard into a device element.

Parameters   DWORD   *dwFlags*

The following flags apply to all devices supporting **MCI_PASTE**:

MCI_NOTIFY

Specifies that MCI should post the **MM_MCINOTIFY** message when this command completes. The window to receive this message is specified in the **dwCallback** field of the data structure identified by *lpPaste*.

MCI_WAIT

Specifies that the device should complete the operation before MCI returns control to the application.

LPMCI_GENERIC_PARMS   *lpPaste*

Specifies a far pointer to the **MCI_GENERIC_PARMS** data structure. (Devices with extended command sets might replace this data structure with a device-specific data structure.)

Return Value   Returns zero if successful. Otherwise, it returns an MCI error code.

Comments   This command is not used by the MCI device drivers supplied with the Multimedia Extensions 1.0.

See Also   **MCI_CUT, MCI_COPY, MCI_DELETE**

MCI_PAUSE

This MCI command message pauses the current action.

Parameters   DWORD   *dwFlags*

The following flags apply to all devices supporting **MCI_PAUSE**:

MCI_NOTIFY

Specifies that MCI should post the **MM_MCINOTIFY** message when this command completes. The window to receive this message is specified in the **dwCallback** field of the data structure identified by *lpDefault*.

MCI_WAIT

Specifies that the device should be paused before MCI returns control to the application.

LPMCI_GENERIC_PARMS   *lpDefault*

Specifies a far pointer to the **MCI_GENERIC_PARMS** data structure. (Devices with extended command sets might replace this data structure with a device-specific data structure.)

Return Value   Returns zero if successful. Otherwise, it returns an MCI error code.

Comments   The difference between **MCI_STOP** and **MCI_PAUSE** depends upon the device. If possible, **MCI_PAUSE** suspends device operation but leaves the device ready to resume play immediately.

See Also   **MCI_PLAY, MCI_RECORD, MCI_RESUME, MCI_STOP**

MCI_PLAY

This MCI command message signals the device to begin transmitting output data. Support of this message by a device is optional. The parameters and flags for this message vary according to the selected device.

Parameters   DWORD   *dwFlags*

The following flags apply to all devices supporting **MCI_PLAY**:

MCI_NOTIFY

Specifies that MCI should post the **MM_MCINOTIFY** message when this command completes. The window to receive this message is specified in the **dwCallback** field of the data structure identified by *lpPlay*.

MCI_WAIT

Specifies that the play operation should finish before MCI returns control to the application.

MCI_FROM

> Specifies that a starting position is included in the **dwFrom** field of the data structure identified by *lpPlay*. The units assigned to the position values is specified with the MCI_SET_TIME_FORMAT flag of the **MCI_SET** command. If MCI_FROM is not specified, the starting position defaults to the current location.

MCI_TO

> Specifies that an ending position is included in the **dwTo** field of the data structure identified by *lpPlay*. The units assigned to the position values is specified with the MCI_SET_TIME_FORMAT flag of the **MCI_SET** command. If MCI_TO is not specified, the end position defaults to the end of the media.

LPMCI_PLAY_PARMS   *lpPlay*

> Specifies a far pointer to an **MCI_PLAY_PARMS** data structure. (Devices with extended command sets might replace this data structure with a device-specific data structure.)

Animation Extensions

DWORD   *dwFlags*

> The following additional flags apply to animation devices:

MCI_ANIM_PLAY_FAST

> Specifies to play fast.

MCI_ANIM_PLAY_REVERSE

> Specifies to play in reverse.

MCI_ANIM_PLAY_SCAN

> Specifies to scan quickly.

> MCIMMP returns MCIERR_UNSUPPORTED_FUNCTION.

MCI_ANIM_PLAY_SLOW

> Specifies to play slowly.

MCI_ANIM_PLAY_SPEED

> Specifies that the play speed is included in the **dwSpeed** field in the data structure identified by *lpPlay*.

> MCIMMP returns MCIERR_UNSUPPORTED_FUNCTION.

LPMCI_ANIM_PLAY_PARMS   *lpPlay*

> Specifies a far pointer to an **MCI_ANIM_PLAY_PARMS** data structure.

Videodisc Extensions

DWORD   *dwFlags*

The following additional flags apply to videodisc devices:

MCI_VD_PLAY_FAST
Specifies to play fast.

MCI_VD_PLAY_REVERSE
Specifies to play in reverse.

MCI_VD_PLAY_SCAN
Specifies to scan quickly.

MCI_VD_PLAY_SLOW
Specifies to play slowly.

MCI_VD_PLAY_SPEED
Specifies that the play speed is included in the **dwSpeed** field in the data structure identified by *lpPlay*.

LPMCI_VD_PLAY_PARMS   *lpPlay*
Specifies a far pointer to an **MCI_VD_PLAY_PARMS** data structure.

Return Value   Returns zero if successful. Otherwise, it returns an MCI error code.

See Also   **MCI_CUE, MCI_PAUSE, MCI_RECORD, MCI_RESUME, MCI_SEEK, MCI_STOP**

MCI_PUT

This MCI command message sets the source, destination, and frame rectangles. The parameters and flags for this message vary according to the selected device.

Parameters   DWORD   *dwFlags*

The following flags apply to all devices supporting **MCI_PUT**:

MCI_NOTIFY
Specifies that MCI should post the **MM_MCINOTIFY** message when this command completes. The window to receive this message is specified in the **dwCallback** field of the data structure identified by *lpDest*.

MCI_WAIT
Specifies that the operation should finish before MCI returns control to the application.

LPMCI_GENERIC_PARMS   *lpDest*

> Specifies a far pointer to an **MCI_GENERIC_PARMS** data structure. (Devices with extended command sets might replace this data structure with a device-specific data structure.)

Animation Extensions

DWORD   *dwFlags*

> The following additional flags apply to animation devices supporting **MCI_PUT**:

> MCI_ANIM_RECT
>
>> Specifies that the **rc** field of the data structure identified by *lpDest* contains a valid rectangle. If this flag is not specified, the default rectangle matches the coordinates of the image or window being clipped.

> MCI_ANIM_PUT_DESTINATION
>
>> Indicates the rectangle defined for MCI_ANIM_RECT specifies the area of the client window used to display an image. The rectangle contains the offset and visible extent of the image relative to the window origin. If the frame is being stretched, the source is stretched to the destination rectangle.

> MCI_ANIM_PUT_SOURCE
>
>> Indicates the rectangle defined for MCI_ANIM_RECT specifies a clipping rectangle for the animation image. The rectangle contains the offset and extent of the image relative to the image origin.
>>
>> MCIMMP returns MCIERR_UNSUPPORTED_FUNCTION.

LPMCI_ANIM_RECT_PARMS   *lpDest*

> Specifies a far pointer to a **MCI_ANIM_RECT_PARMS** data structure. (Devices with extended command sets might replace this data structure with a device-specific data structure.)

Video Overlay Extensions

DWORD   *dwFlags*

> The following additional flags apply to video overlay devices supporting **MCI_PUT**:

> MCI_OVLY_RECT
>
>> Specifies that the **rc** field of the data structure identified by *lpDest* contains a valid display rectangle. If this flag is not specified, the default rectangle matches the coordinates of the video buffer or window being clipped.

> MCI_OVLY_PUT_DESTINATION
>
>> Indicates the rectangle defined for MCI_OVLY_RECT specifies the area of the client window used to display an image. The rectangle contains the offset and

visible extent of the image relative to the window origin. If the frame is being stretched, the source is stretched to the destination rectangle.

MCI_OVLY_PUT_FRAME

Indicates the rectangle defined for MCI_OVLY_RECT specifies the area of the video buffer used to receive the video image. The rectangle contains the offset and extent of the buffer area relative to the video buffer origin.

MCI_OVLY_PUT_SOURCE

Indicates that the rectangle defined for MCI_OVLY_RECT specifies the area of the video buffer used as the source of the digital image. The rectangle contains the offset and extent of the clipping rectangle for the video buffer relative to its origin.

MCI_OVLY_PUT_VIDEO

Indicates that the rectangle defined for MCI_OVLY_RECT specifies the area of the video source capture by the video buffer. The rectangle contains the offset and extent of the clipping rectangle for the video source relative to its origin.

LPMCI_OVLY_RECT_PARMS   *lpDest*

Specifies a far pointer to a **MCI_OVLY_RECT_PARMS** data structure.

Return Value   Returns zero if successful. Otherwise, it returns an MCI error code.

See Also   **MCI_WHERE**

MCI_RECORD

This MCI command message starts recording from the current position or from the specified position until the specified position. Support of this message by a device is optional. The parameters and flags for this message vary according to the selected device.

Parameters   DWORD   *dwFlags*

The following flags apply to all devices supporting **MCI_RECORD**:

MCI_NOTIFY

Specifies that MCI should post the **MM_MCINOTIFY** message when this command completes. The window to receive this message is specified in the **dwCallback** field of the data structure identified by *lpRecord*.

MCI_WAIT

Specifies that recording should finish before MCI returns control to the application.

MCI_RECORD_INSERT

Indicates that newly recorded information should be inserted or pasted into the existing data. (Some devices may not support this.) If supported, this is the default.

MCI_FROM

Specifies that a starting position is included in the **dwFrom** field of the data structure identified by *lpRecord*. The units assigned to the position values is specified with the MCI_SET_TIME_FORMAT flag of the **MCI_SET** command. If MCI_FROM is not specified, the starting position defaults to the current location.

MCI_RECORD_OVERWRITE

Specifies that data should overwrite existing data.

MCIWAVE returns MCIERR_UNSUPPORTED_FUNCTION in response to this flag.

MCI_TO

Specifies that an ending position is included in the **dwTo** field of the data structure identified by *lpRecord*. The units assigned to the position values is specified with the MCI_SET_TIME_FORMAT flag of the **MCI_SET** command. If MCI_TO is not specified, the ending position defaults to the end of the media.

LPMCI_RECORD_PARMS   *lpRecord*

Specifies a far pointer to the **MCI_RECORD_PARMS** data structure. (Devices with extended command sets might replace this data structure with a device-specific data structure.)

Return Value   Returns zero if successful. Otherwise, it returns an MCI error code.

MCISEQ returns MCIERR_UNSUPPORTED_FUNCTION for this command.

Comments   This command is supported by devices that return TRUE to the MCI_GETDEVCAPS_CAN_RECORD query.

See Also   **MCI_CUE, MCI_PAUSE, MCI_PLAY, MCI_RESUME, MCI_SEEK**

MCI_RESUME

This MCI command message resumes a paused device. Support of this message by a device is optional.

Parameters   DWORD   *dwFlags*

The following flags apply to all devices supporting **MCI_RESUME**:

MCI_NOTIFY

> Specifies that MCI should post the **MM_MCINOTIFY** message when this command completes. The window to receive this message is specified in the **dwCallback** field of the data structure identified by *lpDefault*.

MCI_WAIT

> Specifies that the device should resume before MCI returns control to the application.

LPMCI_GENERIC_PARMS   *lpDefault*

> Specifies a far pointer to the **MCI_GENERIC_PARMS** data structure. (Devices with extended command sets might replace this data structure with a device-specific data structure.)

Return Value   Returns zero if successful. Otherwise, it returns an MCI error code.

Comments   This command resumes playing and recording without changing the stop position set with **MCI_PLAY** or **MCI_RECORD**.

See Also   **MCI_STOP, MCI_PLAY, MCI_RECORD**

MCI_SAVE

This MCI command message saves the current file. Devices which modify files should not destroy the original copy until they receive the save message. Support of this message by a device is optional. The parameters and flags for this message vary according to the selected device.

Parameters   DWORD   *dwFlags*

> The following flags apply to all devices supporting **MCI_SAVE**:

MCI_NOTIFY

> Specifies that MCI should post the **MM_MCINOTIFY** message when this command completes. The window to receive this message is specified in the **dwCallback** field of the data structure identified by *lpSave*.

MCI_WAIT

> Specifies that the save operation should finish before MCI returns control to the application.

MCI_SAVE_FILE

> Indicates the **lpfilename** field of the data structure identified by *lpSave* contains a pointer to a buffer containing the destination file name.

LPMCI_SAVE_PARMS   *lpSave*

Specifies a far pointer to the **MCI_SAVE_PARMS** data structure. (Devices with additional parameters might replace this data structure with a device-specific data structure.)

Video Overlay Extensions

DWORD   *dwFlags*

The following additional flags apply to video overlay devices supporting **MCI_SAVE**:

MCI_OVLY_RECT

Specifies that the **rc** field of the data structure identified by *lpSave* contains a valid display rectangle indicating the area of the video buffer to save.

LPMCI_OVLY_SAVE_PARMS   *lpSave*

Specifies a far pointer to a **MCI_OVLY_SAVE_PARMS** data structure.

Return Value   Returns zero if successful. Otherwise, it returns an MCI error code. MCISEQ returns MCIERR_UNSUPPORTED_FUNCTION.

Comments   This command is supported by devices that return true to the MCI_GETDEVCAPS_CAN_SAVE query. MCIWAVE supports this command.

See Also   **MCI_LOAD**

MCI_SEEK

This MCI command message changes the current position of media as quickly as possible. Video and audio output are disable during the seek. After the seek is complete, the device will be stopped. Support of this message by a device is optional. The parameters and flags for this message vary according to the selected device.

Parameters   DWORD   *dwFlags*

The following flags apply to all devices supporting **MCI_SEEK**:

MCI_NOTIFY

Specifies that MCI should post the **MM_MCINOTIFY** message when this command completes. The window to receive this message is specified in the **dwCallback** field of the data structure identified by *lpSeek*.

MCI_WAIT

Specifies that the seek operation should finish before MCI returns control to the application.

MCI_SEEK_TO_END

Specifies to seek to the end of the media.

MCI_SEEK_TO_START

>Specifies to seek to the start of the media.

MCI_TO

>Specifies a position is included in the **dwTo** field of the **MCI_SEEK_PARMS** data structure. The units assigned to the position values is specified with the MCI_SET_TIME_FORMAT flag of the **MCI_SET** command. Do not use this flag with MCI_SEEK_END or MCI_SEEK_START.

LPMCI_SEEK_PARMS *lpSeek*

>Specifies a far pointer to the **MCI_SEEK_PARMS** data structure. (Devices with extended command sets might replace this data structure with a device-specific data structure.)

Videodisc Extensions

DWORD *dwFlags*

>The following additional flag applies to videodisc devices.

MCI_VD_SEEK_REVERSE

>Specifies to seek backward.

LPMCI_SEEK_PARMS *lpSeek*

>Specifies a far pointer to the **MCI_SEEK_PARMS** data structure.

Return Value   Returns zero if successful. Otherwise, it returns an MCI error code.

See Also   **MCI_PLAY**, **MCI_RECORD**

MCI_SET

This MCI command message sets device information. Support of this message by a device is optional. The parameters and flags for this message vary according to the selected device.

Parameters   DWORD *dwFlags*

>The following flags apply to all devices supporting **MCI_SET**:

MCI_NOTIFY

>Specifies that MCI should post the **MM_MCINOTIFY** message when this command completes. The window to receive this message is specified in the **dwCallback** field of the data structure identified by *lpSet*.

MCI_WAIT

>Specifies that the set operation should finish before MCI returns control to the application.

MCI_SET_AUDIO

Specifies an audio channel number is included in the **dwAudio** field of the data structure identified by *lpSet*. This flag must be used with MCI_SET_ON or MCI_SET_OFF. Use one of the following constants to indicate the channel number:

MCI_SET_AUDIO_ALL

Specifies all audio channels.

MCI_SET_AUDIO_LEFT

Specifies the left channel.

MCI_SET_AUDIO_RIGHT

Specifies the right channel.

MCI_SET_DOOR_CLOSED

Instructs the device to close the media cover (if any).

MCI_SET_DOOR_OPEN

Instructs the device to open the media cover (if any).

MCI_SET_TIME_FORMAT

Specifies a time format parameter is included in the **dwTimeFormat** field of the data structure identified by *lpSet*. Specifying MCI_FORMAT_MILLISECONDS indicates that subsequent commands that specify time will use milliseconds for both input and output. Other units are device dependent.

MCI_SET_VIDEO

Sets the video signal on or off. This flag must be used with either MCI_SET_ON or MCI_SET_OFF. Devices that do not have video return MCIERR_UNSUPPORTED_FUNCTION.

MCI_SET_ON

Enables the specified video or audio channel.

MCI_SET_OFF

Disables the specified video or audio channel.

LPMCI_SET_PARMS *lpSet*

Specifies a far pointer to the **MCI_SET_PARMS** data structure. (Devices with extended command sets might replace this data structure with a device-specific data structure.)

Animation Extensions

DWORD   *dwFlags*

The following additional flags apply to animation devices:

MCI_SET_TIME_FORMAT

Specifies a time format parameter is included in the **dwTimeFormat** field of the data structure identified by *lpSet*. The following constants are defined for the time format:

MCI_FORMAT_MILLISECONDS

Changes the time format to milliseconds.

MCIMMP returns MCIERR_UNSUPPORTED_FUNCTION if the time format is set to MCI_FORMAT_MILLISECONDS.

MCI_FORMAT_FRAMES

Changes the time format to frames.

LPMCI_SET_PARMS   *lpSet*

Specifies a far pointer to the **MCI_SET_PARMS** data structure.

CD Audio Extensions

DWORD   *dwFlags*

The following additional flags apply to videodisc devices:

MCI_SET_TIME_FORMAT

Specifies a time format parameter is included in the **dwTimeFormat** field of the data structure identified by *lpSet*. The following constants are defined for the time format:

MCI_FORMAT_MILLISECONDS

Changes the time format to milliseconds.

MCI_FORMAT_MSF

Changes the time format to minutes, seconds, and frames.

MCI_FORMAT_TMSF

Changes the time format to tracks, minutes, seconds, and frames. (MCI uses continuous track numbers.)

LPMCI_SET_PARMS   *lpSet*

Specifies a far pointer to the **MCI_SET_PARMS** structure.

MIDI Sequencer Extensions

DWORD   *dwFlags*

The following additional flags apply to MIDI sequencer devices:

MCI_SEQ_SET_MASTER

Sets the sequencer as a source of synchronization data and indicates that the type of synchronization is specified in the **dwMaster** field of the data structure identified by *lpSet*.

MCISEQ returns MCIERR_UNSUPPORTED_FUNCTION.

The following constants are defined for the synchronization type:

MCI_SEQ_MIDI

The sequencer will send MIDI format synchronization data.

MCI_SEQ_SMPTE

The sequencer will send SMPTE format synchronization data.

MCI_SEQ_NONE

The sequencer will not send synchronization data.

MCI_SEQ_SET_OFFSET

Changes the SMPTE offset of a sequence to that specified by the **dwOffset** field of the data structure identified by *lpSet*. This only affects sequences with a SMPTE division type.

MCI_SEQ_SET_PORT

Sets the output MIDI port of a sequence to that specified by the MIDI device ID in the **dwPort** field of the data structure identified by *lpSet*. The device will close the previous port (if any), and attempt to open and use the new port. If it fails, it will return an error and re-open the previously used port (if any). The following constants are defined for the ports:

MCI_SEQ_NONE

Closes the previously used port (if any). The sequencer will behave exactly the same as if a port were open, except no MIDI message will be sent.

MIDI_MAPPER

Sets the port opened to the MIDI Mapper.

MCI_SEQ_SET_SLAVE

Sets the sequencer to receive synchronization data and indicates that the type of synchronization is specified in the **dwSlave** field of the data structure identified by *lpSet*.

MCISEQ returns MCIERR_UNSUPPORTED_FUNCTION.

The following constants are defined for the synchronization type:

MCI_SEQ_FILE

Sets the sequencer to receive synchronization data contained in the MIDI file.

MCI_SEQ_SMPTE

Sets the sequencer to receive SMPTE synchronization data.

MCI_SEQ_MIDI

Sets the sequencer to receive MIDI synchronization data.

MCI_SEQ_NONE

Sets the sequencer to ignore synchronization data in a MIDI stream.

MCI_SEQ_SET_TEMPO

Changes the tempo of the MIDI sequence to that specified by the **dwTempo** field of the structure pointed to by *lpSet*. For sequences with division type PPQN, tempo is specified in beats per minute; for sequences with division type SMPTE, tempo is specified in frames per second.

MCI_SET_TIME_FORMAT

Specifies a time format parameter is included in the **dwTimeFormat** field of the data structure identified by *lpSet*. The following constants are defined for the time format:

MCI_FORMAT_MILLISECONDS

Changes the time format to milliseconds for both input and output.

MCI_FORMAT_SMPTE_24

Sets the time format to 24 frame SMPTE.

MCI_FORMAT_SMPTE_25

Sets the time format to 25 frame SMPTE.

MCI_FORMAT_SMPTE_30

Sets the time format to 30 frame SMPTE.

MCI_FORMAT_SMPTE_30DROP

Sets the time format to 30 drop-frame SMPTE.

MCI_SEQ_FORMAT_SONGPTR
>   Sets the time format to song-pointer units.

LPMCI_SEQ_SET_PARMS   *lpSet*
>   Specifies a far pointer to the **MCI_SEQ_SET_PARMS** data structure.

Videodisc Extensions

DWORD   *dwFlags*
>   The following additional flags apply to videodisc devices:

MCI_SET_TIME_FORMAT
>   Specifies a time format parameter is included in the **dwTimeFormat** field of
>   the data structure identified by *lpSet*. The following constants are defined for
>   the time format:

MCI_FORMAT_CHAPTERS
>   Changes the time format to chapters.

MCI_FORMAT_FRAMES
>   Changes the time format to frames.

MCI_FORMAT_HMS
>   Changes the time format to hours, minutes, and seconds.

MCI_FORMAT_MILLISECONDS
>   Changes the time format to milliseconds for both input and output.

MCI_VD_FORMAT_TRACK
>   Changes the time format to tracks. MCI uses continuous track numbers.

LPMCI_VD_SET_PARMS   *lpSet*
>   Specifies a far pointer to the **MCI_VD_SET_PARMS** structure. (Devices with
>   additional parameters might replace this data structure with a device-specific
>   data structure.)

Waveform Audio Extensions

DWORD   *dwFlags*
>   The following additional flags apply to waveform audio devices:

MCI_WAVE_INPUT
>   Sets the input used for recording to the **wInput** field of the data structure
>   identified by *lpSet*.

MCI_WAVE_OUTPUT

Sets the output used for playing to the **wOutput** field of the data structure identified by *lpSet*.

MCI_WAVE_SET_ANYINPUT

Specifies that any wave input compatible with the current format can be used for recording.

MCI_WAVE_SET_ANYOUTPUT

Specifies that any wave output compatible with the current format can be used for playing.

MCI_WAVE_SET_AVGBYTESPERSEC

Sets the bytes per second used for playing, recording, and saving to the **nAvgBytesPerSec** field of the data structure identified by *lpSet*.

MCI_WAVE_SET_BITSPERSAMPLE

Sets the bits per sample used for playing, recording, and saving to the **nBitsPerSample** field of the data structure identified by *lpSet*.

MCI_WAVE_SET_BLOCKALIGN

Sets the block alignment used for playing, recording, and saving to the **nBlockAlign** field of the data structure identified by *lpSet*.

MCI_WAVE_SET_CHANNELS

Specifies the number of channels is indicated in the **nChannels** field of the data structure identified by *lpSet*.

MCI_WAVE_SET_FORMATTAG

Sets the format type used for playing, recording, and saving to the **wFormatTag** field of the data structure identified by *lpSet*. Specifying WAVE_FORMAT_PCM changes the format to PCM.

MCI_WAVE_SET_SAMPLESPERSEC

Sets the samples per second used for playing, recording, and saving to the **nSamplesPerSec** field of the data structure identified by *lpSet*.

MCI_SET_TIME_FORMAT

Specifies a time format parameter is included in the **dwTimeFormat** field of the data structure identified by *lpSet*. The following constants are defined for the time format:

MCI_FORMAT_BYTES

Changes the time format to bytes for input or output.

MCI_FORMAT_MILLISECONDS

Changes the time format to milliseconds for input or output.

MCI_FORMAT_SAMPLES

Changes the time format to samples for input or output.

LPMCI_WAVE_SET_PARMS *lpSet*

Specifies a far pointer to the **MCI_WAVE_SET_PARMS** data structure. This parameter replaces the standard default parameter data structure identified by *lpDefault*.

Return Value   Returns zero if successful. Otherwise, it returns an MCI error code.

MCI_SOUND

This MCI command message plays system sounds identified in the [sounds] section of the WIN.INI file. The name of the sound is specified in the buffer pointed to by the **lpstrSoundName** field of the data structure identified by *lpInfo*. This is an MCI system message that is not sent to any device.

Parameters   DWORD *dwFlags*

The following standard and command-specific flags apply to all devices:

MCI_NOTIFY

Specifies that MCI should post the **MM_MCINOTIFY** message when this command completes. The window to receive this message is specified in the **dwCallback** field of the data structure identified by *lpInfo*.

MCI_WAIT

Specifies that the playing of the sound should finish before MCI returns control to the application.

MCI_SOUND_NAME

Indicates that the name of a sound to play is included in the **lpstrSoundName** of the data structure identified by *lpSound*. If omitted, the default sound is played.

LPMCI_SOUND_PARMS *lpInfo*

Specifies a far pointer to the **MCI_SOUND_PARMS** data structure.

Return Value   Returns zero if successful. Otherwise, it returns an MCI error code.

Comments   This command will only play files that fit into available memory. Use the MCI waveform audio device to play longer waveform files.

MCI_STATUS

This MCI command message is used to obtain information about an MCI device. All devices respond to this message. The parameters and flags available for this message depend on the selected device. Information is returned in the **dwReturn** field of the data structure identified by *lpStatus*.

Parameters   DWORD   *dwFlags*

The following standard and command-specific flags apply to all devices:

MCI_NOTIFY

Specifies that MCI should post the **MM_MCINOTIFY** message when this command completes. The window to receive this message is specified in the **dwCallback** field of the data structure identified by *lpStatus*.

MCI_WAIT

Specifies that the status operation should finish before MCI returns control to the application.

MCI_STATUS_ITEM

Specifies that the **dwItem** field of the data structure identified by *lpStatus* contains a constant specifying which status item to obtain. The following constants define which status item to return in the **dwReturn** field of the data structure:

MCI_STATUS_CURRENT_TRACK

The **dwReturn** field is set to the current track number. MCI uses continuous track numbers.

MCI_STATUS_LENGTH

The **dwReturn** field is set to the total media length.

MCI_STATUS_MODE

The **dwReturn** field is set to the current mode of the device. The modes include the following:

- MCI_MODE_NOT_READY
- MCI_MODE_PAUSE
- MCI_MODE_PLAY
- MCI_MODE_STOP
- MCI_MODE_OPEN
- MCI_MODE_RECORD
- MCI_MODE_SEEK

MCI_STATUS_NUMBER_OF_TRACKS

The **dwReturn** field is set to the total number of playable tracks.

MCI_STATUS_POSITION

The **dwReturn** field is set to the current position.

MCI_STATUS_READY

The **dwReturn** field is set to TRUE if the device is ready; otherwise, it is set to FALSE.

MCI_STATUS_TIME_FORMAT

The **dwReturn** field is set to the current time format of the device. The time formats include:

- MCI_FORMAT_BYTES
- MCI_FORMAT_FRAMES
- MCI_FORMAT_HMS
- MCI_FORMAT_MILLISECONDS
- MCI_FORMAT_MSF
- MCI_FORMAT_SAMPLES
- MCI_FORMAT_TMSF

MCI_STATUS_START

Obtains the starting position of the media. To get the starting position, combine this flag with MCI_STATUS_ITEM and set the **dwItem** field of the data structure identified by *lpStatus* to MCI_STATUS_POSITION.

MCI_TRACK

Indicates a status track parameter is included in the **dwTrack** field of the data structure identified by *lpStatus*. You must use this flag with the MCI_STATUS_POSITION or MCI_STATUS_LENGTH constants.

When used with MCI_STATUS_POSITION, MCI_TRACK obtains the starting position of the specified track.

When used with MCI_STATUS_LENGTH, MCI_TRACK obtains the length of the specified track. MCI uses continuous track numbers.

LPMCI_STATUS_PARMS   *lpStatus*

Specifies a far pointer to the **MCI_STATUS_PARMS** data structure. (Devices with extended command sets might replace this data structure with a device-specific data structure.)

Animation Extensions

DWORD   *dwFlags*

The following extensions apply to animation devices:

MCI_STATUS_ITEM

Specifies that the **dwItem** field of the data structure identified by *lpStatus* contains a constant specifying which status item to obtain. The following additional status constants are defined for animation devices and indicate which item to return in the **dwReturn** field of the data structure:

MCI_ANIM_STATUS_FORWARD

The **dwReturn** field is set to TRUE if playing forward; otherwise, it is set to FALSE.

MCI_ANIM_STATUS_HPAL

The **dwReturn** field is set to the handle of the movie palette.

MCI_ANIM_STATUS_HWND

The **dwReturn** field is set to the handle of the playback window.

MCI_ANIM_STATUS_SPEED

The **dwReturn** field is set to the animation speed.

MCI_STATUS_MEDIA_PRESENT

The **dwReturn** field is set to TRUE if the media is inserted in the device; otherwise, it is set to FALSE.

LPMCI_STATUS_PARMS   *lpStatus*

Specifies a far pointer to the **MCI_STATUS_PARMS** data structure.

CD Audio Extensions

DWORD   *dwFlags*

The following extensions applies to CD audio devices:

MCI_STATUS_ITEM

Specifies that the **dwItem** field of the data structure identified by *lpStatus* contains a constant specifying which status item to obtain. The following additional status constants are defined for CD audio devices and indicate which item to return in the **dwReturn** field of the data structure:

MCI_STATUS_MEDIA_PRESENT

The **dwReturn** field is set to TRUE if the media is inserted in the device; otherwise, it is set to FALSE.

LPMCI_STATUS_PARMS   *lpStatus*

Specifies a far pointer to the **MCI_STATUS_PARMS** data structure. This parameter replaces the standard default parameter data structure.

MIDI Sequencer Extensions

DWORD   *dwFlags*

The following extensions apply to sequencers:

MCI_STATUS_ITEM

Specifies that the **dwItem** field of the data structure identified by *lpStatus* contains a constant specifying which status item to obtain. The following additional status constants are defined for sequencers and indicate which item to return in the **dwReturn** field of the data structure:

MCI_SEQ_STATUS_DIVTYPE

The **dwReturn** field is set to one of the following values indicating the current division type of a sequence:

- MCI_SEQ_DIV_PPQN
- MCI_SEQ_DIV_SMPTE_24
- MCI_SEQ_DIV_SMPTE_25
- MCI_SEQ_DIV_SMPTE_30
- MCI_SEQ_DIV_SMPTE_30DROP

MCI_SEQ_STATUS_MASTER

The **dwReturn** field is set to the synchronization type used for master operation.

MCI_SEQ_STATUS_OFFSET

The **dwReturn** field is set to the current SMPTE offset of a sequence.

MCI_SEQ_STATUS_PORT

The **dwReturn** field is set to the MIDI device ID for the current port used by the sequence.

MCI_SEQ_STATUS_SLAVE

The **dwReturn** field is set to the synchronization type used for slave operation.

MCI_SEQ_STATUS_TEMPO

The **dwReturn** field is set to the current tempo of a MIDI sequence in beats-per-minute for PPQN files, or frames-per-second for SMPTE files.

MCI_STATUS_MEDIA_PRESENT

The **dwReturn** field is set to TRUE if the media for the device is present; otherwise, it is set to FALSE.

LPMCI_STATUS_PARMS   *lpStatus*

Specifies a far pointer to the **MCI_STATUS_PARMS** data structure. This parameter replaces the standard default parameter data structure.

Videodisc Extensions

DWORD   *dwFlags*

The following additional flags apply to videodisc devices:

MCI_STATUS_ITEM

Specifies that the **dwItem** field of the data structure identified by *lpStatus* contains a constant specifying which status item to obtain. The following additional status constants are defined for videodisc devices and indicate which item to return in the **dwReturn** field of the data structure:

MCI_STATUS_MEDIA_PRESENT

The **dwReturn** field is set to TRUE if the media is inserted in the device; otherwise, it is set to FALSE.

MCI_VD_STATUS_DISC_SIZE

The **dwReturn** field is set to the size of the loaded disc in inches (8 or 12).

MCI_VD_STATUS_FORWARD

The **dwReturn** field is set to TRUE if playing forward; otherwise, it is set to FALSE.

MCI_VD_STATUS_MEDIA_TYPE

The **dwReturn** field is set to the media type of the inserted media. The following media types can be returned:

- MCI_VD_MEDIA_CAV

- MCI_VD_MEDIA_CLV

- MCI_VD_MEDIA_OTHER

MCI_STATUS_MODE

The **dwReturn** field is set to the current mode of the device. All devices can return the following constants to indicate the current mode:

- MCI_MODE_NOT_READY

- MCI_MODE_PAUSE

- MCI_MODE_PLAY

- MCI_MODE_STOP
- MCI_VD_MODE_PARK (videodisc devices)

MCI_VD_STATUS_SIDE

The **dwReturn** field is set to 1 or 2 to indicate which side of the disc is loaded. Not all videodisc devices support this flag.

MCI_VD_STATUS_SPEED

The **dwReturn** field is set to the play speed in frames per second.

MCIPIONR returns MCIERR_UNSUPPORTED_FUNCTION.

LPMCI_STATUS_PARMS   *lpStatus*

Specifies a far pointer to the **MCI_STATUS_PARMS** data structure. This parameter replaces the standard default parameter data structure.

Waveform Audio Extensions

DWORD   *dwFlags*

The following additional flags apply to waveform audio devices:

MCI_STATUS_ITEM

Specifies that the **dwItem** field of the data structure identified by *lpStatus* contains a constant specifying which status item to obtain. The following additional status constants are defined for waveform audio devices and indicate which item to return in the **dwReturn** field of the data structure:

MCI_STATUS_MEDIA_PRESENT

The **dwReturn** field is set to TRUE if the media is inserted in the device; otherwise, it is set to FALSE.

MCI_WAVE_INPUT

The **dwReturn** field is set to the wave input device used for recording. If no device is in use and no device has been explicitly set, then the error return is MCI_WAVE_INPUTUNSPECIFIED.

MCI_WAVE_OUTPUT

The **dwReturn** field is set to the wave output device used for playing. If no device is in use and no device has been explicitly set, then the error return is MCI_WAVE_OUTPUTUNSPECIFIED.

MCI_WAVE_STATUS_AVGBYTESPERSEC

The **dwReturn** field is set to the current bytes per second used for playing, recording, and saving.

MCI_WAVE_STATUS_BITSPERSAMPLE

The **dwReturn** field is set to the current bits per sample used for playing, recording, and saving.

MCI_WAVE_STATUS_BLOCKALIGN

The **dwReturn** field is set to the current block alignment used for playing, recording, and saving.

MCI_WAVE_STATUS_CHANNELS

The **dwReturn** field is set to the current channel count used for playing, recording, and saving.

MCI_WAVE_FORMATTAG

The **dwReturn** field is set to the current format tag used for playing, recording, and saving.

MCI_WAVE_STATUS_LEVEL

The **dwReturn** field is set to the current record or playback level. The value is returned as an 8- or 16-bit value, depending on the sample size used. The right or mono channel level is returned in the low-order word. The left channel level is returned in the high-order word.

MCI_WAVE_STATUS_SAMPLESPERSEC

The **dwReturn** field is set to the current samples per second used for playing, recording, and saving.

LPMCI_STATUS_PARMS   *lpStatus*

Specifies a far pointer to the **MCI_STATUS_PARMS** data structure.

Video Overlay Extensions

DWORD   *dwFlags*

The following additional flags apply to video overlay devices:

MCI_OVLY_STATUS_HWND

The **dwReturn** field is set to the handle of the window associated with the video overlay device.

MCI_STATUS_ITEM

Specifies that the **dwItem** field of the data structure identified by *lpStatus* contains a constant specifying which status item to obtain. The following additional status constants are defined for video overlay devices and indicate which item to return in the **dwReturn** field of the data structure:

MCI_STATUS_MEDIA_PRESENT

The **dwReturn** field is set to TRUE if the media is inserted in the device; otherwise, it is set to FALSE.

LPMCI_STATUS_PARMS   *lpStatus*
> Specifies a far pointer to the **MCI_STATUS_PARMS** data structure.

Return Value   Returns zero if successful. Otherwise, it returns an MCI error code.

MCI_STEP

This MCI command message steps the player one or more frames.

Parameters   DWORD   *dwFlags*
> The following flags apply to all devices supporting **MCI_STEP**:

> MCI_NOTIFY
> > Specifies that MCI should post the **MM_MCINOTIFY** message when this command completes. The window to receive this message is specified in the **dwCallback** field of the data structure identified by *lpStep*.

> MCI_WAIT
> > Specifies that the step operation should finish before MCI returns control to the application.

Animation Extensions

DWORD   *dwFlags*
> The following additional flag applies to animation devices.

> MCI_ANIM_STEP_FRAMES
> > Indicates that the **dwFrames** field of the data structure identified by *lpStep* specifies the number of frames to step.

> MCI_ANIM_STEP_REVERSE
> > Steps in reverse.

LPMCI_ANIM_STEP_PARMS   *lpStep*
> Specifies a far pointer to the **MCI_ANIM_STEP_PARMS** data structure.

Videodisc Extensions

DWORD   *dwFlags*
> The following additional flag applies to videodisc devices.

> MCI_VD_STEP_FRAMES
> > Indicates that the **dwFrames** field of the data structure identified by *lpStep* specifies the number of frames to step.

MCI_VD_STEP_REVERSE

Steps in reverse.

LPMCI_VD_STEP_PARMS   *lpStep*

Specifies a far pointer to the **MCI_VD_STEP_PARMS** data structure.

Return Value   Returns zero if successful. Otherwise, it returns an MCI error code.

Comments   Only devices that return TRUE to the MCI_GETDEVCAPS_HAS_VIDEO capability query support this command at present.

See Also   **MCI_CUE, MCI_PLAY, MCI_SEEK**

MCI_STOP

This MCI command message stops all play and record sequences, unloads all play buffers, and ceases display of video images. Support of this message by a device is optional. The parameters and flags for this message vary according to the selected device.

Parameters   DWORD   *dwFlags*

The following flags apply to all devices supporting **MCI_STOP**:

MCI_NOTIFY

Specifies that MCI should post the **MM_MCINOTIFY** message when this command completes. The window to receive this message is specified in the **dwCallback** field of the data structure identified by *lpStop*.

MCI_WAIT

Specifies that the device should stop before MCI returns control to the application.

LPMCI_GENERIC_PARMS   *lpStop*

Specifies a far pointer to the **MCI_GENERIC_PARMS** data structure. (Devices with extended command sets might replace this data structure with a device-specific data structure.)

Return Value   Returns zero if successful. Otherwise, it returns an MCI error code.

Comments   The difference between **MCI_STOP** and **MCI_PAUSE** depends upon the device. If possible, **MCI_PAUSE** suspends device operation but leaves the device ready to resume play immediately.

See Also   **MCI_PAUSE, MCI_PLAY, MCI_RECORD, MCI_RESUME**

MCI_SYSINFO

This MCI command message returns information about MCI devices. MCI supports this message directly rather than passing it to the devices. String information is returned in the application-supplied buffer pointed to by the **lpstrReturn** field of the data structure identified by *lpSysInfo*. Numeric information is returned as a DWORD placed in the application-supplied buffer. The **dwReturnSize** field specifies the buffer length.

Parameters

DWORD *dwFlags*

The following standard and command-specific flags apply to all devices:

MCI_SYSINFO_INSTALLNAME

Obtains the name (listed in the SYSTEM.INI file) used to install the device.

MCI_SYSINFO_NAME

Obtains a device name corresponding to the device number specified in the **dwNumberField** of the data structure identified by *lpSysInfo* . If the MCI_SYSINFO_OPEN flag is set, MCI returns the names of open devices.

MCI_SYSINFO_OPEN

Obtains the quantity or name of open devices.

MCI_SYSINFO_QUANTITY

Obtains the number of devices of the specified type that are listed in the [mci] section of the SYSTEM.INI file. If the MCI_SYSINFO_OPEN flag is set, the number of open devices is returned.

LPMCI_SYSINFO_PARMS   *lpSysInfo*

Specifies a far pointer to the **MCI_SYSINFO_PARMS** structure.

Return Value

Returns zero if successful. Otherwise, it returns an MCI error code.

Comments

The **wDeviceType** element of the *lpSysInfo* structure is used to indicate the device type of the query. If the *wDeviceID* parameter is set to MCI_ALL_DEVICE_ID it will override the value of **wDeviceType**.

Integer return values are DWORDS returned in the buffer pointed to by the **lpstrReturn** field of **MCI_SYSINFO_PARMS**.

String return values are NULL-terminated strings returned in the buffer pointed to by the **lpstrReturn** field.

MCI_UNFREEZE (VIDEO OVERLAY)

This MCI command message restores motion to an area of the video buffer frozen with **MCI_FREEZE**. This command is part of the video overlay command set. The parameters and flags for this message vary according to the selected device.

Parameters   DWORD *dwFlags*

The following flags apply to all devices supporting **MCI_UNFREEZE**:

MCI_NOTIFY

Specifies that MCI should post the **MM_MCINOTIFY** message when this command completes. The window to receive this message is specified in the **dwCallback** field of the data structure identified by *lpFreeze*.

MCI_WAIT

Specifies that the unfreeze operation should finish before MCI returns control to the application.

MCI_OVLY_RECT

Specifies that the **rc** field of the data structure identified by *lpFreeze* contains a valid display rectangle. This is a required parameter.

LPMCI_OVLY_RECT_PARMS *lpFreeze*

Specifies a far pointer to a **MCI_OVLY_RECT_PARMS** data structure. (Devices with additional parameters might replace this data structure with a device-specific data structure.)

Return Value   Returns zero if successful. Otherwise, it returns an MCI error code.

Comments   This command applies to video overlay devices.

See Also   **MCI_FREEZE**

MCI_WHERE (ANIMATION/VIDEO OVERLAY)

This MCI command message obtains the clipping rectangle for the video device. The top and left fields of the returned rectangle contain the origin of the clipping rectangle, and the right and bottom fields contain the width and height of the clipping rectangle. The parameters and flags for this message vary according to the selected device.

Parameters   DWORD *dwFlags*

The following flags apply to all devices supporting **MCI_WHERE**:

MCI_NOTIFY

Specifies that MCI should post the **MM_MCINOTIFY** message when this command completes. The window to receive this message is specified in the **dwCallback** field of the data structure identified by *lpQuery*.

MCI_WAIT

> Specifies that the operation should complete before MCI returns control to the application.

DWORD   *lpQuery*

Specifies a far pointer to a device-specific data structure. For a description of this parameter, see the *lpQuery* description included with the device extensions.

Animation Extensions

DWORD   *dwFlags*

The following additional flags apply to animation devices supporting **MCI_WHERE**:

MCI_ANIM_WHERE_DESTINATION

> Obtains the destination display rectangle. The rectangle coordinates are placed in the **rc** field of the data structure identified by *lpQuery*.

MCI_ANIM_WHERE_SOURCE

> Obtains the animation source rectangle. The rectangle coordinates are placed in the **rc** field of the data structure identified by *lpQuery*.

LPMCI_ANIM_RECT_PARMS   *lpQuery*

> Specifies a far pointer to a **MCI_ANIM_RECT_PARMS** data structure.

Video Overlay Extensions

DWORD   *dwFlags*

The following additional flags apply to video overlay devices supporting **MCI_WHERE**:

MCI_OVLY_WHERE_DESTINATION

> Obtains the destination display rectangle. The rectangle coordinates are placed in the **rc** field of the data structure identified by *lpQuery*.

MCI_OVLY_WHERE_FRAME

> Obtains the overlay frame rectangle. The rectangle coordinates are placed in the **rc** field of the data structure identified by *lpQuery*.

MCI_OVLY_WHERE_SOURCE

> Obtains the source rectangle. The rectangle coordinates are placed in the **rc** field of the data structure identified by *lpQuery*.

MCI_OVLY_WHERE_VIDEO

> Obtains the video rectangle. The rectangle coordinates are placed in the **rc** field of the data structure identified by *lpQuery*.

LPMCI_OVLY_RECT_PARMS *lpQuery*

Specifies a far pointer to a **MCI_OVLY_RECT_PARMS** data structure.

Return Value   Returns zero if successful. Otherwise, it returns an MCI error code.

Comments   This command applies to animation and video overlay devices.

See Also   **MCI_PUT**

MCI_WINDOW

This MCI command message specifies the window and the window characteristics for graphic devices. Graphic devices should create a default window when a device is opened but should not display it until they receive the play command. The window command is used to supply an application-created window to the device and to change the display characteristics of an application-supplied or default display window. If the application supplies the display window, it should be prepared to update an invalid rectangle on the window.

Support of this message by a device is optional. The parameters and flags for this message vary according to the selected device.

Parameters   DWORD *dwFlags*

The following flags apply to all devices supporting **MCI_WINDOW**:

MCI_NOTIFY

Specifies that MCI should post the **MM_MCINOTIFY** message when this command completes. The window to receive this message is specified in the **dwCallback** field of the data structure identified by *lpWindow*.

MCI_WAIT

Specifies that the operation should finish before MCI returns control to the application.

DWORD *lpWindow*

Specifies a far pointer to a device specific data structure. For a description of this parameter, see the *lpWindow* description included with the device extensions.

Animation Extensions

DWORD *dwFlags*

The following additional flags apply to animation devices supporting **MCI_WINDOW**:

MCI_ANIM_WINDOW_HWND

> Indicates the handle of the window to use for the destination is included in the **hWnd** field of the data structure identified by *lpWindow*. Set this to MCI_ANIM_WINDOW_DEFAULT to return to the default window.

MCI_ANIM_WINDOW_STATE

> Indicates the **nCmdShow** field of the **MCI_ANIM_WINDOW_PARMS** data structure contains parameters for setting the window state. This flag is equivalent to calling **ShowWindow** with the state parameter. The constants are the same as the ones in WINDOWS.H (such as SW_HIDE, SW_MINIMIZE, or SW_SHOWNORMAL.)

MCI_ANIM_WINDOW_TEXT

> Indicates the **lpstrText** field of the **MCI_ANIM_WINDOW_PARMS** data structure contains a pointer to a buffer containing the caption used for the window.

LPMCI_ANIM_WINDOW_PARMS   *lpWindow*

> Specifies a far pointer to a **MCI_ANIM_WINDOW_PARMS** data structure. (Devices with additional parameters might replace this data structure with a device-specific data structure.)

Video Overlay Extensions

DWORD   *dwFlags*

> The following additional flags apply to video overlay devices supporting **MCI_WINDOW**:

MCI_OVLY_WINDOW_HWND

> Indicates the handle of the window used for the destination is included in the **hWnd** field of the **MCI_OVLY_WINDOW_PARMS** data structure. Set this to MCI_OVLY_WINDOW_DEFAULT to return to the default window.

MCI_OVLY_WINDOW_STATE

> Indicates the **nCmdShow** field of the *lpWindow* data structure contains parameters for setting the window state. This flag It is equivalent to calling **showwindow** with the state parameter. The constants are the same as those defined in WINDOWS.H (such as SW_HIDE, SW_MINIMIZE, or SW_SHOWNORMAL.)

MCI_OVLY_WINDOW_TEXT

> Indicates the **lpstrText** field of the **MCI_OVLY_WINDOWS_PARMS** data structure contains a pointer to buffer containing the caption used for the window.

LPMCI_OVLY_WINDOW_PARMS *lpWindow*
Specifies a far pointer to a **MCI_OVLY_WINDOW_PARMS** data structure.
(Devices with additional parameters might replace this data structure with a
device-specific data structure.)

Return Value Returns zero if successful. Otherwise, it returns an MCI error code.

Comments This command applies to animation, and video overlay devices.

MIM_CLOSE

This message is sent to a MIDI input callback function when a MIDI input device is
closed. The device handle is no longer valid once this message has been sent.

Parameters DWORD *dwParam1*
Currently unused.

DWORD *dwParam2*
Currently unused.

Return Value None

See Also **MM_MIM_CLOSE**

MIM_DATA

This message is sent to a MIDI input callback function when a MIDI message is received
by a MIDI input device.

Parameters DWORD *dwParam1*
Specifies the MIDI message that was received. The message is packed into a
DWORD with the first byte of the message in the low-order byte.

DWORD *dwParam2*
Specifies the time that the message was received by the input device driver. The
timestamp is specified in milliseconds, beginning at 0 when **midiInStart** was called.

Return Value None

Comments MIDI messages received from a MIDI input port have running status disabled; each
message is expanded to include the MIDI status byte.

This message is not sent when a MIDI system-exclusive message is received.

See Also **MM_MIM_DATA, MIM_LONGDATA**

MIM_ERROR

This message is sent to a MIDI input callback function when an invalid MIDI message is received.

Parameters   DWORD   *dwParaml*

Specifies the invalid MIDI message that was received. The message is packed into a DWORD with the first byte of the message in the low-order byte.

DWORD   *dwParam2*

Specifies the time that the message was received by the input device driver. The timestamp is specified in milliseconds, beginning at 0 when **midiInStart** was called.

Return Value   None

See Also   **MM_MIM_ERROR**

MIM_LONGDATA

This message is sent to a MIDI input callback function when an input buffer has been filled with MIDI system-exclusive data and is being returned to the application.

Parameters   DWORD   *dwParaml*

Specifies a far pointer to a **MIDIHDR** structure identifying the input buffer.

DWORD   *dwParam2*

Specifies the time that the data was received by the input device driver. The timestamp is specified in milliseconds, beginning at 0 when **midiInStart** was called.

Return Value   None

Comments   The returned buffer may not be full. The **dwBytesRecorded** field of the **MIDIHDR** structure specified by *dwParaml* will specify the number of bytes recorded into the buffer.

See Also   **MIM_DATA, MM_MIM_LONGDATA**

MIM_LONGERROR

This message is sent to a MIDI input callback function when an invalid MIDI system-exclusive message is received.

Parameters   DWORD   *dwParaml*

Specifies a pointer to a **MIDIHDR** structure identifying the buffer containing the invalid message.

DWORD   *dwParam2*
> Specifies the time that the data was received by the input device driver. The timestamp is specified in milliseconds, beginning at 0 when **midiInStart** was called.

Return Value   None

Comments   The returned buffer may not be full. The **dwBytesRecorded** field of the **MIDIHDR** structure specified by *dwParam1* will specify the number of bytes recorded into the buffer.

See Also   **MM_MIM_LONGERROR**

MIM_OPEN

This message is sent to a MIDI input callback function when a MIDI input device is opened.

Parameters   DWORD   *dwParam1*
> Currently unused.

DWORD   *dwParam2*
> Currently unused.

Return Value   None

See Also   **MM_MIM_OPEN**

MM_JOY1BUTTONDOWN

This message is sent to the window that has captured joystick 1 when a button is pressed.

Parameters   WORD   *wParam*
> Indicates which button has changed state. It can be any one of the following combined with any of the flags defined in MM_JOY1MOVE.

> JOY_BUTTON1CHG
>> Set if first joystick button has changed.

> JOY_BUTTON2CHG
>> Set if second joystick button has changed.

> JOY_BUTTON3CHG
>> Set if third joystick button has changed.

> JOY_BUTTON4CHG
>> Set if fourth joystick button has changed.

DWORD   *lParam*

The low-order word contains the current *x*-position of the joystick. The high-order word contains the current *y*-position.

Return Value   None

See Also   **MM_JOY1BUTTONUP**

MM_JOY1BUTTONUP

This message is sent to the window that has captured joystick 1 when a button is released.

Parameters   WORD   *wParam*

Indicates which button has changed state. It can be any one of the following combined with any of the flags defined in MM_JOY1MOVE.

JOY_BUTTON1CHG

Set if first joystick button has changed.

JOY_BUTTON2CHG

Set if second joystick button has changed.

JOY_BUTTON3CHG

Set if third joystick button has changed.

JOY_BUTTON4CHG

Set if fourth joystick button has changed.

DWORD   *lParam*

The low-order word contains the current *x*-position of the joystick. The high-order word contains the current *y*-position.

Return Value   None

See Also   **MM_JOY1BUTTONDOWN**

MM_JOY1MOVE

This message is sent to the window that has captured joystick 1 when the joystick position changes.

Parameters   WORD   *wParam*

Indicates which joystick buttons are pressed. It can be any combination of the following values:

JOY_BUTTON1
> Set if first joystick button is pressed.

JOY_BUTTON2
> Set if second joystick button is pressed.

JOY_BUTTON3
> Set if third joystick button is pressed.

JOY_BUTTON4
> Set if fourth joystick button is pressed.

DWORD *lParam*
> The low-order word contains the current *x*-position of the joystick. The high-order word contains the current *y*-position.

Return Value   None

See Also   **MM_JOY1ZMOVE**

MM_JOY1ZMOVE

This message is sent to the window that has captured joystick 1 when the *z*-axis position changes.

Parameters   WORD *wParam*
> Indicates which joystick buttons are pressed. It can be any combination of the following values:

JOY_BUTTON1
> Set if first joystick button is pressed.

JOY_BUTTON2
> Set if second joystick button is pressed.

JOY_BUTTON3
> Set if third joystick button is pressed.

JOY_BUTTON4
> Set if fourth joystick button is pressed.

DWORD *lParam*
> The low-order word contains the current *z*-position of the joystick.

Return Value   None

See Also   **MM_JOY1MOVE**

MM_JOY2BUTTONDOWN

This message is sent to the window that has captured joystick 2 when a button is pressed.

Parameters   WORD   *wParam*

Indicates which button has changed state. It can be any one of the following combined with any of the flags defined in MM_JOY1MOVE.

JOY_BUTTON1CHG

Set if first joystick button has changed.

JOY_BUTTON2CHG

Set if second joystick button has changed.

JOY_BUTTON3CHG

Set if third joystick button has changed.

JOY_BUTTON4CHG

Set if fourth joystick button has changed.

DWORD   *lParam*

The low-order word contains the current *x*-position of the joystick.
The high-order word contains the current *y*-position.

Return Value   None

See Also   **MM_JOY2BUTTONUP**

MM_JOY2BUTTONUP

This message is sent to the window that has captured joystick 2 when a button is released.

Parameters   WORD   *wParam*

Indicates which button has changed state. It can be any one of the following combined with any of the flags defined in MM_JOY1MOVE.

JOY_BUTTON1CHG

Set if first joystick button has changed.

JOY_BUTTON2CHG

Set if second joystick button has changed.

JOY_BUTTON3CHG

Set if third joystick button has changed.

JOY_BUTTON4CHG

> Set if fourth joystick button has changed.

DWORD   *lParam*

> The low-order word contains the current *x*-position of the joystick. The high-order word contains the current *y*-position.

Return Value   None

See Also   **MM_JOY2BUTTONDOWN**

MM_JOY2MOVE

This message is sent to the window that has captured joystick 2 when the joystick position changes.

Parameters   WORD   *wParam*

> Indicates which joystick buttons are pressed. It can be any combination of the following values:

JOY_BUTTON1

> Set if first joystick button is pressed.

JOY_BUTTON2

> Set if second joystick button is pressed.

JOY_BUTTON3

> Set if third joystick button is pressed.

JOY_BUTTON4

> Set if fourth joystick button is pressed.

DWORD   *lParam*

> The low-order word contains the current *x*-position of the joystick. The high-order word contains the current *y*-position.

Return Value   None

See Also   **MM_JOY2ZMOVE**

MM_JOY2ZMOVE

This message is sent to the window that has captured joystick 2 when the z-axis position changes.

Parameters   WORD   *wParam*

Indicates which joystick buttons are pressed. It can be any combination of the following values:

JOY_BUTTON1

Set if first joystick button is pressed.

JOY_BUTTON2

Set if second joystick button is pressed.

JOY_BUTTON3

Set if third joystick button is pressed.

JOY_BUTTON4

Set if fourth joystick button is pressed.

DWORD   *lParam*

The low-order word contains the current z-position of the joystick.

Return Value   None

See Also   **MM_JOY2MOVE**

MM_MCINOTIFY

This message is sent to a window to notify an application that an MCI device has completed an operation. MCI devices send this message only when the MCI_NOTIFY flag is used with an MCI command message or when the **notify** flag is used with an MCI command string.

Parameters   WORD   *wParam*

Contains one of the following flags:

MCI_NOTIFY_ABORTED

Specifies that the device received a command that prevented the current conditions for initiating the callback from being met. If a new command interrupts the current command and it also requests notification, the device sends only this message and not MCI_NOTIFY_SUPERCEDED.

MCI_NOTIFY_SUCCESSFUL

Specifies that the conditions initiating the callback have been met.

MCI_NOTIFY_SUPERSEDED

Specifies that the device received another command with the MCI_NOTIFY flag set and the current conditions for initiating the callback have been superseded.

MCI_NOTIFY_FAILURE

Specifies that a device error occurred while the device was executing the command.

LONG   *lParam*

The low-order word specifies the ID of the device initiating the callback.

Return Value   Returns zero if successful. Otherwise, it returns an MCI error code.

Comments   A device returns the flag MCI_NOTIFY_SUCCESSFUL with MM_MCINOTIFY when the action for a command finishes. For example, a CD audio device uses this flag for notification for MCI_PLAY when the device finishes playing. The MCI_PLAY command completes successfully only when it reaches the specified end position or reaches the end of the media. Similarly, MCI_SEEK and MCI_RECORD do not return MCI_NOTIFY_SUCCESSFUL until they reach the specified end position or reach the end of the media.

A device returns the flag MCI_NOTIFY_ABORTED with MM_MCINOTIFY only when it receives a command that prevents it from meeting the notification conditions. For example, the command MCI_PLAY would not abort notification for a previous play command provided that the new command does not change the play direction or change the ending position for the play command with an active notify. The MCI_RECORD and MCI_SEEK commands behave similarly.

MCI also does not send MCI_NOTIFY_ABORTED when MCI_PLAY or MCI_RECORD is paused with MCI_PAUSE. Sending the MCI_RESUME command will let them continue to meet the callback conditions.

When your application requests notification for a command, check the error return of **mciSendMessage** or **mciSendCommand**. If these functions encounter an error and return a nonzero value, MCI will not set notification for the command.

MM_MIM_CLOSE

This message is sent to a window when a MIDI input device is closed. The device handle is no longer valid once this message has been sent.

Parameters   WORD   *wParam*

Specifies a handle to the MIDI input device that was closed.

LONG   *lParam*

Currently unused.

Return Value   None

See Also   **MIM_CLOSE**

MM_MIM_DATA

This message is sent to a window when a MIDI message is received by a MIDI input device.

Parameters   WORD   *wParam*

Specifies a handle to the MIDI input device that received the MIDI message.

LONG   *lParam*

Specifies the MIDI message that was received. The message is packed into a DWORD with the first byte of the message in the low-order byte.

Return Value   None

Comments   MIDI messages received from a MIDI input port have running status disabled; each message is expanded to include the MIDI status byte.

This message is not sent when a MIDI system-exclusive message is received. No timestamp is available with this message. For timestamped input data, you must use the messages that are sent to low-level callback functions.

See Also   **MIM_DATA, MM_MIM_LONGDATA**

MM_MIM_ERROR

This message is sent to a window when an invalid MIDI message is received.

Parameters   WORD   *wParam*

Specifies a handle to the MIDI input device that received the invalid message.

LONG   *lParam*

Specifies the invalid MIDI message. The message is packed into a DWORD with the first byte of the message in the low-order byte.

Return Value   None

See Also   **MIM_ERROR**

MM_MIM_LONGDATA

This message is sent to a window when an input buffer has been filled with MIDI system-exclusive data and is being returned to the application.

Parameters
WORD   *wParam*
Specifies a handle to the MIDI input device that received the data.

LONG   *lParam*
Specifies a far pointer to a **MIDIHDR** structure identifying the buffer.

Return Value   None

Comments
The returned buffer may not be full. The **dwBytesRecorded** field of the **MIDIHDR** structure specified by *lParam* will specify the number of bytes recorded into the buffer.

No timestamp is available with this message. For timestamped input data, you must use the messages that are sent to low-level callback functions.

See Also   **MM_MIM_DATA, MIM_LONGDATA**

MM_MIM_LONGERROR

This message is sent to a window when an invalid MIDI system-exclusive message is received.

Parameters
WORD   *wParam*
Specifies a handle to the MIDI input device that received the invalid message.

LONG   *lParam*
Specifies a far pointer to a **MIDIHDR** structure identifying buffer containing the invalid message.

Return Value   None

Comments
The returned buffer may not be full. The **dwBytesRecorded** field of the **MIDIHDR** structure specified by *lParam* will specify the number of bytes recorded into the buffer.

See Also   **MIM_LONGERROR**

MM_MIM_OPEN

This message is sent to a window when a MIDI input device is opened.

Parameters   WORD   *wParam*
Specifies the handle to the MIDI input device that was opened.

LONG   *lParam*
Currently unused.

Return Value   None

See Also   **MIM_OPEN**

MM_MOM_CLOSE

This message is sent to a window when a MIDI output device is closed. The device handle is no longer valid once this message has been sent.

Parameters   WORD   *wParam*
Specifies the handle to the MIDI output device.

LONG   *lParam*
Currently unused.

Return Value   None

See Also   **MOM_CLOSE**

MM_MOM_DONE

This message is sent to a window when the specified system-exclusive buffer has been played and is being returned to the application.

Parameters   WORD   *wParam*
Specifies a handle to the MIDI output device that played the buffer.

LONG   *lParam*
Specifies a far pointer to a **MIDIHDR** structure identifying the buffer.

Return Value   None

See Also   **MOM_DONE**

MM_MOM_OPEN

This message is sent to a window when a MIDI output device is opened.

Parameters   WORD   *wParam*
Specifies the handle to the MIDI output device.

LONG   *lParam*
Currently unused.

Return Value   None

See Also   **MOM_OPEN**

MM_WIM_CLOSE

This message is sent to a window when a waveform input device is closed. The device handle is no longer valid once this message has been sent.

Parameters   WORD   *wParam*
Specifies a handle to the waveform input device that was closed.

LONG   *lParam*
Currently unused.

Return Value   None

See Also   **WIM_CLOSE**

MM_WIM_DATA

This message is sent to a window when waveform data is present in the input buffer and the buffer is being returned to the application. The message can be sent either when the buffer is full, or after the **waveInReset** function is called.

Parameters   WORD   *wParam*
Specifies a handle to the waveform input device that received the waveform data.

LONG   *lParam*
Specifies a far pointer to a WAVEHDR structure identifying the waveform data buffer.

Return Value   None

Comments   The returned buffer may not be full. The **dwBytesRecorded** field of the **WAVEHDR** structure specified by *lParam* will specify the number of bytes recorded into the buffer.

See Also   **WIM_DATA**

MM_WIM_OPEN

This message is sent to a window when a waveform input device is opened.

Parameters   WORD   *wParam*
                        Specifies a handle to the waveform input device that was opened.

                        LONG   *lParam*
                        Currently unused.

Return Value   None

See Also   **WIM_OPEN**

MM_WOM_CLOSE

This message is sent to a window when a waveform output device is closed. The device handle is no longer valid once this message has been sent.

Parameters   WORD   *wParam*
                        Specifies a handle to the waveform output device that was closed.

                        LONG   *lParam*
                        Currently unused.

Return Value   None

See Also   **WOM_CLOSE**

MM_WOM_DONE

This message is sent to a window when the specified output buffer is being returned to the application. Buffers are returned to the application when they have been played, or as the result of a call to **waveOutReset**.

Parameters   WORD   *wParam*
                        Specifies a handle to the waveform output device that played the buffer.

                        LONG   *lParam*
                        Specifies a far pointer to a **WAVEHDR** structure identifying the buffer.

Return Value   None

See Also   **WOM_DONE**

MM_WOM_OPEN

This message is sent to a window when a waveform output device is opened.

Parameters   WORD   *wParam*

Specifies a handle to the waveform output device that was opened.

LONG   *lParam*

Currently unused.

Return Value   None

See Also   **WOM_OPEN**

MMIOM_CLOSE

This message is sent to an I/O procedure by **mmioClose** to request that a file be closed.

Parameters   LONG   *lParam1*

Specifies options contained in the *wFlags* parameter of **mmioClose**.

LONG   *lParam2*

Is not used.

Return Value   The return value is zero if the file is successfully closed. Otherwise, the return value specifies an error code.

See Also   **mmioClose, MMIOM_OPEN**

MMIOM_OPEN

This message is sent to an I/O procedure by **mmioOpen** to request that a file be opened or deleted.

Parameters   LONG   *lParam1*

Specifies a null-terminated string containing the name of the file to open.

LONG   *lParam2*

Is not used.

Return Value   The return value is zero if the operation is successful. Otherwise, the return value specifies an error value. Possible error returns are:

MMIOM_CANNOTOPEN

Specified file could not be opened.

MMIOM_OUTOFMEMORY

Not enough memory to perform operation.

Comments   The **dwFlags** field of the **MMIOINFO** structure contains option flags passed to the **mmioOpen** function. The **lDiskOffset** field of the **MMIOINFO** structure is initialized to zero. If this value is incorrect, then the I/O procedure must correct it.

If the caller passed a **MMIOINFO** structure to **mmioOpen**, the return value will be returned in the **wErrorRet** field.

See Also   **mmioOpen, MMIOM_CLOSE**

MMIOM_READ

This message is sent to an I/O procedure by **mmioRead** to request that a specified number of bytes be read from an open file.

Parameters   LONG   *lParam1*

Specifies a huge pointer to the buffer to be filled with data read from the file.

LONG   *lParam2*

Specifies the number of bytes to read from the file.

Return Value   The return value is the number of bytes actually read from the file. If no more bytes can be read, the return value is zero. If there is an error, the return value is -1.

Comments   The I/O procedure is responsible for updating the **lDiskOffset** field of the **MMIOINFO** structure to reflect the new file position after the read operation.

See Also   **mmioRead, MMIOM_WRITE, MMIOM_WRITEFLUSH**

MMIOM_SEEK

This message is sent to an I/O procedure by **mmioSeek** to request that the current file position be moved.

Parameters   LONG   *lParam1*

Specifies the new file position according to the option flag specified in *lParam2*.

LONG   *lParam2*

Specifies how the file position is changed. Only one of the following flags c an be specified:

SEEK_SET

Move the file position to be *lParam1* bytes from the beginning of the file.

SEEK_CUR

> Move the file position to be *lParam1* bytes from the current position. *lParam1* may be positive or negative.

SEEK_END

> Move the file position to be *lParam1* bytes from the end of the file.

Return Value   The return value is the new file position. If there is an error, the return value is -1.

Comments   The I/O procedure is responsible for maintaining the current file position in the **lDiskOffset** field of the **MMIOINFO** structure.

See Also   **mmioSeek**

MMIOM_WRITE

This message is sent to an I/O procedure by **mmioWrite** to request that data be written to an open file.

Parameters   LONG *lParam1*

> Specifies a huge pointer to a buffer containing the data to write to the file.

LONG *lParam2*

> Specifies the number of bytes to write to the file.

Return Value   The return value is the number of bytes actually written to the file. If there is an error, the return value is -1.

Comments   The I/O procedure is responsible for updating the **lDiskOffset** field of the **MMIOINFO** structure to reflect the new file position after the write operation.

See Also   **mmioWrite, MMIOM_READ, MMIOM_WRITEFLUSH**

MMIOM_WRITEFLUSH

This message is sent to an I/O procedure by **mmioWrite** to request that data be written to an open file and then that any internal buffers used by the I/O procedure be flushed to disk.

Parameters   LONG *lParam1*

> Specifies a huge pointer to a buffer containing the data to write to the file.

LONG *lParam2*

> Specifies the number of bytes to write to the file.

Return Value   The return value is the number of bytes actually written to the file. If there is an error, the return value is -1.

Comments   The I/O procedure is responsible for updating the **lDiskOffset** field of the **MMIOINFO** structure to reflect the new file position after the write operation.

Note that this message is equivalent to the **MMIOM_WRITE** message except that it additionally requests that the I/O procedure flush its internal buffers, if any. Unless an I/O procedure performs internal buffering, this message can be handled exactly like the **MMIOM_WRITE** message.

See Also   **mmioWrite, mmioFlush, MMIOM_READ, MMIOM_WRITE**

MMP_HOOK_FRAME

This message is passed to a Movie Player frame-hook callback function after the Movie Player completes screen updates for the specified frame or subframe.

Parameters   WORD   *wParam*
Specifies the frame index.

LONG   *lParam*
Specifies the subframe index.

Return Value   Not used.

See Also   **mmpSetFrameHook, mmpGetFrameHook, MMP_HOOK_SCRIPT**

MMP_HOOK_SCRIPT

This message is passed to a Movie Player frame-hook callback function before the Movie Player processes the text in the movie script channel.

Parameters   WORD   *wParam*
Specifies the frame index.

LONG   *lParam*
Specifies a far pointer to a null-terminated character buffer containing the script-channel text for this frame.

Return Value   Return FALSE to direct the Movie Player to process the script text for the frame. Return TRUE to indicate that the callback function handled the script text and that the Movie Player should ignore it.

See Also   **mmpSetFrameHook, mmpGetFrameHook, MMP_HOOK_FRAME**

MOM_CLOSE

This message is sent to a MIDI output callback function when a MIDI output device is closed. The device handle is no longer valid once this message has been sent.

Parameters DWORD *dwParam1*
Currently unused.

DWORD *dwParam2*
Currently unused.

Return Value None

See Also **MM_MOM_CLOSE**

MOM_DONE

This message is sent to a MIDI output callback function when the specified system-exclusive buffer has been played and is being returned to the application.

Parameters DWORD *dwParam1*
Specifies a far pointer to a **MIDIHDR** structure identifying the buffer.

DWORD *dwParam2*
Currently unused.

Return Value None

See Also **MM_MOM_DONE**

MOM_OPEN

This message is sent to a MIDI output callback function when a MIDI output device is opened.

Parameters DWORD *dwParam1*
Currently unused.

DWORD *dwParam2*
Currently unused.

Return Value None

See Also **MM_MOM_OPEN**

WIM_CLOSE

This message is sent to a waveform input callback function when a waveform input device is closed. The device handle is no longer valid once this message has been sent.

Parameters

DWORD   *dwParam1*
  Currently unused.

DWORD   *dwParam2*
  Currently unused.

Return Value   None

See Also   **MM_WIM_CLOSE**

WIM_DATA

This message is sent to a waveform input callback function when waveform data is present in the input buffer and the buffer is being returned to the application. The message can be sent either when the buffer is full, or after the **waveInReset** function is called.

Parameters

DWORD   *dwParam1*
  Specifies a far pointer to a **WAVEHDR** structure identifying the buffer containing the waveform data.

DWORD   *dwParam2*
  Currently unused.

Return Value   None

Comments   The returned buffer may not be full. Use the **dwBytesRecorded** field of the **WAVEHDR** structure specified by *dwParam1* to determine the number of bytes recorded into the returned buffer.

See Also   **MM_WIM_DATA**

WIM_OPEN

This message is sent to a waveform input callback function when a waveform input device is opened.

Parameters

DWORD *dwParam1*
   Currently unused.

DWORD *dwParam2*
   Currently unused.

Return Value   None

See Also   **MM_WIM_OPEN**

WM_SYSCOMMAND

This message is sent when the user selects a command from the System menu, when the user selects the minimize or maximize box, or when the screen saver is preparing to blank the screen.

Parameters

WORD *wParam*
   Specifies the type of system command. Windows defines a series of system-command types. The Multimedia extensions add the following system-command type:

SC_SCREENSAVE
   Screen saver will be invoked. Return a nonzero value to prevent the screen saver from being invoked; otherwise, pass the message to **DefWindowProc**.

DWORD *lParam*
   Not used with the SC_SCREENSAVE command.

Return Value   Depends on system-command type.

Comments   Refer to the Windows SDK documentation for a description of the other WM_SYSCOMMAND command types.

WOM_CLOSE

This message is sent to a waveform output callback function when a waveform output device is closed. The device handle is no longer valid once this message has been sent.

Parameters   DWORD   *dwParam1*
Currently unused.

DWORD   *dwParam2*
Currently unused.

Return Value   None

See Also   **MM_WOM_CLOSE**

WOM_DONE

This message is sent to a waveform output callback function when the specified output buffer is being returned to the application. Buffers are returned to the application when they have been played, or as the result of a call to **waveOutReset**.

Parameters   DWORD   *dwParam1*
Specifies a far pointer to a **WAVEHDR** structure identifying the buffer.

DWORD   *dwParam2*
Currently unused.

Return Value   None

See Also   **MM_WOM_DONE**

WOM_OPEN

This message is sent to a waveform output callback function when a waveform output device is opened.

Parameters   DWORD   *dwParam1*
Currently unused.

DWORD   *dwParam2*
Currently unused.

Return Value   None

See Also   **MM_WOM_OPEN**

Chapter 6
Data Types and Structures

This chapter describes data types and data structures used in the Multimedia extensions to Windows. For information about standard Windows data types, see the *Microsoft Windows Software Development Kit Reference Volume 2*. This chapter contains three parts:

- An alphabetical list of all Multimedia extensions data types

- An overview of all data structures, organized by category. This overview includes brief descriptions of all data structures.

- Detailed descriptions of all data structures, organized alphabetically. These descriptions list the structure definition and the type and contents of each field in the structure.

You can also refer to the MMSYSTEM.H and MMP.H header files to see the actual data structure definitions.

Data Types

The Multimedia extensions use the following data types:

FOURCC

A 32-bit value representing a four-character code.

HPSTR

A huge pointer to a character string.

HMIDIIN

A handle to a MIDI input device.

HMIDIOUT

A handle to a MIDI output device.

HMMIO

A handle to an open file.

HWAVEIN

A handle to a waveform input device.

HWAVEOUT

A handle to a waveform output device.

MMPID

An instance identifier for the Multimedia Movie Player.

The MMSYSTEM.H and MMP.H header files also define a series of pointer types associated with Multimedia extensions data structures. Each of these pointer types is named with an LP prefix followed by the name of the corresponding data structure. For example, the **MMTIME** data structure has an associated **LPMMTIME** pointer type.

Data Structure Overview

The Multimedia extensions data structures are grouped as follows:

- Auxiliary audio data structures
- Joystick data structures
- Media Control Interface (MCI) data structures
- MIDI audio data structures
- Multimedia Movie Player data structures
- Multimedia file I/O data structures
- Timer data structures
- Waveform audio data structures

Each data structure has an associated long pointer data type with prefix LP.

Auxiliary Audio Data Structures

The following data structure is used with auxiliary audio devices:

AUXCAPS

A data structure that describes the capabilities of an auxiliary audio device.

Joystick Data Structures

The following data structures are used with joystick functions:

JOYCAPS

A data structure that defines joystick capabilities.

JOYINFO

A data structure for joystick information.

Media Control Interface (MCI) Data Structures

The MCI data structures are divided into the following categories:

- Data structures used with system commands
- Data structures used with required commands
- Data structures used with basic commands
- Data structures used with extended commands

Some MCI commands have several associated data structures; for example, the **MCI_PLAY** command message is used with a generic **MCI_PLAY_PARMS** structure and three extended data structures for the multimedia movie, video overlay, and waveform audio devices. Also, the **MCI_GENERIC_PARMS** data structure is used with several MCI command message.

Data Structures for MCI System Commands

The following data structures are used to specify parameter blocks for system command messages (message handled directly by MCI):

MCI_BREAK_PARMS

A data structure that specifies parameters for the **MCI_BREAK** command.

MCI_SOUND_PARMS

A data structure that specifies parameters for the **MCI_SOUND** command.

MCI_SYSINFO_PARMS

A data structure that specifies parameters for the **MCI_SYSINFO** command.

Data Structures for MCI Required Commands

The following data structures are used to specify parameter blocks for required command messages (messages handled by all MCI devices):

MCI_GENERIC_PARMS

A data structure that specifies parameters for the **MCI_CLOSE** command.

MCI_GETDEVCAPS_PARMS

A data structure that specifies parameters for the **MCI_GETDEVCAPS** command.

MCI_INFO_PARMS

A data structure that specifies parameters for the **MCI_INFO** command.

MCI_OPEN_PARMS
MCI_ANIM_OPEN_PARMS (multimedia movie device)
MCI_OVLY_OPEN_PARMS (video overlay device)
MCI_WAVE_OPEN_PARMS (waveform audio device)

Data structures that specify parameters for the **MCI_OPEN** command.

MCI_STATUS_PARMS

A data structure that specifies parameters for the **MCI_STATUS** command.

Data Structures for MCI Basic Commands

The following data structures are used to specify parameter blocks for basic command messages (messages recognized by all MCI devices):

MCI_GENERIC_PARMS

A data structure that specifies parameters for the **MCI_PAUSE, MCI_RESUME,** and **MCI_STOP** commands.

MCI_LOAD_PARMS
MCI_OVLY_LOAD_PARMS (video overlay device)

A data structure that specifies parameters for the **MCI_LOAD** command.

MCI_PLAY_PARMS
MCI_ANIM_PLAY_PARMS (multimedia movie device)
MCI_VD_PLAY_PARMS (videodisc device)

Data structures that specify parameters for the **MCI_PLAY** command.

MCI_RECORD_PARMS

A data structure that specifies parameters for the **MCI_RECORD** command.

MCI_SAVE_PARMS
MCI_OVLY_SAVE_PARMS (video overlay device)

A data structure that specifies parameters for the **MCI_SAVE** command.

MCI_SEEK_PARMS

A data structure that specifies parameters for the **MCI_SEEK** command.

MCI_SET_PARMS
MCI_SEQ_SET_PARMS (sequencer device)
MCI_WAVE_SET_PARMS (waveform audio device)
>   Data structures that specify parameters for the **MCI_SET** command.

Data Structures for MCI Extended Commands

The following data structures are used to specify parameter blocks for MCI extended command messages (messages defined for specific MCI device types):

MCI_WAVE_DELETE_PARMS (waveform audio device)
>   A data structure that specifies parameters for the **MCI_DELETE** command.

MCI_VD_ESCAPE_PARMS (video overlay device)
>   A data structure that specifies parameters for the **MCI_ESCAPE** command.

MCI_ANIM_RECT_PARMS (multimedia movie device)
MCI_OVLY_RECT_PARMS (video overlay device)
>   Data structures that specify parameters for the **MCI_PUT** and **MCI_WHERE** commands.

MCI_ANIM_STEP_PARMS (multimedia movie device)
MCI_VD_STEP_PARMS (videodisc device)
>   Data structures that specify parameters for the **MCI_STEP** command used with the multimedia movie and video overlay devices.

MCI_ANIM_UPDATE_PARMS (multimedia movie device)
MCI_OVLY_UPDATE_PARMS (video overlay device)
>   A data structure that specifies parameters for the **MCI_UPDATE** command used with the multimedia movie and video overlay devices.

MCI_ANIM_WINDOW_PARMS (multimedia movie device)
MCI_OVLY_WINDOW_PARMS (video overlay device)
>   Data structures that specify parameters for the **MCI_WINDOW** command used with the multimedia movie and video overlay devices.

MIDI Audio Data Structures

The following data structures are used with MIDI functions:

MIDIHDR

A data structure representing a header for MIDI input and output data blocks.

MIDIINCAPS

A data structure that describes the capabilities of a MIDI input device.

MIDIOUTCAPS

A data structure that describes the capabilities of a MIDI output device.

Movie Playback Data Structures

The following data structures are used with movie playback functions:

MMPACTION

A data structure that contains a Movie Player action entry (script-channel command).

MMPLABEL

A data structure that contains a Movie Player label entry.

MMPMOVIEINFO

A data structure that describes a multimedia movie file.

Multimedia File I/O Data Structures

The following data structures are used with the multimedia file I/O functions:

MMIOINFO

A data structure for information about an open file.

MMCKINFO

A data structure for information about a RIFF chunk in an open file.

Timer Data Structures

The following data structures are used with timer functions:

MMTIME

A data structure that represents time in one of several different formats.

TIMECAPS

A data structure that defines timer capabilities.

Waveform Audio Data Structures

The following data structures are used with waveform functions:

MMTIME

A data structure used to represent time to waveform functions.

PCMWAVEFORMAT

A data structure representing the format of PCM waveform data.

WAVEFORMAT

A data structure representing generic format information common to all types of waveform data.

WAVEHDR

A data structure representing a header for waveform input and output data blocks.

WAVEINCAPS

A data structure that describes the capabilities of a waveform input device.

WAVEOUTCAPS

A data structure that describes the capabilities of a waveform output device.

Data Structures Reference

This section lists the Multimedia extensions data structures alphabetically. Each structure description shows the definition of the structure type and a description of each structure field.

AUXCAPS_LRVOLUME

Supports separate left and right volume control.

Comments

If a device supports volume changes, the AUXCAPS_VOLUME flag will be set for the **dwSupport** field. If a device supports separate volume changes on the left and right channels, both the AUXCAPS_VOLUME and the AUXCAPS_LRVOLUME flags will be set for this field.

See Also

auxGetDevCaps

JOYCAPS

Structure for storing joystick capability information.

```
typedef struct joyinfo_tag {
    WORD   wMid;
    WORD   wPid;
    char   szPname[MAXPNAMELEN];
    WORD   wXmin;
    WORD   wXmax;
    WORD   wYmin;
    WORD   wYmax;
    WORD   wZmin;
    WORD   wZmax;
    WORD   wNumButtons;
    WORD   wPeriodMin;
    WORD   wPeriodMax;
} JOYCAPS;
```

Fields

The **JOYCAPS** structure has the following fields:

wMid

Specifies the manufacturer ID of the joystick. Manufacturer IDs are listed in Appendix B, "Manufacturer ID and Product ID Lists."

wPid

Specifies the product ID of the joystick. Product IDs are listed in Appendix B, "Manufacturer ID and Product ID Lists."

szPname[MAXPNAMELEN]

Specifies the product name of the joystick, stored as a NULL-terminated string.

wXmin

Specifies the minimum x-position value of the joystick.

wXmax

Specifies the maximum x-position value of the joystick.

wYmin

Specifies the minimum y-position value of the joystick.

wYmax

Specifies the maximum y-position value of the joystick.

wZmin

Specifies the minimum z-position value of the joystick.

wZmax

Specifies the maximum z-position value of the joystick.

wNumButtons

Specifies the number of buttons on the joystick.

wPeriodMin

Specifies the smallest polling interval supported when captured by **joySetCapture**.

wPeriodMax

Specifies the largest polling interval supported when captured by **joySetCapture**.

See Also   **joyGetDevCaps**

JOYINFO

Structure for storing joystick position and button state information.

```
typedef struct joyinfo_tag {
    WORD   wXpos;
    WORD   wYpos;
    WORD   wZpos;
    WORD   wButtons;
} JOYINFO;
```

Fields   The **JOYINFO** structure has the following fields:

wXpos

Specifies the current x-position of joystick.

wYpos

Specifies the current y-position of joystick.

wZpos

Specifies the current z-position of joystick.

wButtons

Specifies the current state of joystick buttons. It can be any combination of the following bit flags:

JOY_BUTTON1

Set if button 1 is pressed.

JOY_BUTTON2

Set if button 2 is pressed.

JOY_BUTTON3

Set if button 3 is pressed.

JOY_BUTTON4

Set if button 4 is pressed.

See Also   **joyGetPos**

MCI_ANIM_OPEN_PARMS

The **MCI_ANIM_OPEN_PARMS** structure contains information for MCI_OPEN message. When assigning data to the fields in this data structure, set the corresponding MCI flags in the *dwFlags* parameter of **mciSendCommand** to validate the fields. You can use the **MCI_OPEN_PARMS** data structure in place of **MCI_ANIM_OPEN_PARMS** if you are not using the extended data fields.

```
typedef struct {
    DWORD  dwCallback;
    WORD   wDeviceID;
    WORD   wReserved0;
    LPSTR  lpstrDeviceType;
    LPSTR  lpstrElementName;
    LPSTR  lpstrAlias;
    DWORD  dwStyle;
    WORD   hWndParent;
    WORD   wReserved1;
} MCI_ANIM_OPEN_PARMS;
```

Fields   The **MCI_ANIM_OPEN_PARMS** structure has the following fields:

dwCallback

The low-order word specifies a window handle used for the MCI_NOTIFY flag.

wDeviceID

Specifies the device ID returned to user.

wReserved0

Reserved field.

lpstrDeviceType

Specifies the name or constant ID of the device type.

lpstrElementName

Specifies the device element name (usually a pathname).

lpstrAlias

Specifies an optional device alias.

dwStyle

Specifies the window style.

hWndParent

Specifies the handle to use as the window parent.

wReserved1

Reserved.

See Also   **MCI_OPEN**

MCI_ANIM_PLAY_PARMS

The **MCI_ANIM_PLAY_PARMS** structure contains parameters for the **MCI_PLAY** message for animation devices. When assigning data to the fields in this data structure, set the corresponding MCI flags in the *dwFlags* parameter of **mciSendCommand** to validate the fields. You can use the **MCI_PLAY_PARMS** data structure in place of **MCI_ANIM_PLAY_PARMS** if you are not using the extended data fields.

```
typedef struct {
    DWORD   dwCallback;
    DWORD   dwFrom;
    DWORD   dwTo;
    DWORD   dwSpeed;
} MCI_ANIM_PLAY_PARMS;
```

Fields   The **MCI_ANIM_PLAY_PARMS** structure has the following fields:

dwCallback

The low-order word specifies a window handle used for the MCI_NOTIFY flag.

dwFrom

Specifies the position to play from.

dwTo

Specifies the position to play to.

dwSpeed

Specifies the play rate in frames per second.

See Also   **MCI_PLAY**

MCI_ANIM_RECT_PARMS

The **MCI_ANIM_RECT_PARMS** structure contains parameters for the **MCI_PUT** and **MCI_WHERE** messages for animation devices. When assigning data to the fields in this data structure, set the corresponding MCI flags in the *dwFlags* parameter of **mciSendCommand** to validate the fields.

```
typedef struct {
    DWORD  dwCallback;
    RECT   rc;
} MCI_ANIM_RECT_PARMS;
```

Fields   The **MCI_ANIM_RECT_PARMS** structure has the following fields:

dwCallback

The low-order word specifies a window handle used for the MCI_NOTIFY flag.

rc

Specifies a rectangle.

See Also   **MCI_PUT**, **MCI_WHERE**

MCI_ANIM_STEP_PARMS

The **MCI_ANIM_STEP_PARMS** structure contains parameters for the **MCI_STEP** message for animation devices. When assigning data the fields in this data structure, set the corresponding MCI flags in the *dwFlags* parameter of **mciSendCommand** to validate the fields.

```
typedef struct {
    DWORD  dwCallback;
    DWORD  dwFrames;
} MCI_ANIM_STEP_PARMS;
```

Fields   The **MCI_ANIM_STEP_PARMS** structure has the following fields:

dwCallback

The low-order word specifies a window handle used for the MCI_NOTIFY flag.

dwFrames

Specifies the number of frames to step.

See Also   MCI_STEP

MCI_ANIM_UPDATE_PARMS

The **MCI_ANIM_UPDATE_PARMS** structure contains parameters for the **MCI_UPDATE** message for animation devices. When assigning data to the fields in this data structure, set the corresponding MCI flags in the *dwFlags* parameter of **mciSendCommand** to validate the fields.

```
typedef struct {
    DWORD  dwCallback;
    RECT   rc;
    HDC    hDC;
} MCI_ANIM_UPDATE_PARMS;
```

Fields   The **MCI_ANIM_UPDATE_PARMS** structure has the following fields:

dwCallback

The low-order word specifies a window handle used for the MCI_NOTIFY flag.

rc

Specifies a window rectangle.

hDC

Specifies a handle to the device context.

See Also   MCI_UPDATE

MCI_ANIM_WINDOW_PARMS

The **MCI_ANIM_WINDOW_PARMS** structure contains parameters for the **MCI_WINDOW** message for animation devices. When assigning data to the fields in this data structure, set the corresponding MCI flags in the *dwFlags* parameter of **mciSendCommand** to validate the fields.

```
typedef struct {
    DWORD  dwCallback;
    WORD   hWnd;
    WORD   wReserved1;
    WORD   nCmdShow;
    WORD   wReserved2;
    LPSTR  lpstrText;
} MCI_ANIM_WINDOW_PARMS;
```

Fields   The **MCI_ANIM_WINDOW_PARMS** structure has the following fields:

dwCallback
The low-order word specifies a window handle used for the MCI_NOTIFY flag.

hWnd
Specifies a handle to the display window.

wReserved1
Reserved.

nCmdShow
Specifies how the window is displayed.

wReserved2
Reserved.

lpstrText
Specifies a long pointer to a null-terminated string containing the window caption.

See Also   **MCI_WINDOW**

MCI_BREAK_PARMS

The **MCI_BREAK_PARMS** structure contains parameters for the **MCI_BREAK** message. When assigning data to the fields in this data structure, set the corresponding MCI flags in the *dwFlags* parameter of **mciSendCommand** to validate the fields.

```
typedef struct {
    DWORD  dwCallback;
    int  nVirtKey;
    WORD  wReserved0;
    HWND  hwndBreak;
    WORD  wReserved1;
} MCI_BREAK_PARMS;
```

Fields   The **MCI_BREAK_PARMS** structure has the following fields:

dwCallback
The low-order word specifies a window handle used for the MCI_NOTIFY flag.

nVirtKey
Specifies the virtual key code used for the break key.

wReserved0
Reserved.

hwndBreak

Specifies a window handle of the window that must be the current window for break detection.

wReserved1

Reserved.

See Also   **MCI_BREAK**

MCI_GENERIC_PARMS

The **MCI_GENERIC_PARMS** structure contains the information for MCI command messages that have empty parameter lists. When assigning data to the fields in this data structure, set the corresponding MCI flags in the *dwFlags* parameter of **mciSendCommand** to validate the fields.

```
typedef struct {
    DWORD  dwCallback;
} MCI_GENERIC_PARMS;
```

Fields   The **MCI_GENERIC_PARMS** structure has the following fields:

dwCallback

The low-order word specifies a window handle used for the MCI_NOTIFY flag.

MCI_GETDEVCAPS_PARMS

The **MCI_GETDEVCAPS_PARMS** structure contains parameters for the **MCI_GETDEVCAPS** message. When assigning data to the fields in this data structure, set the corresponding MCI flags in the *dwFlags* parameter of **mciSendCommand** to validate the fields.

```
typedef struct {
    DWORD  dwCallback;
    DWORD  dwReturn;
    DWORD  dwItem;
} MCI_GETDEVCAPS_PARMS;
```

Fields   The **MCI_GETDEVCAPS_PARMS** structure has the following fields:

dwCallback

The low-order word specifies a window handle used for the MCI_NOTIFY flag.

dwReturn

Contains the return information on exit.

dwItem

Identifies the capability being queried.

See Also   **MCI_GETDEVCAPS**

MCI_INFO_PARMS

The **MCI_INFO_PARMS** structure contains parameters for the **MCI_INFO** message. When assigning data to the fields in this data structure, set the corresponding MCI flags in the *dwFlags* parameter of **mciSendCommand** to validate the fields.

```
typedef struct {
    DWORD  dwCallback;
    LPSTR  lpstrReturn;
    DWORD  dwRetSize;
} MCI_INFO_PARMS;
```

Fields   The **MCI_INFO_PARMS** structure has the following fields:

dwCallback

The low-order word specifies a window handle used for the MCI_NOTIFY flag.

lpstrReturn

Specifies a long pointer to a user-supplied buffer for the return string.

dwRetSize

Specifies the size in bytes of the buffer for the return string.

See Also   **MCI_INFO**

MCI_LOAD_PARMS

The **MCI_LOAD_PARMS** structure contains the information for **MCI_LOAD** message. When assigning data to the fields in this data structure, set the corresponding MCI flags in the *dwFlags* parameter of **mciSendCommand** to validate the fields.

```
typedef struct {
    DWORD  dwCallback;
    LPSTR  lpfilename;
} MCI_LOAD_PARMS;
```

Fields   The **MCI_LOAD_PARMS** structure has the following fields:

dwCallback

The low-order word specifies a window handle used for the MCI_NOTIFY flag.

lpfilename

Specifies a far pointer to a null-terminated string containing the filename of the device element to load.

See Also   MCI_LOAD

MCI_OPEN_PARMS

The **MCI_OPEN_PARMS** structure contains information for MCI open message. When assigning data to the fields in this data structure, set the corresponding MCI flags in the *dwFlags* parameter of **mciSendCommand** to validate the fields.

```
typedef struct {
    DWORD  dwCallback;
    WORD   wDeviceID;
    WORD   wReserved0;
    LPSTR  lpstrDeviceType;
    LPSTR  lpstrElementName;
    LPSTR  lpstrAlias;
} MCI_OPEN_PARMS;
```

Fields   The **MCI_OPEN_PARMS** structure has the following fields:

dwCallback

The low-order word specifies a window handle used for the MCI_NOTIFY flag.

wDeviceID

Contains the device ID returned to user.

wReserved0

Reserved.

lpstrDeviceType

Specifies the name or constant ID of the device type.

lpstrElementName

Specifies the device element name (usually a pathname).

lpstrAlias

Specifies an optional device alias.

See Also   MCI_OPEN

MCI_OVLY_LOAD_PARMS

The **MCI_OVLY_LOAD_PARMS** structure contains parameters for the MCI_LOAD message for video overlay devices. When assigning data to the fields in this data structure, set the corresponding MCI flags in the *dwFlags* parameter of **mciSendCommand** to validate the fields.

```
typedef struct {
    DWORD  dwCallback;
    DWORD  lpfilename;
    RECT  rc;
} MCI_OVLY_LOAD_PARMS;
```

Fields

The **MCI_OVLY_LOAD_PARMS** structure has the following fields:

dwCallback

The low-order word specifies a window handle used for the MCI_NOTIFY flag.

lpfilename

Specifies a far pointer to the buffer containing a null-terminated string.

rc

Specifies a rectangle.

See Also   **MCI_LOAD**

MCI_OVLY_OPEN_PARMS

The **MCI_OVLY_OPEN_PARMS** structure contains information for **MCI_OPEN** message for video overlay devices. When assigning data to the fields in this data structure, set the corresponding MCI flags in the *dwFlags* parameter of **mciSendCommand** to validate the fields. You can use the **MCI_OPEN_PARMS** data structure in place of **MCI_OVLY_OPEN_PARMS** if you are not using the extended data fields.

```
typedef struct {
    DWORD  dwCallback;
    WORD   wDeviceID;
    WORD   wReserved0;
    LPSTR  lpstrDeviceType;
    LPSTR  lpstrElementName;
    LPSTR  lpstrAlias;
    DWORD  dwStyle;
    DWORD  hWndParent;
    WORD   wReserved1;
} MCI_OVLY_OPEN_PARMS;
```

Fields

The **MCI_OVLY_OPEN_PARMS** structure has the following fields:

dwCallback

The low-order word specifies a window handle used for the MCI_NOTIFY flag.

wDeviceID

Specifies the device ID returned to user.

wReserved0

Reserved.

lpstrDeviceType

Specifies the name or contstant ID of the device type obtained from the SYSTEM.INI file.

lpstrElementName

Specifies the device element name (usually a pathname).

lpstrAlias

Specifies an optional device alias.

dwStyle

Specifies the window style.

hWndParent

Specifies the handle to use as the window parent.

wReserved1

Reserved.

See Also   **MCI_OPEN**

MCI_OVLY_RECT_PARMS

The **MCI_OVLY_RECT_PARMS** structure contains parameters for the **MCI_PUT** and **MCI_WHERE** messages for video overlay devices. When assigning data to the fields in this data structure, set the corresponding MCI flags in the *dwFlags* parameter of **mciSendCommand** to validate the fields.

```
typedef struct {
    DWORD  dwCallback;
    RECT   rc;
} MCI_OVLY_RECT_PARMS;
```

Fields   The **MCI_OVLY_RECT_PARMS** structure has the following fields:

dwCallback

The low-order word specifies a window handle used for the MCI_NOTIFY flag.

rc
> Specifies a rectangle.

See Also   **MCI_PUT, MCI_WHERE**

MCI_OVLY_SAVE_PARMS

The **MCI_OVLY_SAVE_PARMS** structure contains parameters for the **MCI_SAVE** message for video overlay devices. When assigning data to the fields in this data structure, set the corresponding MCI flags in the *dwFlags* parameter of **mciSendCommand** to validate the fields.

```
typedef struct {
    DWORD  dwCallback;
    DWORD  lpfilename;
    RECT   rc;
} MCI_OVLY_SAVE_PARMS;
```

Fields   The **MCI_OVLY_SAVE_PARMS** structure has the following fields:

dwCallback
> The low-order word specifies a window handle used for the MCI_NOTIFY flag.

lpfilename
> Specifies a far pointer to the buffer containing a null-terminated string.

rc
> Specifies a rectangle.

See Also   **MCI_SAVE**

MCI_OVLY_WINDOW_PARMS

The **MCI_OVLY_WINDOW_PARMS** structure contains parameters for the **MCI_WINDOW** message for video overlay devices. When assigning data to the fields in this data structure, set the corresponding MCI flags in the *dwFlags* parameter of **mciSendCommand** to validate the fields.

```
typedef struct {
    DWORD  dwCallback;
    WORD   hWnd;
    WORD   wReserved1;
    WORD   nCmdShow;
    WORD   wReserved2;
    LPSTR  lpstrText;
} MCI_OVLY_WINDOW_PARMS;
```

Fields

The **MCI_OVLY_WINDOW_PARMS** structure has the following fields:

dwCallback

The low-order word specifies a window handle used for the MCI_NOTIFY flag.

hWnd

Specifies a handle to the display window.

wReserved1

Reserved.

nCmdShow

Specifies how the window is displayed.

wReserved2

Reserved.

lpstrText

Specifies a long pointer to a null-terminated buffer containing the window caption.

See Also

MCI_WINDOW

MCI_PLAY_PARMS

The **MCI_PLAY_PARMS** structure contains parameters for the **MCI_PLAY** message. When assigning data to the fields in this data structure, set the corresponding MCI flags in the *dwFlags* parameter of **mciSendCommand** to validate the fields.

```
typedef struct {
    DWORD   dwCallback;
    DWORD   dwFrom;
    DWORD   dwTo;
} MCI_PLAY_PARMS;
```

Fields

The **MCI_PLAY_PARMS** structure has the following fields:

dwCallback

The low-order word specifies a window handle used for the MCI_NOTIFY flag.

dwFrom

Specifies the position to play from.

dwTo

Specifies the position to play to.

See Also

MCI_PLAY

MCI_RECORD_PARMS

The **MCI_RECORD_PARMS** structure contains parameters for the **MCI_RECORD** message. When assigning data to the fields in this data structure, set the corresponding MCI flags in the *dwFlags* parameter of **mciSendCommand** to validate the fields.

```
typedef struct {
    DWORD  dwCallback;
    DWORD  dwFrom;
    DWORD  dwTo;
} MCI_RECORD_PARMS;
```

Fields

The **MCI_RECORD_PARMS** structure has the following fields:

dwCallback

The low-order word specifies a window handle used for the MCI_NOTIFY flag.

dwFrom

Specifies the position to play from.

dwTo

Specifies the position to play to.

See Also

MCI_RECORD

MCI_SAVE_PARMS

The **MCI_SAVE_PARMS** structure contains the information for **MCI_SAVE** message. When assigning data to the fields in this data structure, set the corresponding MCI flags in the *dwFlags* parameter of **mciSendCommand** to validate the fields.

```
typedef struct {
    DWORD  dwCallback;
    DWORD  lpfilename;
} MCI_SAVE_PARMS;
```

Fields

The **MCI_SAVE_PARMS** structure has the following fields:

dwCallback

The low-order word specifies a window handle used for the MCI_NOTIFY flag.

lpfilename

Specifies a far pointer to the buffer containing a null-terminated string.

See Also

MCI_SAVE

MCI_SEEK_PARMS

The **MCI_SEEK_PARMS** structure contains parameters for the **MCI_SEEK** message. When assigning data to the fields in this data structure, set the corresponding MCI flags in the *dwFlags* parameter of **mciSendCommand** to validate the fields.

```
typedef struct {
    DWORD   dwCallback;
    DWORD   dwTo;
} MCI_SEEK_PARMS;
```

Fields

The **MCI_SEEK_PARMS** structure has the following fields:

dwCallback

The low-order word specifies a window handle used for the MCI_NOTIFY flag.

dwTo

Specifies the position to seek to.

See Also   **MCI_SEEK**

MCI_SEQ_SET_PARMS

The **MCI_SEQ_SET_PARMS** structure contains parameters for the **MCI_SET** message for MIDI sequencer devices. When assigning data to the fields in this data structure, set the corresponding MCI flags in the *dwFlags* parameter of **mciSendCommand** to validate the fields.

```
typedef struct {
    DWORD   dwCallback;
    DWORD   dwTimeFormat;
    DWORD   dwAudio;
    DWORD   dwTempo;
    DWORD   dwPort;
    DWORD   dwSlave;
    DWORD   dwMaster;
    DWORD   dwOffset;
} MCI_SEQ_SET_PARMS;
```

Fields

The **MCI_SEQ_SET_PARMS** structure has the following fields:

dwCallback

The low-order word specifies a window handle used for the MCI_NOTIFY flag.

dwTimeFormat

Specifies the time format of the sequencer.

dwAudio

Specifies the audio output channel.

dwTempo

Specifies the tempo.

dwPort

Specifies the output port.

dwSlave

Specifies the type of synchronization used by the sequencer for slave operation.

dwMaster

Specifies the type of synchronization used by the sequencer for master operation.

dwOffset

Specifies the data offset.

See Also   **MCI_SET**

MCI_SET_PARMS

The **MCI_SET_PARMS** structure contains parameters for the **MCI_SET** message. When assigning data to the fields in this data structure, set the corresponding MCI flags in the *dwFlags* parameter of **mciSendCommand** to validate the fields.

```
typedef struct {
    DWORD  dwCallback;
    DWORD  dwTimeFormat;
    DWORD  dwAudio;
} MCI_SET_PARMS;
```

Fields   The **MCI_SET_PARMS** structure has the following fields:

dwCallback

The low-order word specifies a window handle used for the MCI_NOTIFY flag.

dwTimeFormat

Specifies the time format used by the device.

dwAudio

Specifies the audio output channel.

See Also   **MCI_SET**

MCI_SOUND_PARMS

The **MCI_SOUND_PARMS** structure contains parameters for the **MCI_SOUND** message. When assigning data to the fields in this data structure, set the corresponding MCI flags in the *dwFlags* parameter of **mciSendCommand** to validate the fields.

```
typedef struct {
    DWORD  dwCallback;
    LPSTR  lpstrSoundName;
} MCI_SOUND_PARMS;
```

Fields

The **MCI_SOUND_PARMS** structure has the following fields:

dwCallback

The low-order word specifies a window handle used for the MCI_NOTIFY flag.

lpstrSoundName

Specifies a far pointer to a null-terminated string containing the name of the sound or the name of the file containing the sound to be played.

See Also

MCI_SOUND

MCI_STATUS_PARMS

The **MCI_STATUS_PARMS** structure contains parameters for the **MCI_STATUS** message. When assigning data to the fields in this data structure, set the corresponding MCI flags in the *dwFlags* parameter of **mciSendCommand** to validate the fields.

```
typedef struct {
    DWORD  dwCallback;
    DWORD  dwReturn;
    DWORD  dwItem;
    DWORD  dwTrack;
} MCI_STATUS_PARMS;
```

Fields

The **MCI_STATUS_PARMS** structure has the following fields:

dwCallback

The low-order word specifies a window handle used for the MCI_NOTIFY flag.

dwReturn

Contains the return information on exit.

dwItem

Identifies the capability being queried.

dwTrack

Specifies the length or number of tracks.

See Also   MCI_STATUS

MCI_SYSINFO_PARMS

The **MCI_SYSINFO_PARMS** structure contains parameters for the **MCI_SYSINFO** message. When assigning data to the fields in this data structure, set the corresponding MCI flags in the *dwFlags* parameter of **mciSendCommand** to validate the fields.

```
typedef struct {
    DWORD  dwCallback;
    LPSTR  lpstrReturn;
    DWORD  dwRetSize;
    DWORD  dwNumber;
    WORD   wDeviceType;
    WORD   wReserved0;
} MCI_SYSINFO_PARMS;
```

Fields   The **MCI_SYSINFO_PARMS** structure has the following fields:

dwCallback

The low-order word specifies a window handle used for the MCI_NOTIFY flag.

lpstrReturn

Specifies a long pointer to a user-supplied buffer for the return string. It is also used to return a DWORD when the MCI_SYSINFO_QUANTITY flag is used.

dwRetSize

Specifies the size in bytes of the buffer for the return string.

dwNumber

Specifies a number indicating the device position in the MCI device table or in the list of open devices if the MCI_SYSINFO_OPEN flag is set.

wDeviceType

Specifies the type of device.

wReserved0

Reserved.

See Also   MCI_SYSINFO

MCI_VD_ESCAPE_PARMS

The **MCI_VD_ESCAPE_PARMS** structure contains parameters for the **MCI_ESCAPE** message for videodisc devices. When assigning data to the fields in this data structure, set the corresponding MCI flags in the *dwFlags* parameter of **mciSendCommand** to validate the fields.

```
typedef struct {
    DWORD  dwCallback;
    LPSTR  lpstrCommand;
} MCI_VD_ESCAPE_PARMS;
```

Fields

The **MCI_VD_ESCAPE_PARMS** structure has the following fields:

dwCallback

The low-order word specifies a window handle used for the MCI_NOTIFY flag.

lpstrCommand

Specifies a far pointer to a null-terminated buffer containing the command to send to the device.

See Also

MCI_ESCAPE

MCI_VD_PLAY_PARMS

The **MCI_VD_PLAY_PARMS** structure contains parameters for the **MCI_PLAY** message for videodiscs. When assigning data to the fields in this data structure, set the corresponding MCI flags in the *dwFlags* parameter of **mciSendCommand** to validate the fields. You can use the **MCI_PLAY_PARMS** data structure in place of **MCI_VD_PLAY_PARMS** if you are not using the extended data fields.

```
typedef struct {
    DWORD  dwCallback;
    DWORD  dwFrom;
    DWORD  dwTo;
    DWORD  dwSpeed;
} MCI_VD_PLAY_PARMS;
```

Fields

The **MCI_VD_PLAY_PARMS** structure has the following fields:

dwCallback

The low-order word specifies a window handle used for the MCI_NOTIFY flag.

dwFrom

Specifies the position to play from.

dwTo

Specifies the position to play to.

dwSpeed

Specifies the playing speed in frames per second.

See Also   **MCI_PLAY**

MCI_VD_STEP_PARMS

The **MCI_VD_STEP_PARMS** structure contains parameters for the **MCI_STEP** message for videodiscs. When assigning data to the fields in this data structure, set the corresponding MCI flags in the *dwFlags* parameter of **mciSendCommand** to validate the fields.

```
typedef struct {
    DWORD   dwCallback;
    DWORD   dwFrames;
} MCI_VD_STEP_PARMS;
```

Fields   The **MCI_VD_STEP_PARMS** structure has the following fields:

dwCallback

The low-order word specifies a window handle used for the MCI_NOTIFY flag.

dwFrames

Specifies the number of frames to step.

See Also   **MCI_STEP**

MCI_WAVE_DELETE_PARMS

The **MCI_WAVE_DELETE_PARMS** structure contains parameters for the **MCI_DELETE** message for waveform audio devices. When assigning data to the fields in this data structure, set the corresponding MCI flags in the *dwFlags* parameter of **mciSendCommand** to validate the fields.

```
typedef struct {
    DWORD   dwCallback;
    DWORD   dwFrom;
    DWORD   dwTo;
} MCI_WAVE_DELETE_PARMS;
```

Fields   The **MCI_WAVE_DELETE_PARMS** structure has the following fields:

dwCallback

The low-order word specifies a window handle used for the MCI_NOTIFY flag.

dwFrom

Specifies the starting position for the delete.

dwTo

Specifies the end position for the delete.

See Also   **MCI_DELETE**

MCI_WAVE_OPEN_PARMS

The **MCI_WAVE_OPEN_PARMS** structure contains information for **MCI_OPEN** message for waveform audio devices. When assigning data to the fields in this data structure, set the corresponding MCI flags in the *dwFlags* parameter of **mciSendCommand** to validate the fields. You can use the **MCI_OPEN_PARMS** data structure in place of **MCI_WAVE_OPEN_PARMS** if you are not using the extended data fields.

```
typedef struct {
    DWORD  dwCallback;
    WORD   wDeviceID;
    WORD   wReserved0;
    LPSTR  lpstrDeviceType;
    LPSTR  lpstrElementName;
    LPSTR  lpstrAlias;
    DWORD  dwBufferSeconds;
} MCI_WAVE_OPEN_PARMS;
```

Fields

The **MCI_WAVE_OPEN_PARMS** structure has the following fields:

dwCallback

The low-order word specifies a window handle used for the MCI_NOTIFY flag.

wDeviceID

Specifies the device ID returned to user.

wReserved0

Reserved.

lpstrDeviceType

Specifies the name or constant ID of the device type obtained.

lpstrElementName

Specifies the device element name (usually a pathname).

lpstrAlias

Specifies an optional device alias.

dwBufferSeconds

Specifies the buffer length in seconds.

See Also   **MCI_OPEN**

MCI_WAVE_SET_PARMS

The **MCI_WAVE_SET_PARMS** structure contains parameters for the **MCI_SET** message for waveform audio devices. When assigning data to the fields in this data structure, set the corresponding MCI flags in the *dwFlags* parameter of **mciSendCommand** to validate the fields.

```
typedef struct {
    DWORD  dwCallback;
    DWORD  dwTimeFormat;
    DWORD  dwAudio;
    WORD   wInput;
    WORD   wReserved0;
    WORD   wOutput;
    WORD   wReserved1;
    WORD   wFormatTag;
    WORD   wReserved2;
    WORD   nChannels;
    WORD   wReserved3;
    DWORD  nSamplesPerSec;
    DWORD  nAvgBytesPerSec;
    WORD   nBlockAlign;
    WORD   wReserved4;
    WORD   wBitsPerSample;
    WORD   wReserved5;
} MCI_WAVE_SET_PARMS;
```

Fields   The **MCI_WAVE_SET_PARMS** structure has the following fields:

dwCallback

The low-order word specifies a window handle used for the MCI_NOTIFY flag.

dwTimeFormat

Specifies the time format used by by the device.

dwAudio

Specifies the channel used for audio output.

wInput

Specifies the channel used for audio input.

wReserved0

Reserved.

wOutput

Specifies the channel used for output.

wReserved1

Reserved.

wFormatTag

Species the interpretation of the waveform data.

wReserved2

Reserved.

nChannels

Specifies mono (1) or stereo (2).

wReserved3

Reserved.

nSamplesPerSec

Specifies the samples per second used for the waveform.

nAvgBytesPerSec

Specifies the sample rate in bytes per second.

nBlockAlign

Specifies the block alignment of the data.

wReserved4

Reserved.

wBitsPerSample

Specifies the number of bits per sample.

wReserved5

Reserved.

See Also   **MCI_SET**

MIDIHDR

The **MIDIHDR** structure defines the header used to identify a MIDI system-exclusive data buffer.

```
typedef struct midihdr_tag {
    LPSTR  lpData;
    DWORD  dwBufferLength;
    DWORD  dwBytesRecorded;
    DWORD  dwUser;
    DWORD  dwFlags;
    struct midihdr_tag far *  lpNext;
    DWORD  reserved;
} MIDIHDR;
```

Fields

The **MIDIHDR** structure has the following fields:

lpData

Specifies a far pointer to the system-exclusive data buffer.

dwBufferLength

Specifies the length of the data buffer.

dwBytesRecorded

When the header is used in input, this specifies how much data is in the buffer.

dwUser

Specifies user data.

dwFlags

Specifies flags giving information about the data buffer.

MHDR_DONE

Set by the device driver to indicate that it is finished with the data buffer and is returning it to the application.

MHDR_PREPARED

Set by Windows to indicate that the data buffer has been prepared with **midiInPrepareHeader** or **midiOutPrepareHeader**.

lpNext

Is reserved and should not be used.

reserved

Is reserved and should not be used.

MIDIINCAPS

The **MIDIINCAPS** structure describes the capabilities of a MIDI input device.

```
typedef struct midiincaps_tag {
    WORD  wMid;
    WORD  wPid;
    VERSION  vDriverVersion;
    char  szPname[MAXPNAMELEN];
} MIDIINCAPS;
```

Fields

The **MIDIINCAPS** structure has the following fields:

wMid

Specifies a manufacturer ID for the device driver for the MIDI input device. Manufacturer IDs are defined in Appendix B, "Manufacturer ID and Product ID Lists."

wPid

Specifies a product ID for the MIDI input device. Product IDs are defined in Appendix B, "Manufacturer ID and Product ID Lists."

vDriverVersion

Specifies the version number of the device driver for the MIDI input device. The high-order byte is the major version number, and the low-order byte is the minor version number.

szPname[MAXPNAMELEN]

Specifies the product name in a NULL-terminated string.

See Also

midiInGetDevCaps

MIDIOUTCAPS

The **MIDIOUTCAPS** structure describes the capabilities of a MIDI output device.

```
typedef struct midioutcaps_tag {
    WORD   wMid;
    WORD   wPid;
    VERSION   vDriverVersion;
    char   szPname[MAXPNAMELEN];
    WORD   wTechnology;
    WORD   wVoices;
    WORD   wNotes;
    WORD   wChannelMask;
    DWORD   dwSupport;
} MIDIOUTCAPS;
```

Fields

The **MIDIOUTCAPS** structure has the following fields:

wMid

Specifies a manufacturer ID for the device driver for the MIDI output device. Manufacturer IDs are defined in Appendix B, "Manufacturer ID and Product ID Lists."

wPid

Specifies a product ID for the MIDI output device. Product IDs are defined in Appendix B, "Manufacturer ID and Product ID Lists."

vDriverVersion

Specifies the version number of the device driver for the MIDI output device. The high-order byte is the major version number, and the low-order byte is the minor version number.

szPname[MAXPNAMELEN]

Specifies the product name in a NULL-terminated string.

wTechnology

Describes the type of the MIDI output device according to one of the following flags:

MOD_MIDIPORT

Indicates the device is a MIDI hardware port.

MOD_SQSYNTH

Indicates the device is a square wave synthesizer.

MOD_FMSYNTH

Indicates the device is an FM synthesizer.

MOD_MAPPER

Indicates the device is the Microsoft MIDI Mapper.

wVoices

Specifies the number of voices supported by an internal synthesizer device. If the device is a port, the field is not meaningful and will be set to 0.

wNotes

Specifies the maximum number of simultaneous notes that may be played by an internal synthesizer device. If the device is a port, the field is not meaningful and will be set to 0.

wChannelMask

Specifies the channels that an internal synthesizer device responds to, where the least significant bit refers to channel 0 and the most significant bit to channel 15. Port devices transmit on all channels and so will set this field to 0xFFFF.

dwSupport

Specifies optional functionality supported by the device.

MIDICAPS_VOLUME

Supports volume control.

MIDICAPS_LRVOLUME

Supports separate left and right volume control.

MIDICAPS_CACHE

Supports patch caching.

Comments   If a device supports volume changes, the MIDICAPS_VOLUME flag will be set for the **dwSupport** field. If a device supports separate volume changes on the left and right channels, both the MIDICAPS_VOLUME and the MIDICAPS_LRVOLUME flags will be set for this field.

See Also   **midiOutGetDevCaps**

MMCKINFO

This structure contains information about a chunk in a RIFF file.

```
typedef struct _MMCKINFO {
    FOURCC  ckid;
    DWORD   cksize;
    FOURCC  fccType;
    DWORD   dwDataOffset;
    DWORD   dwFlags;
} MMCKINFO;
```

Fields

The **MMCKINFO** structure has the following fields:

ckid

Specifies the chunk ID of the chunk.

cksize

Specifies the size of the data field of the chunk. The size of the data field does not include the four-byte chunk ID, the four-byte chunk size, or the optional pad byte at the end of the data field.

fccType

Specifies the form type for "RIFF" chunks or the list type for "LIST" chunks.

dwDataOffset

Specifies the file offset of the beginning of the chunk's data field, relative to the beginning of the file.

dwFlags

Specifies flags giving additional information about the chunk. Contains zero or more of the following flags:

MMIO_DIRTY

Indicates that the length of the chunk may have changed and should be updated by **mmioAscend**. This flag is set when a chunk is created by **mmioCreateChunk**.

MMIOINFO

This structure contains the current state of a file opened with **mmioOpen**.

```
typedef struct _MMIOINFO {
    DWORD  dwFlags;
    FOURCC fccIOProc;
    LPMMIOPROC pIOProc;
    WORD   wErrorRet;
    WORD   wReserved;
    LONG   cchBuffer;
    HPSTR  pchBuffer;
    HPSTR  pchNext;
    HPSTR  pchEndRead;
    HPSTR  pchEndWrite;
    LONG   lBufOffset;
    LONG   lDiskOffset;
    DWORD  adwInfo[4];
    DWORD  dwReserved1;
    DWORD  dwReserved2;
    HMMIO  hmmio;
} MMIOINFO;
```

Fields

The **MMIOINFO** structure has the following fields:

dwFlags

Specifies options indicating how a file was opened:

MMIO_READ

The file was opened only for reading.

MMIO_WRITE

The file was opened only for writing.

MMIO_READWRITE

The file was opened for both reading and writing.

MMIO_COMPAT

The file was opened with compatibility mode, allowing any process on a given machine to open the file any number of times.

MMIO_EXCLUSIVE

The file was opened with exclusive mode, denying other processes both read and write access to the file.

MMIO_DENYWRITE

Other processes are denied write access to the file.

MMIO_DENYREAD

Other processes are denied read access to the file.

MMIO_DENYNONE

Other processes are not denied read or write access to the file.

MMIO_CREATE

mmioOpen was directed to create the file, or truncate it to zero length if it already existed.

MMIO_ALLOCBUF

The file's I/O buffer was allocated by **mmioOpen** or **mmioSetBuffer**.

fccIOProc

Specifies the four-character code identifying the file's I/O procedure. If the I/O procedure is not an installed I/O procedure, **fccIOProc** is NULL.

pIOProc

Specifies the address of the file's I/O procedure.

wErrorRet

Holds the extended error value from **mmioOpen** if **mmioOpen** returns NULL. Is not used to return extended error information from any other functions.

wReserved

Reserved for future use.

cchBuffer

Specifies the size of the file's I/O buffer in bytes. If the file does not have an I/O buffer, this field is zero.

pchBuffer

Specifies the address of the file's I/O buffer. If the file is unbuffered, **pchBuffer** is NULL.

pchNext

Specifies a huge pointer to the next location in the I/O buffer to be read or written. If no more bytes can be read without calling **mmioAdvance** or **mmioRead**, then this field points to **pchEndRead**. If no more bytes can be written without calling **mmioAdvance** or **mmioWrite**, then this field points to **pchEndWrite**.

pchEndRead

Specifies a pointer to the location that is one byte past the last location in the buffer that can be read.

pchEndWrite

Specifies a pointer to the location that is one byte past the last location in the buffer that can be written.

lBufOffset

Reserved for internal use by MMIO functions.

lDiskOffset

Specifies the current file position. The current file position is an offset in bytes from the beginning of the file. I/O procedures are responsible for maintaining this field.

adwInfo[4]

Contained state information maintained by the I/O procedure. I/O procedures can also use these fields to transfer information from the caller to the I/O procedure when the caller opens a file.

dwReserved1

Reserved for internal use by MMIO functions.

dwReserved2

Reserved for internal use by MMIO functions.

hmmio

Specifies the MMIO handle to the open file. I/O procedures can use this handle when calling other MMIO functions.

See Also   mmioGetInfo

MMPACTION

The **MMPACTION** structure contains information about a movie file script-channel command.

```
typedef struct tagMMPACTION {
    BYTE  bMenuItem;
    BYTE  bActionCode;
    WORD  wTextOffset;
} MMPACTION;
```

Fields   The **MMPACTION** structure has the following fields:

bMenuItem

Specifies the menu item number from the script-channel window.

bActionCode

Not used by Movie Player.

wTextOffset

> Specifies the offset of the script-channel text from the start of the action text block.

Comments The action text is stored in packed format, without terminating NULL characters. To determine the length of an action-text entry, subtract the **wTextOffset** value of the action entry from the **wTextOffset** value of the next action entry in the list. The action-entry list contains one action entry beyond the count of action-code entries returned by the **mmpGetInfo** function. The **wTextOffset** value of the last **MMPACTION** structure indexes one byte beyond the end of the action-code text.

See Also **mmpGetInfo, mmpSetInfo**

MMPLABEL

The **MMPLABEL** structure contains information about a movie file label entry.

```
typedef struct tagMMPLABEL {
    WORD  wFrameNum;
    WORD  wTextOffset;
} MMPLABEL;
```

Fields The **MMPLABEL** structure has the following fields:

wFrameNum

> Specifies the frame number associated with the label.

wTextOffset

> Specifies the offset of the label text from the start of the label text block.

Comments The label text is stored in packed format without terminating NULL characters. To determine the length of a label entry, subtract the **wTextOffset** value of the label entry from the **wTextOffset** value of the next label entry. The label list contains one label entry beyond the count of label entries returned by the **mmpGetInfo** function. The **wTextOffset** value of the last **MMPLABEL** structure indexes one byte beyond the end of the label text.

See Also **mmpGetInfo, mmpSetInfo**

MMPMOVIEINFO

The **MMPMOVIEINFO** structure contains information about a movie file.

```
typedef struct tagMMPMOVIEINFO {
    DWORD  dwFileVersion;
    DWORD  dwTotalFrames;
    DWORD  dwInitialFramesPerSecond;
    WORD  wPixelDepth;
    DWORD  dwMovieExtentX;
    DWORD  dwMovieExtentY;
    char  chFullMacName[128];
} MMPMOVIEINFO;
```

Fields

The **MMPMOVIEINFO** structure has the following fields:

dwFileVersion

Specifies the version of the authoring system used to create the file. The high-order word contains the major version number, and the low-order word contains the minor version number.

dwTotalFrames

Specifies the number of frames in the movie.

dwInitialFramesPerSecond

Specifies the initial tempo of the movie in frames per second. This field is set to zero if the **mmpGetFileInfo** function was used to retrieve the movie information.

wPixelDepth

Specifies the number of bits per pixel under which the movie was authored (either 1, 4, or 8).

dwMovieExtentX

Specifies the pixel width of the movie playback area.

dwMovieExtentY

Specifies the pixel length of the movie playback area.

chFullMacName[128]

Specifies the movie title in a NULL-terminated string.

See Also   **mmpGetFileInfo, mmpGetMovieInfo**

MMTIME

General purpose structure for timing information.

```
typedef struct mmtime_tag {
    WORD  wType;
    union {
        DWORD  ms;
        DWORD  sample;
        DWORD  cb;
        struct {
            BYTE  hour;
            BYTE  min;
            BYTE  sec;
            BYTE  frame;
            BYTE  fps;
            BYTE  dummy;
        } smpte;
        struct {
            DWORD  songptrpos;
        } midi;
    } u;
} MMTIME;
```

Fields

The **MMTIME** structure has the following fields:

wType

Specifies the type of the union.

TIME_MS

Time counted in milliseconds.

TIME_SAMPLES

Number of wave samples.

TIME_BYTES

Current byte offset.

TIME_SMPTE

SMPTE time.

TIME_MIDI

MIDI time.

u

The contents of the union. The following fields are contained in union **u**:

ms

Milliseconds. Used when **wType** is TIME_MS.

sample

Samples. Used when **wType** is TIME_SAMPLES.

cb

Byte count. Used when **wType** is TIME_BYTES.

smpte

SMPTE time. Used when **wType** is TIME_SMPTE. The following fields are contained in structure **smpte**:

hour

Hours.

min

Minutes.

sec

Seconds.

frame

Frames.

fps

Frames per second (24, 25, 29(30 drop) or 30).

dummy

Dummy byte for alignment.

midi

MIDI time. Used when **wType** is TIME_MIDI. The following fields are contained in structure **midi**:

songptrpos

Song pointer position.

PCMWAVEFORMAT

The **PCMWAVEFORMAT** structure describes the data format for PCM waveform data.

```
typedef struct pcmwaveformat_tag {
    WAVEFORMAT  wf;
    WORD  wBitsPerSample;
} PCMWAVEFORMAT;
```

Fields

The **PCMWAVEFORMAT** structure has the following fields:

wf

Specifies a **WAVEFORMAT** structure containing general information about the format of the waveform data.

wBitsPerSample

Specifies the number of bits per sample.

See Also

WAVEFORMAT

TIMECAPS

Structure for returning information about the resolution of the timer.

```
typedef struct timecaps_tag {
    WORD  wPeriodMin;
    WORD  wPeriodMax;
} TIMECAPS;
```

Fields

The **TIMECAPS** structure has the following fields:

wPeriodMin

Minimum period supported by timer.

wPeriodMax

Maximum period supported by timer.

See Also

timeGetDevCaps

WAVEFORMAT

The **WAVEFORMAT** structure describes the format of waveform data. Only format information common to all waveform data formats is included in this structure. For formats that require additional information, this structure is included as a field in another data structure along with the additional information.

```
typedef struct waveformat_tag {
    WORD   wFormatTag;
    WORD   nChannels;
    DWORD  nSamplesPerSec;
    DWORD  nAvgBytesPerSec;
    WORD   nBlockAlign;
} WAVEFORMAT;
```

Fields

The **WAVEFORMAT** structure has the following fields:

wFormatTag

Specifies the format type. Currently defined format types are as follows:

WAVE_FORMAT_PCM
Waveform data is PCM.

nChannels

Specifies the number of channels in the waveform data. Mono data uses 1 channel and stereo data uses 2 channels.

nSamplesPerSec

Specifies the sample rate in samples per second.

nAvgBytesPerSec

Specifies the required average data transfer rate in bytes per second.

nBlockAlign

Specifies the block alignment in bytes. The block alignment is the minimum atomic unit of data.

Comments

For PCM data, the block alignment is the number of bytes used by a single sample, including data for both channels if the data is stereo. For example, the block alignment for 16-bit stereo PCM is 4 bytes (2 channels, 2 bytes per sample).

See Also

PCMWAVEFORMAT

WAVEHDR

The **WAVEHDR** structure defines the header used to identify a waveform data buffer.

```
typedef struct wavehdr_tag {
    LPSTR  lpData;
    DWORD  dwBufferLength;
    DWORD  dwBytesRecorded;
    DWORD  dwUser;
    DWORD  dwFlags;
    DWORD  dwLoops;
    struct wavehdr_tag far *  lpNext;
    DWORD  reserved;
} WAVEHDR;
```

Fields

The **WAVEHDR** structure has the following fields:

lpData

Specifies a far pointer to the waveform data buffer.

dwBufferLength

Specifies the length of the data buffer.

dwBytesRecorded

When the header is used in input, this specifies how much data is in the buffer.

dwUser

Specifies 32 bits of user data.

dwFlags

Specifies flags giving information about the data buffer.

WHDR_DONE

Set by the device driver to indicate that it is finished with the data buffer and is returning it to the application.

WHDR_BEGINLOOP

Specifies that this buffer is the first buffer in a loop. This flag is only used with output data buffers.

WHDR_ENDLOOP

Specifies that this buffer is the last buffer in a loop. This flag is only used with output data buffers.

WHDR_PREPARED

Set by Windows to indicate that the data buffer has been prepared with **waveInPrepareHeader** or **waveOutPrepareHeader**.

dwLoops

Specifies the number of times to play the loop. This parameter is used only with output data buffers.

lpNext

Is reserved and should not be used.

reserved

Is reserved and should not be used.

Comments   Use the WHDR_BEGINLOOP and WHDR_ENDLOOP flags in the **dwFlags** field to specify the beginning and ending data blocks for looping. To loop on a single block, specify both flags for the same block. Use the **dwLoops** field in the **WAVEHDR** structure for the first block in the loop to specify the number of times to play the loop.

WAVEINCAPS

The **WAVEINCAPS** structure describes the capabilities of a waveform input device.

```
typedef struct waveincaps_tag {
    WORD   wMid;
    WORD   wPid;
    VERSION  vDriverVersion;
    char   szPname[MAXPNAMELEN];
    DWORD  dwFormats;
    WORD   wChannels;
} WAVEINCAPS;
```

Fields   The **WAVEINCAPS** structure has the following fields:

wMid

Specifies a manufacturer ID for the device driver for the waveform input device. Manufacturer IDs are defined in Appendix B, "Manufacturer ID and Product ID Lists."

wPid

Specifies a product ID for the waveform input device. Product IDs are defined in Appendix B, "Manufacturer ID and Product ID Lists."

vDriverVersion

Specifies the version number of the device driver for the waveform input device. The high-order byte is the major version number, and the low-order byte is the minor version number.

szPname[MAXPNAMELEN]

Specifies the product name in a NULL-terminated string.

dwFormats

Specifies which standard formats are supported. The supported formats are specified with a logical OR of the following flags:

WAVE_FORMAT_1M08
    11.025 kHz, Mono, 8-bit

WAVE_FORMAT_1S08
    11.025 kHz, Stereo, 8-bit

WAVE_FORMAT_1M16
    11.025 kHz, Mono, 16-bit

WAVE_FORMAT_1S16
    11.025 kHz, Stereo, 16-bit

WAVE_FORMAT_2M08
    22.05 kHz, Mono, 8-bit

WAVE_FORMAT_2S08
    22.05 kHz, Stereo, 8-bit

WAVE_FORMAT_2M16
    22.05 kHz, Mono, 16-bit

WAVE_FORMAT_2S16
    22.05 kHz, Stereo, 16-bit

WAVE_FORMAT_4M08
    44.1 kHz, Mono, 8-bit

WAVE_FORMAT_4S08
    44.1 kHz, Stereo, 8-bit

WAVE_FORMAT_4M16
    44.1 kHz, Mono, 16-bit

WAVE_FORMAT_4S16
    44.1 kHz, Stereo, 16-bit

wChannels

Specifies whether the device supports mono (1) or stereo (2) input.

See Also   **waveInGetDevCaps**

WAVEOUTCAPS

The **WAVEOUTCAPS** structure describes the capabilities of a waveform output device.

```
typedef struct waveoutcaps_tag {
    WORD   wMid;
    WORD   wPid;
    VERSION  vDriverVersion;
    char   szPname[MAXPNAMELEN];
    DWORD  dwFormats;
    WORD   wChannels;
    DWORD  dwSupport;
} WAVEOUTCAPS;
```

Fields

The **WAVEOUTCAPS** structure has the following fields:

wMid

Specifies a manufacturer ID for the device driver for the waveform output device. Manufacturer IDs are defined in Appendix B, "Manufacturer ID and Product ID Lists."

wPid

Specifies a product ID for the waveform output device. Product IDs are defined in Appendix B, "Manufacturer ID and Product ID Lists."

vDriverVersion

Specifies the version number of the device driver for the waveform output device. The high-order byte is the major version number, and the low-order byte is the minor version number.

szPname[MAXPNAMELEN]

Specifies the product name in a NULL-terminated string.

dwFormats

Specifies which standard formats are supported. The supported formats are specified with a logical OR of the following flags:

WAVE_FORMAT_1M08
    11.025 kHz, Mono, 8-bit

WAVE_FORMAT_1S08
    11.025 kHz, Stereo, 8-bit

WAVE_FORMAT_1M16
    11.025 kHz, Mono, 16-bit

WAVE_FORMAT_1S16
11.025 kHz, Stereo, 16-bit

WAVE_FORMAT_2M08
22.05 kHz, Mono, 8-bit

WAVE_FORMAT_2S08
22.05 kHz, Stereo, 8-bit

WAVE_FORMAT_2M16
22.05 kHz, Mono, 16-bit

WAVE_FORMAT_2S16
22.05 kHz, Stereo, 16-bit

WAVE_FORMAT_4M08
44.1 kHz, Mono, 8-bit

WAVE_FORMAT_4S08
44.1 kHz, Stereo, 8-bit

WAVE_FORMAT_4M16
44.1 kHz, Mono, 16-bit

WAVE_FORMAT_4S16
44.1 kHz, Stereo, 16-bit

wChannels

Specifies whether the device supports mono (1) or stereo (2) output.

dwSupport

Specifies optional functionality supported by the device.

WAVECAPS_PITCH
Supports pitch control.

WAVECAPS_PLAYBACKRATE
Supports playback rate control.

WAVECAPS_VOLUME
Supports volume control.

WAVECAPS_LRVOLUME
Supports separate left and right volume control.

Comments   If a device supports volume changes, the WAVECAPS_VOLUME flag will be set for the **dwSupport** field. If a device supports separate volume changes on the left and right channels, both the WAVECAPS_VOLUME and the WAVECAPS_LRVOLUME flags will be set for this field.

See Also   **waveOutGetDevCaps**

Chapter 7

MCI Command Strings

There are two ways to communicate with the Media Control Interface: the command-message interface and the command-string interface. Chapter 4, "Message Overview," and Chapter 5, "Message Directory" cover the command-message interface to MCI. This chapter covers the command-string interface to MCI.

It covers the following topics:

- About MCI Commands

- Creating and using MCI command strings

- Using MCITEST to experiment with MCI command strings

- Tables of MCI command strings for MCI devices

About MCI Commands

MCI command strings are sent to MCI device drivers with the **mciSendString** and **mciExecute** functions. The commands divide into the following categories:

- *System commands* are interpreted directly by MCI rather than being relayed to a device.

- *Required commands* are supported by all MCI devices.

- *Basic commands* are optional commands. If a device uses a basic command, it must respond to all options for that command. If a device does not use a basic command, it will return "Action not available for this device."

- *Extended commands* are specific to a device type or device class, for example, videodisc players. These commands contain both unique commands and extensions to the required and basic commands.

System Commands

The following list summarizes the system commands. MCI supports these commands directly rather than passing them to MCI devices.

Message	Description
break	Sets a break key for an MCI device.
sound	Play sounds from the [sounds] section of the WIN.INI file.
sysinfo	Returns information about MCI devices.

Required Commands

The following list summarizes the required commands. All devices support these commands.

Message	Description
capability	Obtains the capabilities of a device.
close	Closes the device.
info	Obtains textual information from a device.
open	Initializes the device.
status	Obtains status information from the device.

Basic Commands

The following list summarizes the basic commands. The use of these messages by a device is optional.

Message	Description
load	Recalls data from a disk file.
pause	Stops playing.
play	Starts transmitting output data.
record	Starts recording input data.
resume	Resumes playing or recording on a paused device.

Message	Description
save	Saves data to a disk file.
seek	Seeks forward or backward.
set	Sets the operating state of the device.
status	Obtains status information about the device. (The flags for this command supplement the flags for the command in the required command group.)
stop	Stops playing.

Extended Commands

MCI devices can have additional commands or extend the definition of the required and basic commands. While some extended commands only apply to a specific device driver, most of them apply to all devices of a particular type. For example, the MIDI sequencer command set extends the **set** command to add time formats that are needed by MIDI sequencers. You can find descriptions of extended commands in the command tables in this chapter. You can find a summary of the syntax used for the commands strings in Appendix A, "MCI Command String Syntax Summary."

Creating a Command String

There are three components associated with each command string: the command, the name of the device receiving the command, and the command arguments. A command string has the following form:

command   device_name   arguments

These components contain the following information:

- The *command* includes a command from the system, required, basic, or extended command set. Examples of commands include **open**, **close**, and **play**.

- The *device_name* designates the target of the *command*. MCI accepts the names of MCI device types and names of device elements for the *device_name*. An example of a name of device type is **cdaudio**. Other device types are listed in the following section.

- The *arguments* specify the flags and parameters used by the *command*. The flags in the argument consist of the key words supported by the MCI command. Parameters consist of variable numeric or string data which apply to either the MCI command or flag. For example, the **play** command uses the arguments **from** *position* and **to** *position* to indicate the positions to start and end playing. (The key words used as flags are indicated by bold font and variables parameters are indicated by the italic font.) You can list the flags used with a command in any order. When you use a flag that has a parameter associated with it, you must supply a value for the parameter.

You can use the following data types for the parameters in a string command:

- Strings—String data types are delimited by leading and trailing white space and quotation marks ("). MCI removes single quotation marks from a string. If you want to put a quotation mark in a string, use a set of two quotation marks where you want to embed your quotation mark. If you want to use an empty string, use two quotation marks to delimit the empty string.

- Signed long integers—Signed long integer data types are delimited by leading and trailing white space. Unless otherwise specified, integers can be positive or negative. If using negative integers, do not put any white space between the negative sign and the first digit.

- Rectangles—Rectangle data types are an ordered list of four signed short values. White space delimits this data type as well as separates each integer in the list.

For example, the following command string instructs the CD audio player "cdaudio" to play the disc sequence located between 5000 milliseconds and 15000 milliseconds from the start of the disc:

```
play cdaudio from 5000 to 15000
```

Unspecified command arguments assume a default value. For example, if the flag *from* was unspecified in the previous example, the CD audio player would start playing at the current position.

About MCI Device Types

Your application identifies an MCI device by specifying an MCI *device type*. A device type indicates the physical type of device. The following table lists the MCI device types currently defined:

Device Type	Description
cdaudio	CD audio player
dat	Digital audio tape player
digitalvideo	Digital video in a window (not GDI based)
MMMovie	Multimedia movie player
other	Undefined MCI device
overlay	Overlay device (analog video in a window)
scanner	Image scanner
sequencer	MIDI sequencer
vcr	Videotape recorder or player

Device Type	Description
videodisc	Videodisc player
waveaudio	Audio device that plays digitized waveform files

The system software includes device drivers and command sets for the device types that are fundamental to many multimedia presentations. The system software includes the following MCI device drivers:

Device Type	Device Driver	Description
cdaudio	MCICDA.DRV	An MCI device driver for controlling compact disc audio.
MMMovie	MCIMMP.DRV	An MCI device driver for playing multimedia movie files.
sequencer	MCISEQ.DRV	An MCI device driver for playing MIDI audio files.
videodisc	MCIPIONR.DRV	An MCI device driver for controlling the Pioneer LD-V4200 videodisc player.
waveaudio	MCIWAVE.DRV	An MCI device driver for playing and recording waveform audio files.

The [mci] section of the SYSTEM.INI file lists the device types installed in the system. If you have a particular device type installed more than once, the device type names in the SYSTEM.INI file have integers appended to them. This creates unique names for each MCI device type entry. For example, if the "cdaudio" device type is installed twice, the names "cdaudio" and "cdaudio1" are used to create unique names for each occurrence of the device type. Each name usually refers to a different CD audio player in the system.

Using MCI Command Strings

The tables at the end of this chapter contain all of the command strings for the MCI devices. Most applications will use only a subset of these commands. The following sections describe the command strings used most often.

Opening a Device

Before using a device, you must initialize it with the **open** command. The number of devices you can have open depends on the amount of available memory. The syntax for the **open** command has the following form:

open *device_name*   **shareable**   **type** *device_type*   **alias** *alias*

The parameters for the **open** command are:

Parameters	Description
device_name	Specifies the destination device or an MCI element (file) name.
shareable	Allows applications to share a common device or device element.
type *device_type*	Specifies the device type when the *device_name* refers to an MCI element.
alias *alias*	Specifies a replacement name for the device.

MCI classifies device drivers as *compound* and *simple*. Compound device drivers use a *device element*–a media element associated with a device–during operation. For most compound device drivers, the device element is the source or destination data file. For these file elements, the element name references a file and its path. Compound devices include animation devices, waveform audio devices, and MIDI sequencers.

Simple device drivers do not require a device element for playback. Simple devices include CD audio devices and videodisc devices.

Opening Simple Devices

Simple devices require only the *device_name* for operation. You don't need to provide any additional information (such as a name of a data file) to open these devices. For these devices, substitute the name of a device type obtained from the [mci] section of SYSTEM.INI for the *device_name*. For example, you can open a videodisc device with "open videodisc1."

If you want to open a specific simple device, you can use the filename of the device driver for the *device_name*. Opening a device with the filename will make an application device dependent and can prevent the application from running if the system configuration changes. When you specify the filename of the device driver, you can optionally include the .DRV extension but do not include the path to the file.

Opening Compound Devices

Depending upon your needs, there are three ways you can open a compound device:

- By specifying just the device type
- By specifying both the element name and the device type
- By specifying just the element name

To determine the capabilities of a device, you can open a device by specifying only the device type. When opened this way, most compound devices will only let you determine their capabilities and close them. For example, you can open the sequencer with "open sequencer."

You can specify the device type either by using the device type from the SYSTEM.INI file or by using the filename of the device driver. Opening a device with the filename of the device driver will make an application device dependent and can prevent the application from running if the system configuration changes. If you specify the filename of the device driver, you can optionally include the .DRV extension but do not include the path to the file.

To associate a device element with a particular device, you must specify the element name and device type. In the **open** command, substitute the element name for the *device_name*, add the **type** flag, and substitute the name of the device you want to use for *device_type*. This combination lets your application specify the MCI device it needs to use. For example, you can open a device element of the waveaudio device with "open train.wav type waveaudio."

To associate a default MCI device with a device element, you can specify just an element name. In this case, MCI uses the extension of the element name to select the default device from the list in the [mci extensions] section of the SYSTEM.INI file. The entries in the [mci extensions] section use the following form:

file extension = device type

MCI implicitly uses the *device type* if the extension is found. The following fragment shows a typical [mci extensions] section:

```
[mci extensions]
wav=waveaudio
mid=sequencer
rmi=sequencer
mmm=mmmovie
```

With these definitions, MCI opens the default waveaudio device if you use "open train.wav."

Using the Shareable Flag

The **shareable** flag lets multiple applications or tasks access the same device (or element) and device instance concurrently. If your application opens a device or device element without the **shareable** flag, no other application can access it simultaneously. If your application opens a device or device element as shareable, other applications can also access it by also opening it as shareable. The shared device or device element gives each application the ability to change the parameters governing the operating state of the device or device element. Each time a device or device element is opened as shareable, MCI returns a unique device ID even though the IDs refer to the same instance.

If you make a device or device element shareable, your application should not make any assumptions about the state of a device. When working with shared devices, your application might need to compensate for changes made by other applications using the same services.

If a device can service only one open instance it will fail an open with the **shareable** flag.

While most compound device elements are not shareable, you can open multiple elements (where each element is unique), or you can open a single element multiple times. If you open a single file element multiple times, MCI creates an independent instance for each of them. Each file element you open this way must have a unique name. The **alias** flag described in the next section lets you use a unique name for each element.

Using the Alias Flag

The **alias** flag specifies an alternate name for the given device. The alias provides a shorthand notation for compound devices with lengthy pathnames, and it lets you open multiple instances of the same file. If your application creates a device alias, it must use the alias rather than the device name for all subsequent references.

Opening New Device Elements

If you wish to create a new device element without specifying an element name, you can specify **new** as a *device_name*. MCI does not save a new file element until you save it with the **save** command. When creating a new file, you must include a device alias with the **open** command. The following commands open a new waveaudio device element, start and stop recording, save the file element, and close the device element:

```
open new type waveaudio alias capture
record capture
stop capture
save capture orca.wav
close capture
```

Closing a Device

The **close** command releases access to a device or device element. To help MCI manage the devices, your application must explicitly close each device or device element when it is finished with it.

Shortcuts and Variations for MCI Commands

The MCI string interface lets you use several shortcuts when working with MCI devices.

Using All as a Device Name

You can specify **all** as a *device_name* for any command that does not return information. When you specify **all**, MCI sequentially sends the command to all devices opened by the current application. For example, "close all" closes all open devices and "play all" starts playing all devices opened by the task. Because MCI sequentially sends the commands to the MCI devices, there is a delay between when the first device receives the command and when the last device receives the command.

Combining the Device Type and Device Element Name

You can eliminate the **type** flag in the **open** command if you combine the device type with the device element name. MCI recognizes this combination when you use the following syntax:

device_type ! *element_name*

The exclamation mark separates the device type from the element name. The following example opens the right.wav element with the waveaudio device:

```
open waveaudio ! right.wav
```

Automatic Open

If MCI cannot identify the *device_name* of a command as an open device, MCI tries to automatically open the specified device. The following items apply to devices automatically opened:

- Automatic open works only with the command-string interface.

- Automatic open does not let your application specify the **type** flag. Without the device type, MCI determines the device type from the [mci extensions] section of the WIN.INI file. If you want to use a specific device, you can combine the device type name with the device element name using the exclamation mark.

- Automatic open will fail for commands that are specific to custom device drivers. For example, the command to unlock the front panel of the Pioneer videodisc player will fail an automatic open. The command for unlocking the front panel is specific only to this videodisc player.

- A device automatically opened will not respond to a command that uses **all** as a device name.

Automatic Close

MCI automatically closes any device automatically opened using the command-string interface. MCI closes a device when the command completes, when you abort the command, when you request notification in a subsequent command, or when MCI detects a failure.

Using Notify and Wait Flags

Normally, MCI commands return to the user immediately, even if it takes several minutes to complete the action initiated by the command. For example, after a VCR device receives a rewind command, the command returns when the tape starts to rewind and it does not wait for the tape to finish rewinding. You can use either of the following required MCI flags to modify this default behavior:

Flag	Description
notify	Directs the device to post an MM_MCINOTIFY message to a specified window when the requested action is complete.
wait	Directs the device to wait until the requested action is complete before returning to the application.

Using the Notify Flag

The **notify** flag directs the device to post an MM_MCINOTIFY message when the device completes an action. Your application must have a window procedure to process the MM_MCINOTIFY message for notification to have any effect. The *Programmer's Workbook* includes examples of window procedures that process the **MM_MCINOTIFY** message.

While the results of a notification are application dependant, the application's window procedure can act upon four possible conditions associated with the notify message:

- The notification will occur when the notification conditions are satisfied.

- The notification can be superseded.

- The notification can be aborted.

- The notification can fail.

A successful notification occurs when the conditions required for initiating the callback are satisfied and the command completed without interruption.

A notification is superseded when the device has a notification pending and you send it another notify request. When a notification is superseded, MCI resets the callback conditions to correspond to the notify request of the new command.

A notification is aborted when you send a new command that prevents the callback conditions set by a previous command from being satisfied. For example, sending the stop command cancels a notification pending for the "play to 500 notify" command. If your command interrupts a command that has a notification pending, and your command also requests notification, MCI will abort the first notification immediately and respond to the second notification normally.

A notification fails if a device error occurs while a device is executing the MCI command. For example, a notification fails when a hardware error occurs during a play command.

Using the Wait Flag and Break Command

When a command uses the **wait** flag, MCI returns control to the calling application when the target device completes the command. You can cancel a wait operation by pressing a break key. By default, MCI defines this key as CTRL+BREAK. (You can redefine this key with the **break** command.) When you cancel the wait operation, if possible, MCI returns control to the application and does not interrupt the command associated with the **wait** flag. For example, breaking the command "play to 500 wait" cancels the wait operation without interrupting the play operation.

Obtaining Information From MCI Devices

Every device responds to the **capability**, **status**, and **info** commands. These commands obtain information about the device. For example, your application can determine if a videodisc requires a device element by using the command "capability videodisc compound file." (This example returns **false**.) The flags listed for the required and basic commands provide a minimum amount of information about a device. Many devices supplement the required and basic flags with extended flags to provide additional information about the device.

When you request information with the **capability**, **status**, or **info** command, the argument list can contain only one flag requesting information. The string interface can only return one string or value in response to a command requesting information.

The Play Command

The **play** command starts playing a device. Without any flags, the **play** command starts playing from the current position and plays until the command is halted or until the end of the media or file is reached. For example, "play cdaudio" starts playing an audio disc from the position where it was stopped.

Most devices that support the **play** command also support the **from** and **to**. These flags indicate the position at which the device should start and stop playing. For example, "play cdaudio from 0" plays the audio disc from the beginning of the first track. The units assigned to the position value depend on the device. For example, the position is normally specified in frames for CAV videodiscs, and in milliseconds for digital audio.

As an extended command, devices add flags to use the capabilities of a particular device. For example, the **play** command for videodisc devices adds the flags **fast**, **slow**, **reverse,** and **scan**.

Stop, Pause, and Resume Commands

The **stop** command suspends the playing or recording of a device. Many devices include the basic command **pause**, which also suspends these sessions. The difference between **stop** and **pause** depends on the device. Usually **pause** suspends operation but leaves the device ready to resume playing or recording immediately.

Using **play** or **record** to restart a device will reset the **to** and **from** positions specified before the device was paused or stopped. Without the **from** flag, these commands reset the start position to the current position. Without the **to** flag, they reset the end position to the end of the media. If you want to continue playing or recording but want to stop at a position previously specified, use the **to** flag with these commands and repeat the position value.

Some devices include the **resume** command to restart a paused device. This command does not change the **to** and **from** positions specified with the **play** or **record** command which preceded the **pause** command.

Experimenting with Command Strings

The sample application MCITEST provides a simple way to experiment with the MCI commands and devices compatible with MCI. MCITEST uses the command-string interface of MCI. When you run MCITEST, it displays the following dialog box:

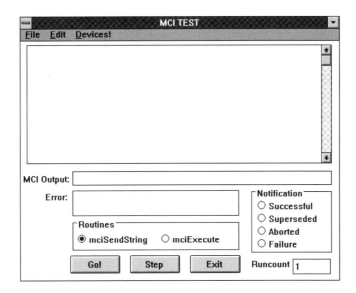

To try an MCI command, enter the command string in the large edit box. MCITEST sends the string directly to the MCI command-string interface when you press RETURN. Any MCI response to the command is displayed in the control labeled "MCI Output." Any errors returned by MCI appear in the control labeled "Error."

The "Routines" options select the function used to send the command strings to MCI.

The GO! button sequentially sends all commands in the edit box to the MCI command-string interface. You can have MCITEST execute the entire command list multiple times by specifying a number in the "Runcount" entry field.

The STEP button sends the selected MCI command, then moves the cursor bar to the next command. The EXIT button ends MCITEST.

MCI sets the indicators in the "Notification" box in response to the notify flag.

The File menu displays a menu for saving and recalling the contents of the edit box. The Edit menu displays a menu for editing the contents of the edit box. The Device! menu displays a list box of open device instances.

MCITEST Examples

The following examples show some of the commands used to control a variety of MCI devices. The examples assume that the WIN.INI and SYSTEM.INI files reflect the proper operating environment for the devices and the sample files are in the \WINDOWS\MMDATA directory.

You can use MCITEST to play digital audio data files. To open the file TRAIN.WAV enter:

```
open \windows\mmdata\train.wav type waveaudio alias sounds
```

Then, to hear the file, enter:

```
play sounds
```

If your audio card is configured properly and your volume is on, you will hear the a train.

If you wish to replay the file, enter:

```
play sounds from 0
```

The flag "from 0" resets the file pointer to the start of the file.

Close the file with:

```
close sounds
```

You can play a compact audio disc with the cdaudio device and the following script:

```
open cdaudio
play cdaudio
stop cdaudio
close cdaudio
```

As a last example you can use the sequencer to play MIDI files with the following script:

```
open \windows\mmdata\canyon.mid type sequencer alias song
play song wait
close song
```

If you wish to replay the song before closing the device, enter the command "play song from 0." If you wish to hear the song at a different speed, enter the command "set song tempo 200" before playing the song.

When you are finished using MCITEST, close all the MCI devices you opened before exiting. Closing an application with open MCI devices can make those devices unaccessible to other applications until the system is rebooted.

MCI System Commands

The following commands are interpreted directly by MCI. The remaining command tables list the commands interpreted by the devices.

Command	Description
break *item*	Specifies a key to abort a **wait** command. One of the following *items* modifies **break**:
	on *virtual_key* Specifies the *virtual_key* code of the that aborts the **wait**. When the key is pressed, the device returns control to the application. If possible, the command continues execution. Substitute a Windows virtual key code for *virtual_key*.
	off Disables the current break key.
sound	The device name field of this command specifies a sound from the [sounds] section of WIN.INI to play. If it is not found, MCI uses the SystemDefault sound.
sysinfo *item*	Obtains MCI system information. One of the following *items* modifies **sysinfo**:
	installname Returns the name listed in the SYSTEM.INI file used to install the device.
	quantity Returns the number of MCI devices listed in the SYSTEM.INI file of the type specified in the device name field. The device name must be a standard MCI device type. Any digits after the name are ignored. The special device name **all** returns the total number of MCI devices in the system.
	quantity open Returns the number of open MCI devices of the type specified in the device name field. The device name must be a standard MCI device type. Any digits after the name are ignored. The name **all** returns the total number of MCI devices in the system that are open.
	name *index* Returns the name of an MCI device. The *index* ranges from 1 to the number of devices of that type. If **all** is specified for the device name, *index* ranges from 1 to the total number of devices in the system.

Command	Description
	name *index* **open** Returns the name of an open MCI device. The *index* ranges from 1 to the number of open devices of that type. If **all** is specified for the device name, *index* ranges from 1 to the total number of open devices in the system.

Required Commands for All Devices

The following required commands are recognized by all devices. Extended commands can add other options to these commands.

Commands Supported by All MCI Devices

Command	Description
capability *item*	Requests information about a particular capability of a device. While other capabilities are defined for specific devices and device types, the following *items* are always available:
	can eject Returns **true** if the device can eject the media.
	can play Returns **true** if the device can play.
	can record Returns **true** if the device supports recording.
	can save Returns **true** if the device can save data.
	compound device Returns **true** if the device requires an element name.
	device type Returns one of the following:
	animation **cdaudio** **dat** **digitalvideo** **other** **overlay** **scanner** **sequencer** **vcr** **videodisc** **waveaudio**
	has audio Returns **true** if the device supports audio playback.
	has video Returns **true** if the device supports video.
	uses files Returns **true** if the element of a compound device is a file pathname.
close	When sent to a simple device, closes the device. When sent to a compound device element, closes the element.

Commands Supported by All MCI Devices

Command	Description
info *item*	Fills a user-supplied buffer with information. One of the following *items* modifies **info**:
	product Returns a null-terminated string with description of the hardware associated with a device. This usually includes the manufacturer and model information.
open *items*	Initializes the device. The following optional *items* modify **open**:
	alias *device_ alias* Specifies an alternate name for the given device. If specified, it must be used for subsequent references to the device.
	shareable Initializes the device or element as shareable. Subsequent attempts to open it fail unless you specify **shareable** in both the original and later **open** commands. MCI returns an error if it is already open and not shareable.
	type *device_ type* Specifies the device type of a device element. As an alternative to **type**, MCI can use the [mci extension] entries in the SYSTEM.INI file to select the device based on the extension used by the device element.
status *item*	Obtains status information for the device. One of the following *items* modifies **status**:
	mode Returns the current mode of the device. All devices can return: **not ready**, **paused**, **playing**, and **stopped**. The modes **open**, **parked**, **recording**, and **seeking** are device dependent.
	ready Returns **true** if the device is ready.

Basic Commands for Specific Device Types

In addition to the commands described previously, each device supports a set of commands specific to its device type. Where possible, these type-specific commands are identical between types. When type-specific commands are common to multiple devices, they are considered basic commands. For example, the basic **play** command is identical for videodisc and videotape devices. Other basic commands are listed in the following table.

Although these commands are optional for a device, if a device supports a command it must respond to the options listed in this table. The options provide a minimum set of capabilities for most devices. If an option does not apply to device, the device must return "Action not available for this device."

Basic Commands

Command	Description
load	Load a device element from disk. The following optional *item* modifies **load**:
	filename Specifies the source path and file.
pause	Stop playing.
play *items*	Start playing the device. The following optional *items* modify **play**:
	from *position* **to** *position* Specifies the position to start and stop playing. If **from** is omitted, the play starts from the current position; if **to** is omitted, the play stops at the end of the media.
record *items*	Start recording data. All data recorded after a file is opened is discarded if the file is closed without saving it. The following optional *items* modify **record**:
	insert Specifies that new data is added to the device element at the current position.
	from *position* **to** *position* Specifies the positions to start and stop recording. If **from** is omitted, the device starts recording at the current position; if **to** is omitted, the device records until a **stop** or **pause** command is received.
	overwrite Specifies that new data will replace data in the device element.
resume	Resumes playing or recording on a paused device.
save *item*	Saves the MCI element. The following optional *item* modifies **save**:
	filename Specifies the destination path and file.
seek *item*	Moves to the specified position and stops. One of the following is required for *item*:
	to *position* Specifies the position to stop the seek.
	to start Specifies to seek to the start of the media or device element.
	to end Specifies to seek to the end of the media or device element.
set *items*	Sets the various control *items*:
	audio all off, audio all on Enables or disables audio output.

Basic Commands

Command	Description
	audio left off, **audio left on** Enables or disables output to the left audio channel.
	audio right off, **audio right on** Enables or disables output to the right audio channel.
	door closed Loads the media and closes the door if possible.
	door open Opens the door and ejects the media if possible.
	time format milliseconds Sets the time format to milliseconds. All position information is this format after this command. You can abbreviate milliseconds as **ms**.
	video off, **video on** Enables or disables video output.
status *item*	Obtains status information for the device. One of the following *items* modifies **status**:
	current track Returns the current track.
	length Returns the total length of the media.
	length track *track_number* Returns the length of the track specified by *track_number*.
	number of tracks Returns the number of tracks on the media.
	position Returns the current position.
	position track *track_number* Returns the position of the start of the track specified by *track_number*.
	start position Returns the starting position of the media or device element.
	time format Returns the time format.
stop	Stops the device.

Animation and Movie Player Commands

The animation and movie player devices share a common command set for operation. This command set provides a common method for displaying animation sequences and movies in the Windows environment. The MCIMMP.DRV device driver for the multimedia movie player uses this command set for operation. Animation and movie player devices use the following command set:

Animation and Movie Player Commands

Command	Description
capability *item*	Requests information about the capabilities of the graphics driver. The *item* is one of the following:
	can eject Returns **true** if the device can eject the media. The MCIMMP movie player returns **false**.
	can play Returns **true** if the device can play. The MCIMMP movie player returns **true**.
	can record Returns **false**. Animation and movie player devices cannot record.
	can reverse Returns **true** if the animation or movie player device can play in reverse.
	can save Returns **false**. Animation and movie player devices cannot save data.
	can stretch Returns **true** if the device can stretch frames to fill a given display rectangle. The MCIMMP movie player returns **false**.
	compound device Returns **true** if the device requires an element name.
	device type Animation and movie player devices return **animation**.
	fast play rate Returns fast play rate in frames per second.
	has audio Returns **true** if the device supports audio playback. The MCIMMP movie player has audio.
	has video Returns **true**. Animation and movie devices are video devices.
	normal play rate Returns normal play rate in frames per second.
	slow play rate Returns the slow play rate in frames per second.

Animation and Movie Player Commands

Command	Description
	uses files Returns **true** if the element of a compound device is a file pathname.
	uses palettes Returns **true** if the device uses palettes. The MCIMMP movie player returns **true**.
	windows Returns the number of windows the device can support. The MCIMMP movie player returns 8.
close	Closes a device element and any resources associated with it.
info *item*	Fills a user-supplied buffer with information. One of the following optional *item* modifies **info**:
	file Returns the name of the file used by the animation device or movie player in a null-terminated string.
	product Returns the product name and model of the current device in a null-terminated string. The MCIMMP movie player returns **Microsoft Multimedia Movie Player**.
	window text Returns the caption of the window used by the device.
open *items*	Initializes the animation device. The following optional *items* modify **open**:
	alias *device_alias* Specifies an alternate name for the animation or movie player element. If specified, it must also be used for subsequent references.
	nostatic Indicates that the device should reduce the number of static (system) colors in the palette. Reducing the number of static colors increases the number of colors controlled by the animation. The MCIMMP movie player reduces the static colors to black and white while in the foreground.
	parent *hwnd* Specifies the window handle of the parent window.
	shareable Initializes a device element as shareable. Subsequent attempts to open it fail unless you specify **shareable** in both the original and subsequent **open** commands. MCI returns an invalid device error if it is already open and not shareable. The MCIMMP movie player does not allow shared files.
	style *style_type* Indicates a window style.
	style child Opens a window with a child window style.

Animation and Movie Player Commands

Command	Description
	style overlapped Opens a window with an overlapped window style.
	style popup Opens a window with a popup window style.
	type *device_ type* Specifies the device type of the device element. MCI reserves MMMovie for the movie player device type. As an alternative to **type**, MCI can use the [mci extension] entries in the SYSTEM.INI file to select the controlling device based on the extension used by the device element.
pause	Pauses playback of the animation if it is playing. If the animation is stopped, **pause** displays the animation if it is not visible and in the foreground.
play *items*	Starts playing the animation sequence. The following optional *items* modify **play**:
	fast Plays the animation sequence at a fast rate.
	from *position* **to** *position* Specifies the frame at which to start and/or stop playing. If **from** is omitted, play starts at the current frame; if **to** is omitted, play stops at the end frame.
	reverse Indicates that the play direction is backwards.
	scan Plays the animation sequence as fast as possible without disabling video.
	slow Plays the animation sequence at a slow rate.
	speed *fps* Plays the animation sequence at the specified speed *fps*. Speed is specified in frames per second.
put *items*	Defines the area of the source image and destination window used for display. One of the following *items* modify **put**:
	destination Sets the whole window as the destination window.
	destination at *rectangle* Specifies a rectangle for the area of the window used to display the image. The *rectangle* coordinates are relative to the window origin and are specified as *X1 Y1 X2 Y2*. The coordinates *X1*, *Y1* specify the top, left corner, and the coordinates *X2*, *Y2* specify the width and height of the rectangle. When an area of the display window is specified, and the device supports stretching, the source image is stretched to the destination offset and extent.

Animation and Movie Player Commands

Command	Description
	source Selects the whole image for display in the destination window.
	source at *rectangle* Specifies a rectangle for the image area used for display. The *rectangle* coordinates are relative to the image origin and are specified as *X1 Y1 X2 Y2*. The coordinates *X1*, *Y1* specify the top, left corner, and the coordinates *X2, Y2* specify the width and height of the rectangle. When an area of the source image is specified, and the device supports stretching, the source image is stretched to the destination offset and extent.
realize *item*	Tells the device to select and realize its palette into a display context of the displayed window. One of the following *items* modifies **realize**:
	background Realizes the palette as a background palette. The MCIMMP movie player does not support this option.
	normal Realizes the palette normally. The MCIMMP movie player does not support this option.
resume	Resumes playing. The MCIMMP movie player does not support this option.
seek *item*	Moves to the specified position and stops. One of the following is required for *item*:
	to *position* Specifies the position to stop the seek.
	to start Specifies to seek to the start of the device element.
	to end Specifies to seek to the end of the device element.
set *items*	Sets the various control *items*:
	audio all off, audio all on Enables or disables audio output.
	audio left off, audio left on Enables or disables output to the left audio channel.
	audio right off, audio right on Enables or disables output to the right audio channel.
	time format frames Sets the time format to frames. All position information is specified in frames following this command. When the device is opened, frames is the default mode.

Animation and Movie Player Commands

Command	Description
	time format milliseconds Sets the time format to milliseconds. All position information is this format after this command. You can abbreviate milliseconds as **ms**. The MCIMMP movie player does not support this option.
	video off, **video on** Enables or disables video output. The MCIMMP movie player does not support this option.
status *item*	Obtains status information for the device. One of the following *items* modifies **status**:
	current track Returns the current track. The MCIMMP movie player returns 1.
	forward Returns **true** if the play direction is forward or if the device is not playing.
	length Returns the total number of frames.
	length track *track_number* Returns the total number of frames in the track specified by *track_number*.
	media present Returns **true** if the media is inserted in the device; otherwise it returns **false**.
	mode Returns **not ready, paused, playing, seeking,** or **stopped** for the current mode.
	number of tracks Returns the number of tracks on the media. The MCIMMP movie player returns 1.
	palette handle Returns the handle of the palette used for the animation in the low-order word of the return value.
	position Returns the current position.
	position track *number* Returns the position of the start of the track specified by *number*.
	ready Returns **true** if the device is ready.
	speed Returns the current speed of the device in frames per second.
	start position Returns the starting position of the media or device element.
	time format Returns the current time format.
	window handle Returns the handle of the window used for the animation in the low-order word of the return value.

Animation and Movie Player Commands

Command	Description
step *item*	Step the play one or more frames forward or reverse. The default action is to step one frame forward. The following *items* modify **step**:
	by *frames* Indicates the number of frames to step.
	reverse Step the frames in reverse.
stop	Stops playing.
update *item*	Repaints the current frame into the specified display context. The following *items* modifies **update**:
	at *rectangle* Specifies the clipping rectangle.
	hdc *hdc* Specifies the handle of the display context to paint.
where	Obtains the rectangle specifying the source or destination area. One of the following *items* modifies **where**:
	destination Requests the destination offset and extent.
	source Requests the source offset and extent.
window *item*	Tells the animation or movie player to use a given window to display the images instead of the default window created by the driver. By default, these devices should create a window when opened but should not display it until they receive the **play** command. Applications providing window handles should manage the display issues that result when the window is sized or when the window handle is switched during play.
	Several flags manipulate the window. Since the **status** command can obtain the handle to the current display window, you can use the standard window functions instead. The following *items* modify **window**:
	handle *window_handle* Specifies the handle of the destination window used as an alternate to the default window.
	handle default Specifies that the animation device or movie player should set the current display window back to the driver's default window.
	state hide Hides the current display window.
	state iconic Displays the window as iconic.
	state maximized Maximizes the current display window.

Animation and Movie Player Commands

Command	Description
	state minimize Minimizes the specified window and activates the top-level window in the window-manager's list.
	state minimized Minimizes the current display window.
	state no action Displays a display window in its current state. The window that is currently active remains active.
	state no activate Displays a display window in its most recent size and state. The window that is currently active remains active.
	state normal Activates and displays the current display window in its original size and position.
	state show Shows the current display window.
	text *caption* + Specifies the *caption* for the display window.

CD Audio (Redbook) Commands

The CD audio command set provides a common method for playing CD audio in the Windows environment. This device type includes the MCICDA.DRV device driver which operates with any CD-ROM device supporting the audio services of MSCDEX. CD audio devices support the following set of commands:

CD Audio Commands

Command	Description
capability *item*	Requests information about the capabilities of the CD audio device. One of the following *items* is required:
	can eject Returns **true** if the CD audio device can eject the media.
	can play Returns **true** if the CD audio device can play the media.
	can record Returns **false**. CD audio devices cannot record.
	can save Returns **false**. CD audio devices cannot save data.

CD Audio Commands

Command	Description
	compound device Returns **false**. CD audio devices are simple devices.
	device type Returns **CD audio**.
	has audio Returns **true**.
	has video Returns **false**. CD audio devices do not support video.
	uses files Returns **false**. Simple devices do not use files.
close	Closes the device.
info *item*	Fills a user-supplied buffer with information. One of the following optional *items* modifies **info**:
	product Returns the product name and model of the current audio device. The MCICDA device driver returns **CD Audio Player**.
open *items*	Initializes the device. MCI reserves cdaudio for the compact disc audio device type. The following optional *items* modify **open**:
	alias *device_alias* Specifies an alternate name for the given device. If specified, it must also be used for subsequent references.
	shareable Initializes the device as shareable. Subsequent attempts to open it fail unless you specify **shareable** in both the original and subsequent **open** commands. MCI returns an error if it is already open and not shareable.
pause	Pauses playing. This is the same as the **stop** command for the MCICDA device driver.
play *items*	Starts playing audio. The following optional *items* modify **play**:
	from *position* **to** *position* Specifies the position to start and stop playing. If **from** is omitted, the play starts at the current position; if **to** is omitted, play stops at the end of the disc. If the **from** position is greater than the end position of the disc, or if the **from** position is greater than the **to** position, MCI returns an error. If the **to** position is greater than the length of the disc, MCI returns an error.
resume	Resumes playing of a paused device. The MCICDA device driver does not support this option.

CD Audio Commands

Command	Description
seek *item*	Moves to the specified location on the disc. If already playing or recording, the device stops. One of the following optional *items* modifies **seek**:
	to *position* Specifies the destination position for the seek. If it is greater than the length of disc, MCI returns an out-of-range error.
	to start Specifies seek to the start of the audio data on the disc.
	to end Specifies seek to the end of the audio data on the disc.
set *items*	Sets the various control *items*:
	audio all off, audio all on Enables or disables audio output.
	audio left off, audio left on Enables or disables output to the left audio channel.
	audio right off, audio right on Enables or disables output to the right audio channel.
	door closed Retracts the tray and closes the door if possible.
	door open Opens the door and ejects the tray if possible.
	time format milliseconds Sets the time format to milliseconds. All position information is in this format after this command. You can abbreviate milliseconds as **ms**.
	time format msf Sets the time format to minutes, seconds, and frames. When time or position values are used, they are expressed as *mm:ss:ff*, where *mm* is minutes, *ss* is seconds, and *ff* is frames. This is the default format for CD audio. On input, *ff* can be omitted if 0, and *ss* can be omitted if both it and *ff* are 0. For example, 3, 3:0, and 3:0:0 are valid ways to express 3 minutes. These fields have the following maximum values:

Minutes	99
Seconds	59
Frames	74

CD Audio Commands

Command	Description
	time format tmsf Sets the time format to tracks, minutes, seconds, and frames. When time or position values are used, they are expressed as *tt:mm:ss:ff*, where *tt* is tracks, *mm* is minutes, *ss* is seconds, and *ff* is frames. All position information is in this format after this command. On input, *ff* can be omitted if 0, *ss* can be omitted if both it and *ff* are 0, and *mm* can be omitted if it, *ss*, and *ff* are 0. For example, 3, 3:0, 3:0:0, 3:0:0:0 all specify track 3. These fields have the following maximum values:

Tracks	99
Minutes	99
Seconds	59
Frames	74

Command	Description
status *item*	Obtains status information for the device. One of the following *items* modifies **status**:
	current track Returns the current track.
	length Returns the total length of the disc.
	length track *track_number* Returns the length of the track specified by *track_number*.
	media present Returns **true** if the disc is inserted in the drive; otherwise it returns **false**.
	mode Returns **not ready**, **open**, **paused**, **playing**, **seeking**, or **stopped** for the current mode of the device.
	number of tracks Returns the number of tracks on the disc.
	position Returns the current position.
	position track *track_no* Returns the starting position of the track specified by *track_no*.
	ready Returns **true** if the device is ready.
	start position Returns the starting position of the disc or device element.
	time format Returns the current time format.
stop	Stops playing.

MIDI Sequencer Commands

The MIDI sequencer supports the following set of commands:

MIDI Sequencer

Command	Description
capability *item*	Requests information about the capabilities of the MIDI sequencer. One of the following *items* is required:
	can eject Returns **false**. Sequencers cannot eject.
	can play Returns **true**.
	can record Returns **true** if the sequencer can record MIDI data. The MCISEQ sequencer cannot record and returns **false**.
	can save Returns **true** if the sequencer can save MIDI data. The MCISEQ sequencer cannot save data and returns **false**.
	compound device Returns **true**; sequencers are compound devices.
	device type Returns **sequencer**.
	has audio Returns **true**. Sequencers support playback.
	has video Returns **false**. Sequencers do not support video.
	uses files Returns **true**. Sequencers use files for operation.
close	Closes the sequencer element and the port and file associated with it.
info *item*	Fills a user-supplied buffer with information. One of the following optional *item* modifies **info**:
	product Returns the product name of the sequencer. The MCISEQ sequencer returns **MIDI Sequencer**.
open *items*	Initializes the sequencer. The following optional *items* modify **open**:
	alias *device_alias* Specifies an alternate name for the sequencer element. If specified, it must also be used for subsequent references.

MIDI Sequencer

Command	Description
	shareable Initializes the sequencer element as shareable. Subsequent attempts to open it fail unless you specify shareable in both the original and subsequent **open** commands. MCI returns an invalid device error if it is already open and not shareable. Files cannot be shared when using the MCISEQ sequencer.
	type *device_ type* Specifies the device type of the device element. MCI reserves sequencer for the MIDI sequencer device type. As an alternative to **type**, MCI can use the [mci extension] entries in the SYSTEM.INI file to select the sequencer based on the extension used by the device element.
pause	Pauses playing.
play *items*	Starts playing the sequencer. The following optional *items* modify **play**:
	from *position* **to** *position* Specifies the positions to start and stop playing. If **from** is omitted, play starts at the current position; if **to** is omitted, play stops at the end of the file.
record *items*	Starts recording MIDI data. All data recorded after a file is opened is discarded if the file is closed without saving it. (The MCISEQ sequencer does not support recording.) The following optional *items* modify **record**:
	insert Specifies that new data is added to the device element.
	from *position* **to** *position* Specifies the positions to start and stop recording. If **from** is omitted, the device starts recording at the current position; if **to** is omitted, the device records until a **stop** or **pause** command is received.
	overwrite Specifies that new data will replace data in the device element.
resume	Resumes playing or recording. The MCISEQ sequencer does not support this option.
save *item*	Saves the MCI element. (The MCISEQ sequencer does not support this option.) The following item *modifies* **save**:
	filename The *filename* specifies the destination path and file.

MIDI Sequencer

Command	Description
seek *item*	Moves to the specified position in the file. One of the following *items* is required: **to** *position* Specifies the final position for the seek. **to start** Specifies to seek to the start of the sequence. **to end** Specifies to seek to the end of the sequence.
set *items*	Sets the various control *items*: **audio all off, audio all on** Enables or disables audio output. The MCISEQ sequencer does not support this option. **audio left off, audio left on** Enables or disables output to the left audio channel. The MCISEQ sequencer does not support this option. **audio right off, audio right on** Enables or disables output to the right audio channel. The MCISEQ sequencer does not support this option. **master MIDI** Sets the MIDI sequencer as the synchronization source. Synchronization data is sent in MIDI format. The MCISEQ sequencer does not support this option. **master none** Inhibits the sequencer from sending synchronization data. The MCISEQ sequencer does not support this option. **master SMPTE** Sets the MIDI sequencer as the synchronization source. Synchronization data is sent in SMPTE format. The MCISEQ sequencer does not support this option. **offset** *time* Sets the SMPTE offset *time*. The offset is the beginning time of a SMPTE based sequence. The *time* is expressed as *hh:mm:ss:ff*, where *hh* is hours, *mm* is minutes, *ss* is seconds, and *ff* is frames. **port** *port_number* Sets the MIDI port receiving the MIDI messages. This command will fail if the port you are trying to open is being used by another application. **port mapper** Sets the MIDI mapper as the port receiving the MIDI messages. This command will fail if the MIDI mapper or a port it needs is being used by another application.

MIDI Sequencer

Command	Description
	port none Disables the sending of MIDI messages. This command also closes a MIDI port.
	slave file Sets the MIDI sequencer to use file data as the synchronization source. This is the default.
	slave MIDI Sets the MIDI sequencer to use incoming data MIDI for the synchronization source. The sequencer recognizes synchronization data with the MIDI format. The MCISEQ sequencer does not support this option.
	slave none Sets the MIDI sequencer to ignore synchronization data.
	slave SMPTE Sets the MIDI sequencer to use incoming MIDI data for the synchronization source. The sequencer recognizes synchronization data with the SMPTE format. The MCISEQ sequencer does not support this option.
	tempo *tempo_value* Sets the tempo of the sequence according to the current time format. For a ppqn-based file, the *tempo_value* is interpreted as beats per minute. For a SMPTE-based file, the *tempo_value* is interpreted as frames per second.
	time format milliseconds Sets the time format to milliseconds. All position information is specified as milliseconds following this command. The sequence file sets the default format to ppqn or SMPTE. You can abbreviate milliseconds as **ms**.
	time format song pointer Sets the time format to song pointer (sixteenth notes). This can only be performed for a sequence of division type ppqn.
	time format SMPTE 24 Sets the time format to SMPTE 24 frame rate. All position information is specified in SMPTE format following this command. The sequence file sets the default format to ppqn or SMPTE.
	time format SMPTE 25 Sets the time format to SMPTE 25 frame rate. All position information is specified in SMPTE format following this command. The sequence file sets the default format to ppqn or SMPTE.

MIDI Sequencer

Command	Description
	time format SMPTE 30 Sets the time format to SMPTE 30 frame rate. All position information is specified in SMPTE format following this command. The sequence file sets the default format to ppqn or SMPTE.
	time format SMPTE 30 drop Sets the time format to SMPTE 30 drop frame rate. All position information is specified in SMPTE format following this command. The sequence file sets the default format to ppqn or SMPTE.
status *item*	Obtains status information for the MIDI sequencer. One of the following *items* modifies **status**:
	current track Returns the current track number. The MCISEQ sequencer returns 1.
	division type Returns one of the following file division type: **PPQN**, **SMPTE 24 frame**, **SMPTE 25 frame**, **SMPTE 30 drop frame**, or **SMPTE 30 frame**. Use this information to determine the format of the MIDI file, and the meaning of tempo and position information.
	length Returns the length of a sequence in the current time format. For ppqn files, this will be song pointer units. For SMPTE files, this will be expressed as *hh:mm:ss:ff*, where *hh* is hours, *mm* is minutes, *ss* is seconds, and *ff* is frames.
	length track *track_number* Returns the length of the sequence in the current time format. For ppqn files, this will be song pointer units. For SMPTE files, this will be expressed as *hh:mm:ss:ff*, where *hh* is hours, *mm* is minutes, *ss* is seconds, and *ff* is frames.
	master Returns **midi**, **none**, or **smpte** depending on the type of synchronization set.
	media present The sequencer returns **true**.
	mode Returns **not ready**, **paused**, **playing**, **seeking**, or **stopped**.
	number of tracks Returns the number of tracks. MCISEQ returns 1.
	offset Returns the offset of a SMPTE-based file. The offset is the start time of a SMPTE based sequence. The time is returned as *hh:mm:ss:ff*, where *hh* is hours, *mm* is minutes, *ss* is seconds, and *ff* is frames.

MIDI Sequencer

Command	Description
	port Returns the MIDI port number assigned to the sequence.
	position Returns the current position of a sequence in the current time format. For ppqn files, this will be song pointer units. For SMPTE files, this will be in colon form *hh:mm:ss:ff*, where *hh* is hours, *mm* is minutes, *ss* is seconds, and *ff* is frames.
	position track *track_number* Returns the current position of the track specified by *track_number* in the current time format. For ppqn files, this will be song pointer units. For SMPTE files, this will be in colon form *hh:mm:ss:ff*, where *hh* is hours, *mm* is minutes, *ss* is seconds, and *ff* is frames. The MCISEQ sequencer returns 0.
	ready Returns **true** if the device is ready.
	slave Returns **file**, **midi**, **none**, or **smpte** depending on the type of synchronization set.
	start position Returns the starting position of the media or device element.
	tempo Returns the current tempo of a sequence in the current time format. For files with ppqn format, the tempo is in beats per minute. For files with SMPTE format, the tempo is in frames per second.
	time format Returns the time format.
stop	Stops playing.

Videodisc Player Commands

The videodisc command set provides a common method for playing videodiscs in the Windows environment. This device type includes the MCIPIONR.DRV device driver which operates with the Pioneer LD-V4200 videodisc player. Videodisc players support the following set of commands:

Videodisc Player Commands

Command	Description
capability *item*	Reports the capabilities of the device. The return information is for the type of disc inserted unless **CAV** or **CLV** is used to override the format. If no disc is present then information is returned for **CAV** discs. The following optional *items* modify **capability**:
	can eject Returns **true** if the device can eject the disc. The MCIPIONR device returns **true**.
	can play Returns **true** if the device supports playing. The MCIPIONR device returns **true**.
	can record Returns **true** if the video device can record. The MCIPIONR device returns **false**.
	can reverse Returns **true** if the device can play in reverse, **false** otherwise. CLV discs return **false**.
	can save Returns **false**. MCI videodisc players cannot save data.
	CAV When combined with other items, **CAV** specifies that the return information applies to CAV format discs. This is the default if no disc is inserted.
	CLV When combined with other items, **CLV** specifies that the return information applies to CLV format discs.
	compound device Returns **false**. MCI videodisc players are simple devices.
	device type Returns **videodisc**.
	fast play rate Returns the standard fast play rate of the player in frames per second. Returns 0 if the device cannot play fast.
	has audio Returns **true** if the videodisc player has audio.
	has video Returns **true**.
	normal play rate Returns the normal play rate in frames per second. Returns 0 for CLV discs.

Videodisc Player Commands

Command	Description
	slow play rate Returns the standard slow play rate in frames per second. Returns 0 if the device cannot play slow.
	uses files Returns **false**. Simple devices do not use files.
close	Closes the device.
escape *item*	Sends custom information to a device. The following *item* modifies **escape**:
	string Specifies the custom information sent to the device.
info *item*	Fills a user-supplied buffer with information. The following optional *item* modifies **info**:
	product Returns the product name of the device that the peripheral is controlling. The MCIPIONR device returns **Pioneer LD-V4200.**
open *items*	Initializes the device. MCI reserves videodisc for the videodisc device type. The following optional *items* modify **open**:
	alias *device_alias* Specifies an alternate name for the given device. If specified, it must also be used for subsequent references.
	shareable Initializes the device as shareable. Subsequent attempts to open it fail unless you specify **shareable** in both the original and subsequent **open** commands. MCI returns an invalid device error if it is already open and not shareable.
pause	Stops playing. For CAV discs, the video frame will freeze. For CLV discs, the player is stopped.
play *items*	Starts playing. The following optional *items* modify **play**:
	fast slow Indicates that the device should play faster or slower than normal. To determine the exact speed on a particular player, use the **status speed** command. To specify the speed more precisely, use the **speed** flag. **Slow** applies only to CAV discs.
	from *position* **to** *position* Specifies the positions to start and stop playing. The default positions are in frames for CAV discs and in hours, minutes, and seconds for CLV discs. If **from** is omitted, play starts at the current position; if **to** is omitted, the play stops at the end of the disc.
	reverse Sets the play direction to backwards. This applies only to CAV discs.

Videodisc Player Commands

Command	Description
	scan Indicates the play speed is as fast as possible, possibly with audio disabled. This applies only to CAV discs.
	speed *integer* Specifies the rate of play in frames per second (for example, speed 15 means 15 frames per second). This applies only to CAV discs.
resume	Resumes playing of a paused device. The MCIPIONR device driver does not support this command.
seek *item*	Searches using fast forward or fast reverse with video and audio off. The following optional *items* modify **seek**:
	reverse Indicates the seek direction on CAV discs is backwards. This modifier is invalid if **to** is specified.
	to *position* Specifies the end position to stop the seek. If **to** is not specified, the seek continues until the end of the disc is reached.
	to start Specifies to seek to the start of the disc.
	to end Specifies to seek to the end of the disc.
set *items*	Sets the various control *items*:
	audio all off, audio all on Enables or disables audio output.
	audio left off, audio left on Enables or disables output to the left audio channel.
	audio right off, audio right on Enables or disables output to the right audio channel.
	door open Opens the door and ejects the tray, if possible.
	door closed Retracts the tray and closes the door, if possible.
	time format frames Sets the position format to frames on CAV discs. All position information is specified in this format following this command. This is the default for CAV discs.
	time format hms Sets the time format to hours, minutes, and seconds. When time or position values are used, they are expressed as *h:mm:ss* where *h* is hours, *mm* is minutes, and *ss* is seconds. All position information is specified in this format following this command. On input, *h* may be omitted if 0, and *mm* may be omitted if both it and *h* are 0. This is the default for CLV discs.

Videodisc Player Commands

Command	Description
	time format milliseconds Sets the position format to milliseconds. All position information is specified in this format following this command. You can abbreviate milliseconds as **ms**.
	time format track Sets the position format to tracks. All position information is specified in this format following this command.
	video on, video off Turns the video on or off.
spin *item*	Starts the disc spinning or stops the disc from spinning. One of the following *items* modifies **status**:
	down Stops the disc from spinning.
	up Starts the disc spinning.
status *item*	Obtains status information for the device. One of the following *items* modifies **status**:
	current track Returns the current track (chapter) number.
	disc size Returns either 8 or 12 to indicate the size of the loaded disc in inches.
	forward Returns **true** if the play direction is forward or if the device is not playing; **false** if the play direction is backward.
	length Returns the total length of the disc.
	length track *track_number* Returns the length of the track (chapter) specified by *track_number*.
	media present Returns **true** if a disc is inserted in the device, **false** otherwise.
	media type Returns either **CAV**, **CLV**, or **other** depending on the type of videodisc.
	mode Returns **not ready**, **open**, **paused**, **parked**, **playing**, **seeking**, or **stopped**.
	number of tracks Returns the number of tracks (chapters) on the disc. The MCIPIONR device does not support this option.
	position Returns the current position.
	position track *track_number* Returns the position of the start of the track (chapter) specified by *track_number*. The MCPIONR device does not support this option.
	ready Returns **true** if the device is ready.

Videodisc Player Commands

Command	Description
	side Returns 1 or 2 to indicate which side of the disc is loaded.
	speed Returns the current speed in frames per second. The MCIPIONR videodisc player does not support this option.
	start position Returns the starting position of the disc.
	time format Returns the time format.
step *items*	Step the play one or more frames forward or backward. The default action is to step one frame forward. The **step** command applies only to CAV discs. The following *items* modifies **step**:
	by *frames* Specifies the number of *frames* to step. If a negative value is used, the **reverse** flag is ignored.
	reverse Step backward.
stop	Stop playing.

Video Overlay Commands

The video overlay command set provides a common method for displaying overlay video in the Windows environment. Video overlay devices must support the following set of commands:

Video Overlay Commands

Command	Description
capability *item*	Requests information about the capabilities of the video overlay device. The *item* is one of the following:
	can eject Returns **false**. Video overlay devices have no media to eject.
	can freeze Returns true if the device can freeze data in the frame buffer.
	can play Returns **false**.
	can record Returns **false**.
	can save Returns **true** if the device can save the current contents of the frame buffer to disk.

Video Overlay Commands

Command	Description
	can stretch Returns **true** if the device can stretch frames to fill a given display rectangle.
	compound device Returns **true** if the device requires an element name. Video overlay devices which support multiple windows may be compound devices.
	device type Returns **overlay**.
	has audio Returns **false** if the device supports audio playback.
	has video Returns **true**. Video overlay devices are video devices.
	uses files Returns **true** if the element of a compound device is a file pathname.
	windows Returns the number of simultaneous display windows the device can support.
close	Closes a video overlay element and any resources associated with it.
freeze *item*	Disables video acquisition to the frame buffer. This is supported only if **capability can freeze** returns **true**. The following optional *item* modifies **freeze**:
	at *rectangle* Specifies the rectangular region that will have video acquisition disabled. Irregular acquisition regions can be specified using the **freeze** and **unfreeze** commands. (Some video overlay devices will place limitations on the complexity of the region used for acquisition.) The *rectangle* region is relative to the video buffer origin and is specified as *X1 Y1 X2 Y2*. The coordinates *X1, Y1* specify the top, left corner and the coordinates *X2, Y2* specify the width and height of the rectangle.
info *item*	Fills a user-supplied buffer with information. The following optional *item* modifies **info**:
	file Returns the name of the file used by the video overlay device.
	product Returns the product name and model of the current video overlay device.
	window text Returns the caption of the window used by the video overlay device.

Video Overlay Commands

Command	Description
load *item*	Loads the contents of the video buffer in a device specific format. The following optional *items* modify **load**: *filename* Specifies the file and pathname used to load the data. **at** *rectangle* Specifies a rectangle relative to the video buffer origin. The *rectangle* is specified as *X1 Y1 X2 Y2*. The coordinates *X1*, *Y1* specify the top, left corner and the coordinates *X2*, *Y2* specify the width and height of the rectangle.
open *items*	Initializes the video overlay device. The following optional *items* modify **open**: **alias** *device_alias* Specifies an alternate name for the device element. If specified, it must also be used for subsequent references. **parent** *hwnd* Specifies the window handle of the parent window. **shareable** Initializes the device element as shareable. Subsequent attempts to open it fail unless you specify **shareable** in both the original and subsequent **open** commands. MCI returns an error if it is already open and not shareable. **style** *style_type* Indicates a window style. **style child** Opens a window with a child window style. **style overlapped** Opens a window with an overlapped window style. **style popup** Opens a window with a popup window style. **type** *device_type* Specifies the device type of the device element. MCI reserves overlay for the video overlay device type. As an alternative to **type**, MCI can use the [mci extension] entries in the SYSTEM.INI file to select the controlling device based on the extension used by the device element.

Video Overlay Commands

Command	Description
put *items*	Defines the source, destination, and frame windows. One of the following *items* modify **put**:

destination   Sets the whole window as the destination window.

destination at *rectangle*   Specifies a rectangle for the area of
the window used to display the image. The *rectangle* coordinates
are relative to the window origin and are specified as *X1 Y1 X2
Y2*. The coordinates *X1, Y1* specify the top, left corner, and the
coordinates *X2, Y2* specify the width and height of the rectangle.
When an area of the display window is specified, and the device
supports stretching, the source image is stretched to the
destination offset and extent.

frame   Specifies that the whole video buffer is used to capture
the video image.

frame at *rectangle*   Specifies a rectangle for the area of the
video buffer used to capture the video image. The *rectangle*
coordinates are relative to the video buffer origin and are
specified as *X1 Y1 X2 Y2*. The coordinates *X1, Y1* specify the
top, left corner, and the coordinates *X2, Y2* specify the width and
height of the rectangle. If the device supports stretching, the
video image is stretched to the frame extent.

source   Selects the whole video buffer for display in the
destination window.

source at *rectangle*   Specifies a rectangle for the video buffer
area used to obtain the image for display. The *rectangle*
coordinates are relative to the video buffer origin and are
specified as *X1 Y1 X2 Y2*. The coordinates *X1, Y1* specify the
top, left corner, and the coordinates *X2, Y2* specify the width and
height of the rectangle. When an area of the source image is
specified, and the device supports stretching, the source image is
stretched to the destination offset and extent.

video   Selects the whole input video source for display in the
destination window.

Video Overlay Commands

Command	Description
	video at *rectangle* Specifies a rectangle for the input video source area used to obtain the image for display. The *rectangle* coordinates are relative to the video origin and are specified as *X1 Y1 X2 Y2*. The coordinates *X1, Y1* specify the top, left corner, and the coordinates *X2, Y2* specify the width and height of the rectangle. When an area of the source image is specified, and the device supports stretching, the source image is stretched to the destination offset and extent.
save *item*	Saves the contents of the video buffer in a device specific format. The following optional *item* modifies **save**:
	filename Specifies the file and pathname used to save the data.
	at *rectangle* Specifies a rectangle relative to the video buffer origin. The *rectangle* is specified as *X1 Y1 X2 Y2*. The coordinates *X1, Y1* specify the top, left corner and the coordinates *X2, Y2* specify the width and height of the rectangle.
set *items*	Sets the various control *items*:
	audio all off, audio all on Video overlay devices do not support this option.
	audio left off, audio left on Video overlay devices do not support this option.
	audio right off, audio right on Video overlay devices do not support this option.
	time format milliseconds Video overlay devices do not support this option.
	video off, video on Enables or disables video output.
status *item*	Obtains status information for the device. One of the following *items* modifies **status**:
	media present Returns **true**.
	mode Returns **not ready**, **recording**, or **stopped** for the current mode.
	ready Returns **true** if the video overlay device is ready.
	window handle Returns the handle of the window used for the video overlay display in the low word of the return value.

Video Overlay Commands

Command	Description
unfreeze *item*	Enables the frame buffer to acquire video data. This is supported only if **capability can freeze** returns **true**. The following optional *item* modifies **unfreeze**: **at** *rectangle* Specifies a rectangle relative to the video buffer origin. The *rectangle* is specified as *X1 Y1 X2 Y2*. The coordinates *X1, Y1* specify the top, left corner and the coordinates *X2, Y2* specify the width and height of the rectangle.
where	Obtains the rectangle specifying the source, destination, or frame area. One of the following *items* modifies **where**: **destination** Requests the offset and extent of the destination rectangle. **frame** Requests the offset and extent of the frame buffer rectangle. **source** Requests the offset and extent of the source rectangle. **video** Requests the offset and extent of the video rectangle.
window *item*	Tells the video overlay device to use a given window for display instead of the default window created by the driver. By default, video overlay devices should create a window when opened but should not display it until the device receives the **play** command. Applications providing window handles should manage the display issues that result when the window is sized or when the window handle is switched during play. Since the **status** command can obtain the handle to the current display window, you can use the standard window functions instead. The following *items* modify **window**: **handle** *window_handle* Specifies the handle of the destination window used as an alternate to the default window. **handle default** Specifies that the video overlay device should create and manage its own window. This flag can be used to set the display back to the driver's default window. **state hide** Hides the current display window. **state iconic** Displays the window as an icon. **state maximized** Maximizes the current display window. **state minimize** Minimizes the specified window and activates the top-level window in the window-manager's list.

Video Overlay Commands

Command	Description
state minimized	Minimizes the current display window.
state no action	Displays the display window in its current state. The window currently active remains active.
state no activate	Displays the display window in its most recent size and state. The window that is currently active remains active.
state normal	Displays the current display window as it was created.
state show	Shows the current display window.
text *caption*	Specifies the *caption* for the display window.

Waveform Audio Commands

Waveform audio drivers must support the following set of commands:

Waveform Audio Commands

Command	Description
capability *item*	Requests information about the capabilities of the waveform audio driver. One of the following *items* modify **capability**:
	can eject Returns **false**. Waveform audio devices have no media to eject.
	can play Returns **true** if the device can play. The waveform audio device returns true if an output device is available.
	can record Returns **true** if the device can record.
	can save Returns **true** if the waveform audio device can save data.
	compound device Returns **true**; waveform audio devices are compound devices.
	device type Returns **waveaudio**.
	has audio Returns **true**.

Waveform Audio Commands

Command	Description
	has video Returns **false**. Waveform audio devices do not support video.
	inputs Returns the total number of input devices.
	outputs Returns the total number of output devices.
	uses files Returns **true**. Waveform audio devices use files for operation.
close	Closes the device element and any resources associated with it.
cue *item*	Prepares for playing or recording. The **cue** command does not have to be issued prior to playing or recording. However, depending on the device, it might reduce the delay associated with the **play** or **record** command. This command fails if playing or recording is in progress. The *item* is one of the following:
	input Prepares for recording.
	output Prepares for playing. This is the default.
delete *items*	Deletes a data segment from the MCI element. The following optional *items* modify **cut**:
	from *position* **to** *position* Specifies the positions to start and stop deleting data. If **from** is omitted, deletion starts at the current position; if **to** is omitted, deletion stops at the end of the file or waveform.
info *item*	Fills a user-supplied buffer with information. One of the following *items* modifies **info**:
	input Returns the description of the current waveform audio input device. Returns **none** if an input device is not set. The MCIWAVE driver returns **Wave Audio Input and Output Device.**
	file Returns the current filename.
	output Returns the description of the current waveform audio output device. Returns **none** if an output device is not set. The MCIWAVE driver returns **Wave Audio Input and Output Device.**
	product Returns the description of the current waveform audio output device. The MCIWAVE driver returns **Wave Audio Input and Output Device.**

Waveform Audio Commands

Command	Description
open *items*	Initializes the device. The following *items* are optional:
	alias *device_alias* Specifies an alternate name for the given device. If specified, it must also be used the alias for references.
	buffer *buffer_size* Sets the size in seconds of the buffer used by the waveform audio device. The default size of the buffer is set when the waveform audio device is installed or configured. Typically the buffer size is set to 4 seconds.
	shareable Initializes the device element as shareable. Subsequent attempts to open it fail unless you specify **shareable** in both the original and subsequent **open** commands. MCI returns an error if it is already open and not shareable. The MCIWAVE device does not support shared files.
	type *device_type* Specifies the device type of a device element. MCI reserves waveaudio for the waveform audio device type. As an alternative to **type**, MCI can use the [mci extension] entries in the SYSTEM.INI file to select the controlling device based on the extension used by the device element.
pause	Pauses playing or recording.
play *items*	Starts playing audio. The following optional *items* modify **play**:
	from *position* **to** *position* Specifies the positions to start and stop playing. If **from** is omitted, play starts at the current position; if **to** is omitted, play stops at the end of the file or waveform.
record *items*	Starts recording audio. All data recorded after a file is opened is discarded if the file is closed without saving it. The following optional *items* modify **record**:
	insert Specifies that new data is added to the device element.
	from *position* **to** *position* Specifies the positions to start and stop recording. If **from** is omitted, the device starts recording at the current position; if **to** is omitted, the device records until a **stop** or **pause** command is received.
	overwrite Specifies that new data will replace data in the device element. The MCIWAVE driver does not support this option.

Waveform Audio Commands

Command	Description
resume	Resumes playing or recording of a paused device.
save *item*	Saves the MCI element in its current format. The following item modifies **save**:
	filename Specifies the file and pathname used to save data.
seek *item*	Moves to the specified location in the file. One of the following items modify **seek**:
	to *position* Specifies the stop position.
	to start Specifies to seek to the start of the first sample.
	to end Specifies to seek to the end of the last sample.
set *items*	Sets the various control *items*:
	alignment *integer* Sets the alignment of data blocks relative to the start of waveform data passed to the waveform audio device. The file is saved in this format.
	any input Use any input that supports the current format when recording. This is the default.
	any output Use any output that supports the current format when playing. This is the default.
	audio all off, audio all on Enables or disables audio output. The MCIWAVE driver does not support this option.
	audio left off, audio left on Enables or disables output to the left audio channel. The MCIWAVE driver does not support this option.
	audio right off, audio right on Enables or disables output to the right audio channel. The MCIWAVE driver does not support this option.
	bitspersample *bit_count* Sets the number of bits per sample played or recorded. The file is saved in this format.
	bytespersec *byte_rate* Sets the average number of bytes per second played or recorded. The file is saved in this format.
	channels *channel_count* Sets the channels for playing and recording. The file is saved in this format.
	format tag *tag* Sets the format type for playing and recording. The file is saved in this format.

Waveform Audio Commands

Command	Description
	format tag pcm Sets the format type to PCM for playing and recording. The file is saved in this format.
	input *integer* Sets the audio channel used as the input.
	output *integer* Sets the audio channel used as the output.
	samplespersec *integer* Sets the sample rate for playing and recording. The file is saved in this format.
	time format bytes Sets the time format to bytes. All position information is specified as bytes following this command.
	time format milliseconds Sets the time format to milliseconds. All position information is specified as milliseconds following this command. This is the default. You can abbreviate milliseconds as **ms**.
	time format samples Sets the time format to samples. All position information is specified as samples following this command.
status *item*	Obtains status information for the device. One of the following *items* modifies **status**:
	alignment Returns the block alignment of data in bytes.
	bitspersample Returns the bits per sample.
	bytespersec Returns the average number of bytes per second played or recorded.
	channels Returns the number of channels set (1 for mono, 2 for stereo).
	current track Returns the index for the current track. The MCIWAVE device returns 1.
	format tag Returns the format tag.
	input Returns the input set. If one is not set, the error returned indicates that any device can be used.
	length Returns the total length of the waveform.
	length track *track_number* Returns the length of the specified track.
	level Returns the current audio sample value.
	media present Returns **true**.

Waveform Audio Commands

Command	Description
	mode Returns **not ready, paused, playing, stopped, recording**, or **seeking** for the device mode.
	number of tracks Returns the number of tracks. The MCIWAVE device returns 1.
	output Returns the currently set output. If no output is set, the error returned indicates that any device can be used.
	position Returns the current position.
	position track *track_number* Returns the position of the track specified by *track_number*. The MCIWAVE device returns 0.
	ready Returns **true** if the device is ready.
	samplespersec Returns the number of samples per second played or recorded.
	start position Returns the starting position of the media or device element.
	time format Returns the current time format.
stop	Stops playing or recording.

Chapter 8
Multimedia File Formats

This chapter describes the file formats used with the Multimedia extensions. The chapter describes the structure of each file type and includes detailed lists of the data structures and fields contained in the files. The chapter also presents examples of multimedia files.

Several file formats used with the Multimedia extensions are based on the Resource Interchange File Format (RIFF). This chapter defines RIFF, the preferred format for new multimedia file types. If your application requires a new file format, you should define it using the RIFF tagged file structure described in this chapter.

This chapter describes the following file formats:

- Device Independent Bitmap (DIB) File Format
- RIFF DIB File Format (RDIB)
- Musical Instrument Digital Interface (MIDI) File Format
- RIFF MIDI File Format (RMID)
- Multimedia Movie File Format (MMM)
- Palette File Format (PAL)
- Rich Text Format (RTF)
- Waveform Audio File Format (WAVE)

About the RIFF Tagged File Format

RIFF (Resource Interchange File Format) is the tagged file structure developed for multimedia resource files. The structure of a RIFF file is similar to the structure of an Electronic Arts IFF file. In fact, RIFF is not actually a file format itself (since it does not represent a specific kind of information), but its name contains the words "interchange file format" in recognition of its roots in IFF. Refer to the EA IFF definition document, *EA IFF 85 Standard for Interchange Format Files*, for a list of reasons to use a tagged file format.

The Multimedia file I/O services provide support for working with RIFF files. For information on the file I/O services, see Chapter 9, "Multimedia File I/O Services," in the *Programmer's Workbook*. Also, functions, messages, and data structures provided by the Multimedia file I/O services are described in this Reference.

Chunks

The basic building block of a RIFF file is called a *chunk*, which, defined using C syntax, looks like the following:

```
typedef unsigned long DWORD;
typedef unsigned char BYTE;
typedef DWORD    FOURCC;          // Four-character code

typedef struct {
    FOURCC  ckID;
    DWORD   ckSize;              // the size of field <ckData>
    BYTE    ckData[ckSize];     // the actual data of the chunk
} CK;
```

Four-character codes (FOURCCs) are used extensively in RIFF files; they identify the sections of data contained in the file. A four-character code has the following characteristics:

- A 32-bit quantity represented as a sequence of one to four ASCII alphanumeric characters

- Padded on the right with blank characters (ASCII character value 32)

- Contains no embedded blanks.

For example, the four-character code "FOO" is stored as a sequence of four bytes ('F' 'O' 'O' ' ') in ascending addresses. For quick comparisons, a four-character code may also be treated as a 32-bit number.

The chunk fields are as follows:

Part	Description
ckID	Chunk ID. This four-character code identifies the representation of the chunk data. A program reading a RIFF file can skip over any chunk whose chunk ID it doesn't recognize; it skips the number of bytes specified by the **ckSize** field plus the pad byte, if present.
ckSize	Chunk size. This is a 32-bit unsigned value identifying the size of **ckData**. This size value includes does not include the size of the **ckID** or **ckSize** fields or the pad byte at the end of the **ckData** field.
ckData	Chunk data. This is binary data of fixed or variable size. The start of **ckData** is word-aligned with the start of the RIFF file. If the size of the chunk is an odd number of bytes, a pad byte with value zero is written after **ckData**. Word aligning is done to improve access speed (for chunks resident in memory) and for compatibility with EA IFF. The **ckSize** value does not include the pad byte.

Two types of chunks, the "LIST" and "RIFF" chunks, may contain nested chunks, or subchunks. These special chunk types are discussed later in this document. All other chunk types store a single element of binary data in **ckData**.

Chunks are represented using the following notation (in this example, the **ckSize** field and pad byte are implicit):

```
<ckID> ( <ckData> )
```

For example, a chunk with chunk ID "FOO" might be represented as follows:

```
FOO ( <foo-Data> )
```

It's common to refer to chunks by their chunk ID; the chunk shown above would be called a "FOO" chunk.

RIFF Forms

A RIFF form is a chunk with a "RIFF" chunk ID. The term also refers to a file format that follows the RIFF framework. The following lists currently registered RIFF forms. Each is described later in this document.

Form Type	Description
PAL	Palette File Format
RDIB	RIFF Device Independent Bitmap Format
RMID	RIFF MIDI Format
RMMP	RIFF Multimedia Movie File Format
WAVE	Waveform Audio Format

Using the notation for representing a chunk, a RIFF form looks like the following:

```
RIFF ( <formType> <ck>... )
```

The first four bytes of a RIFF form make up a chunk ID with values 'R' 'I' 'F' 'F'. The chunk size (**ckSize**) field is required, but for simplicity it is omitted from the notation.

Note RIFF has a counterpart, RIFX, that you can use to define RIFF file formats that use the Motorola integer byte-ordering format rather than the Intel format. A RIFX form is the same as a RIFF form, except that the first four bytes contain the character sequence 'R' 'I' 'F' 'X' rather than RIFF. Integer byte ordering is represented in Motorola format.

The first DWORD of chunk data in the "RIFF" chunk (shown above as **<formType>**) is a four-character code value identifying the data representation, or *form type*, of the file. Following the form-type code is a series of subchunks. Which subchunks are present depends on the form type. The definition of a particular RIFF form typically includes the following:

- A unique four-character code identifying the form type

- A list of mandatory chunks

- A list of optional chunks

- Possibly, a required order for the chunks

Defining and Registering RIFF Forms

The form-type code for a RIFF form must be unique. To guarantee this uniqueness, you must register any new form types before release. To register form types, and to get a current list of registered RIFF forms, request a *Multimedia Developer Registration Kit* from the following group:

Microsoft Corporation
Multimedia Systems Group
Product Marketing
One Microsoft Way
Redmond, WA 98052-6399

Like RIFF forms, RIFX forms must also be registered. Registering a RIFF form does not automatically register the RIFX counterpart. No RIFX form types are currently defined.

When you document the RIFF form, you should use the notation described in "Notation for Representing RIFF Files," later in this chapter.

Registered Form and Chunk Types

By convention, the form-type code for registered form types contains only digits and uppercase letters. Form-type codes that are all uppercase denote a registered, unique form type. Use lowercase letters for temporary or prototype chunk types.

Certain chunk types are also globally unique and must also be registered before use. These registered chunk types are not specific to a certain form type; they can be used in any form. If a registered chunk type can be used to store your data, you should use the registered chunk type rather than define your own chunk type containing the same type of information.

For example, a chunk with chunk ID "INAM" always contains the name or title of a file. Also, within all RIFF files, filenames or titles are contained within chunks with ID "INAM" and have a standard data format.

Unregistered (Form-Specific) Chunk Types

Chunks types that are used only in a certain form type use a lowercase chunk ID. A lowercase chunk ID has specific meaning only within the context of a specific form type. After a form designer is allocated a registered form type, the designer can choose lowercase chunk types to use within that form. See the *Multimedia Developers Registration Kit* for details.

For example, a chunk with ID "scln" inside one form type might contain the "number of scan lines." Inside some other form type, a chunk with ID "scln" might mean "secondary lambda number."

Notation for Representing RIFF Files

RIFF is a binary format, but it is easier to comprehend an ASCII representation of a RIFF file. This section defines a standard notation used to present samples of RIFF files. If you define a RIFF form, we urge you to use this notation in any file format samples you provide in your documentation.

Element Notation Conventions

The following table lists notation conventions used to describe elements of RIFF files. Further conventions are presented in the following sections.

Notation	Description
<element label>	RIFF file element with the label "element label"
<element label: TYPE>	RIFF file element with data type "TYPE"
[<element label>]	Optional RIFF file element
<element label>...	One or more copies of the specified element
[<element label>]...	Zero or more copies of the specified element

Basic Notation for Representing RIFF Files

The following table summarizes the elements of the RIFF notation required for representing sample RIFF files:

Notation	Description
<ckID> (<ckData>)	

The chunk with ID **<ckID>** and data **<ckData>**. The **<ckID>** field is a four-character code that may be enclosed by single quotes for emphasis.

For example, the following notation describes a "RIFF" chunk with a form type of "QRST." The data portion of this chunk contains a "FOO" subchunk.

```
RIFF('QRST' FOO(17 23))
```

The following example describes an "ICOP" chunk containing the string "Copyright Encyclopedia International.":

```
'ICOP' ("Copyright Encyclopedia International."Z)
```

Notation	Description

<number>[<modifier>]

A number consisting of an optional sign (+ or −) followed by one or more digits and modified by the optional **<modifier>**. Valid **<modifier>** values follow:

<modifier>	Meaning
none	16-bit number in decimal format
H	16-bit number in hexadecimal format
C	8-bit number in decimal format
CH	8-bit number in hexadecimal format
L	32-bit number in decimal format
LH	32-bit number in hexadecimal format

Several examples follow:

```
0
65535
-1
0L
4a3c89HL
-1C
21HC
```

Note that −1 and 65535 represent the same value. The application reading this file must know whether to interpret the number as signed or unsigned.

'<chars>'

A four-character code (32-bit quantity) consisting of a sequence of zero to four ASCII characters (**<chars>**) in the given order. If **<chars>** is less than four characters long, it is implicitly padded on the right with blanks. Two single quotes is equivalent to four blanks. Examples follow.

```
'RIFF'
'xyz'
''
```

<chars> can include escape sequences, which are combinations of characters introduced by a backslash (\) used to represent other characters. Escape sequences are listed in the following section.

Notation	Description

"<string>"[<modifier>]

The sequence of ASCII characters contained in **<string>** and modified by the optional modifier **<modifier>**. The quoted text can include any of the escape sequences listed in the following section. Valid **<modifier>** values follow:

<modifier>	Meaning
none	No NULL terminator or size prefix.
Z	String is NULL-terminated
B	String has an 8-bit (byte) size prefix
W	String has a 16-bit (word) size prefix
BZ	String has a byte-size prefix and is NULL-terminated
WZ	String has a word-size prefix and is NULL-terminated

NULL-terminated means that the string is followed by a character with ASCII value 0. A size prefix is an unsigned integer, stored as a byte or a word in Intel format preceding the string characters, that specifies the length of the string. In the case of strings with BZ or WZ modifiers, the size prefix specifies the size of the string without the terminating NULL.

The various string formats are described in "Storing Strings in RIFF Chunks," later in this chapter.

Examples follow:

```
"No prefix, no NULL terminator"
"No prefix, NULL terminator"Z
"Byte prefix, NULL terminator"BZ
```

Escape Sequences for Four-Character Codes and String Chunks

The following escape sequences can be used in four-character codes and string chunks:

Escape Sequence	ASCII Value (Decimal)	Description
\n	10	Newline character
\t	9	Horizontal tab character
\b	8	Backspace character
\r	13	Carriage return character
\f	12	Form feed character
\\	92	Backslash
\'	39	Single quote
\"	34	Double quote
\ddd	Octal ddd	Arbitrary character

Extended Notation for Representing RIFF Form Definitions

When documenting RIFF forms that you create, use the notation listed in the preceding section along with the extended notation listed in the following table to unambiguously define the structure of the new form.

Notation	Description
<name>	

A label that refers to some element of the file, where name is the name of the label. Examples follow:

```
<NAME-ck>
<GOBL-form>
<bitmap-bits>
<foo>
```

Conventionally, a label that refers to a chunk is named <ckID-ck>, where *ckID* is the chunk ID. Similarly, a label that refers to a RIFF form is named <formType-form>, where *formType* is the name of the form's type.

Notation	Description

<name> → elements

The actual data represented by **<name>** is defined as **elements**. This states that **<name>** is an abbreviation for **elements**. An example follows.

```
<GOBL-form> → RIFF ('GOBL'<form-data>)
```

This example defines label <GOBL-form> as representing a RIFF form with chunk ID "GOBL" and data equal to <form-data>, where <form-data> is a label that would be defined in another rule. Note that a label may represent any data, not just a RIFF chunk or form.

Note A number of atomic labels are defined in "Atomic Labels," later in this chapter. These labels refer to primitive data types.

<name:type>

This is the same as **<name>**, but it also defines **<name>** to be equivalent to **<type>**. This notation obviates the following rule:

```
<name> → <type>
```

This allows you to give a symbolic name to an element of a file format and to specify the element data type. An example follows:

```
<xyz-coordinate> → <x:INT> <y:INT> <z:INT>
```

This defines <xyz-coordinate> to consist of three parts concatenated together: <x>, <y>, and <z>. The definition also specifies that <x>, <y>, and <z> are integers. This notation is equivalent to the following:

```
<xyz-coordinate> → <x> <y> <z>
<x> → <INT>
<y> → <INT>
<z> → <INT>
```

[elements]

An optional sequence of labels and literal data. Surrounded by square brackets, it may be considered an element itself. An example follows:

```
<FOO-form> → RIFF('FOO'[<header-ck>]<data-ck>)
```

This example defines form "FOO" with an optional <header> chunk followed by a mandatory <data> chunk.

Notation	Description

el1 | el2 | ... | elN

Exactly one of the listed elements must be present. An example follows:

`<hdr-ck> → hdr(<hdr-x> | <hdr-y> | <hdr-z>)`

This example defines the "hdr" chunk's data as containing one of <hdr-x>, <hdr-y>, or <hdr-z>.

element...

One or more occurrences of **element** may be present. Note that an ellipsis has this meaning only if it follows an element; in other cases (such as, A | B | ... | Z), the ellipsis has its ordinary English meaning. If there is any possibility of confusion, an ellipsis should only be used to indicate one or more occurrences. An example follows:

`<data-ck> → data(<count:INT> <item:INT>...)`

This example defines the data of the "data" chunk to contain an integer <count>, followed by one or more occurrences of the integer <item>.

[element]...

Zero or more occurrences of element may be present. An example follows.

`<data-ck> → data(<count:INT> [<item:INT>]...)`

This example defines the data of the "data" chunk to contain an integer <count> followed by zero or more occurrences of an integer <item>.

{ elements }

The group of **elements** within the braces should be considered a single element. An example follows:

`<blorg> → <this> | <that> | <other>...`

This example defines <blorg> to be either <this> or <that> or one or more occurrences of <other>. The next example defines <blorg> to be either <this> or one or more occurrences of <that> or <other>, intermixed in any way.

`<blorg> → <this> | {<that> | <other>}...`

Notation	Description

struct { ... } name

A structure defined using C syntax. This can be used instead of a sequence of labels if a C header (include) file is available that defines the structure. The label used to refer to the structure should be the same as the structure's typedef name. An example follows:

```
<3D_POINT> → struct              {
                 INT x;          // x-coordinate
                 INT y;          // y-coordinate
                 INT z;          // z-coordinate
             } 3D_POINT
```

Wherever possible, the types used in the structure should be the types listed in the following section, "Atomic Labels," because these types are more portable than C types such as int. The structure fields are assumed to be present in the file in the order given, with no padding or forced alignment.

Unless the RIFF chunk ID is "RIFX" integer byte ordering is assumed to be in Intel format.

// comment

An explanatory comment to a rule. An example follows:

```
<weekend> → 'Sat'|'Sun'    // 4-char code for day
```

Atomic Labels

The following are atomic labels, or labels that refer to primitive data types. Where available, the equivalent Microsoft C data type is also listed.

Label	Meaning	MS C Type
<CHAR>	8-bit signed integer	signed char
<BYTE>	8-bit unsigned quantity	unsigned char
<INT>	16-bit signed integer in Intel format	signed int
<WORD>	16-bit unsigned quantity in Intel format	unsigned int
<LONG>	32-bit signed integer in Intel format	signed long
<DWORD>	32-bit unsigned quantity in Intel format	unsigned long
<FLOAT>	32-bit IEEE floating point number	float
<DOUBLE>	64-bit IEEE floating point number	double
<STR>	String (a sequence of characters)	
<ZSTR>	NULL-terminated string	
<BSTR>	String with byte (8-bit) size prefix	
<WSTR>	String with word (16-bit) size prefix	
<BZSTR>	NULL-terminated string with byte size prefix	
<WZSTR>	NULL-terminated string with word size prefix	

NULL-terminated means that the string is followed by a character with ASCII value 0.

A size prefix is an unsigned integer, stored as a byte or a word in Intel format, that specifies the length of the string. In the case of strings with BZ or WZ modifiers, the size prefix specifies the size of the string without the terminating NULL.

Note   The WINDOWS.H header file defines the C types BYTE, WORD, LONG, and DWORD. These types correspond to labels <BYTE>, <WORD>, <LONG>, and <DWORD>, respectively.

A Sample RIFF Form Definition and RIFF Form

The following example defines <GOBL-form>, the hypothetical RIFF form of type "GOBL." To fully document a new RIFF form definition, a developer would also provide detailed descriptions of each file element, including the semantics of each chunk and sample files documented using the standard notation.

```
<GOBL-form> →   RIFF( 'GOBL'                        // RIFF form header
                  [<org-ck>]                        // Origin chunk (default (0,0,0))
                  <obj-list> )                      // Series of graphical objects

<org-ck> →      org( <origin:3D_POINT> )            // Origin of object list

<obj-list> →    LIST('obj' { <sqr-ck>  |           // An object is: a square
                             <circ-ck> |           //   or a circle
                             <poly-ck>  }… )        //   or a polygon

<sqr-ck> →      sqr( <pt1:3D_POINT>                 // one vertex
                     <pt2:3D_POINT>                 // another vertex
                     <pt3:3D_POINT> )               // a third vertex

<circ-ck> →     circ( <center:3D_POINT>            // center of circle
                      <circumPt:3D_POINT> )         // a point on the circumference

<poly-ck> →     poly( <pt:3D_POINT>… )              // list of points in a polygon

<3D_POINT> →    struct                              // defined in "gobl.h"
                {
                    INT x;                          // x-coordinate
                    INT y;                          // y-coordinate
                    INT z;                          // z-coordinate
                } 3D_POINT
```

Sample RIFF Form

The following sample RIFF form adheres to the form definition for form type GOBL. The file contains three subchunks:

- An "INFO" list
- An "org" chunk
- An "obj" chunk

The "INFO" list and "org" chunk each have two subchunks. The "INFO" list is a registered global chunk that can be used within any RIFF file. The "INFO" list is described in the "The INFO List Chunk," later in this chapter.

Since the definition of the GOBL form does not refer to the INFO chunk, software that expects only "org" and "obj" chunks in a GOBL form would ignore the unknown "INFO" chunk.

```
RIFF( 'GOBL'
        LIST('INFO'           // INFO list containing filename and copyright
                INAM("A House"Z)
                ICOP("(C) Copyright Joe Inc. 1991"Z)
            )

        org (2, 0, 0)         // Origin of object list

        LIST('obj'            // Object list containing two polygons
                poly(0,0,0  2,0,0  2,2,0, 1,3,0, 0,2,0)
                poly(0,0,5  2,0,5  2,2,5, 1,3,5, 0,2,5)
            )
    )                         // End of form
```

Storing Strings in RIFF Chunks

This section lists methods for storing text strings in RIFF chunks. While these guidelines may not make sense for all applications, you should follow these conventions if you must make an arbitrary decision regarding string storage.

NULL-Terminated String (ZSTR) Format

A NULL-terminated string (ZSTR) consists of a series of characters followed by a terminating NULL character. The ZSTR is better than a simple character sequence (STR) because many programs are easier to write if strings are NULL-terminated. ZSTR is preferred to a string with a size prefix (BSTR or WSTR) because the size of the string is already available as the <ckSize> value, minus one for the terminating NULL character.

String Table Format

In a string table, all strings used in a structure are stored at the end of the structure in packed format. The structure includes fields that specify the offsets from the beginning of the string table to the individual strings. An example follows:

```
typedef struct
{
    INT     iWidgetNumber;     // the widget number
    WORD    offszWidgetName;   // an offset to a string in <rgchStrTab>
    WORD    offszWidgetDesc;   // an offset to a string in <rgchStrTab>
    INT     iQuantity;         // how many widgets
    CHAR    rgchStrTab[1];     // string table (allocate as large as needed)
}   WIDGET;
```

If multiple chunks within the file need to reference variable-length strings, you can store the strings in a single chunk that acts as a string table. The chunks that refer to the strings contain offsets relative to the beginning of the data part of the string table chunk.

NULL-Terminated, Byte Size Prefix String (BZSTR) Series

In a BZSTR series, a series of strings is stored in packed format. Each string is a BZSTR, with a byte size prefix and a NULL terminator. This format retains the ease-of-use characteristics of the ZSTR while providing the string size, allowing the application to quickly skip unneeded strings.

Multiline String Format

When storing multiline strings, separate lines with a carriage return/line feed pair (ASCII 13/ASCII 10 pair). Although applications vary in their requirements for new line symbols (carriage return only, line feed only, or both), it is generally easier to strip out extra characters than to insert extra ones. Inserting characters might require reallocating memory blocks or pre-scanning the chunk before allocating memory for it.

Choosing a Storage Method

The following lists guidelines for deciding which storage method is appropriate for your application.

Usage	Recommended Format
Chunk data contains nothing except a string	ZSTR (NULL-terminated string) format.
Chunk data contains a number of fields, some of which are variable-length strings	String-table format
Multiple chunks within the file need to reference variable-length strings	String-table format
Chunk data stores a sequence of strings, some of which the application may want to skip	BZSTR (NULL-terminated string with byte size prefix) series
Chunk data contains multiline strings	A multiline string format

LIST Chunk

A LIST chunk is defined as follows:

```
LIST( <list-type> [<chunk>]... )
```

A LIST chunk contains a list, or ordered sequence, of subchunks. The **<list-type>** is a four-character code that identifies the contents of the list.

If an application recognizes the list type, it should know how to interpret the sequence of subchunks. However, since a LIST chunk may contain only subchunks (after the list type), an application that does not know about a specific list type can still walk through the sequence of subchunks.

Like chunk IDs, list types must be registered, and an all-lowercase list type has meaning relative to the form that contains it.

The INFO List Chunk

The "INFO" list is a registered global form type that can store information that helps identify the contents of the chunk. This information is useful but does not affect the way a program interprets the file; examples are copyright information and comments. An "INFO" list is a "LIST" chunk with list type "INFO." The following shows a sample "INFO" list chunk:

```
LIST('INFO' INAM("Two Trees"Z)
        ICMT("A picture for the opening screen"Z) )
```

An "INFO" list should contain only the following chunks. New chunks may be defined, but an application should ignore any chunk it doesn't understand. The chunks listed below may only appear in an "INFO" list. Each chunk contains a ZSTR, or null-terminated text string.

Chunk ID	Description
IARL	*Archival Location.* Indicates where the subject of the file is archived.
IART	*Artist.* Lists the artist of the original subject of the file. For example, "Michaelangelo."
ICMS	*Commissioned.* Lists the name of the person or organization that commissioned the subject of the file. For example, "Pope Julian II."
ICMT	*Comments.* Provides general comments about the file or the subject of the file. If the comment is several sentences long, end each sentence with a period. Do *not* include newline characters.

Chunk ID	Description
ICOP	*Copyright.* Records the copyright information for the file. For example, "Copyright Encyclopedia International 1991." If there are multiple copyrights, separate them by a semicolon followed by a space.
ICRD	*Creation date.* Specifies the date the subject of the file was created. List dates in year-month-day format, padding one-digit months and days with a zero on the left. For example, "1553-05-03" for May 3, 1553.
ICRP	*Cropped.* Describes whether an image has been cropped and, if so, how it was cropped. For example, "lower right corner."
IDIM	*Dimensions.* Specifies the size of the original subject of the file. For example, "8.5 in h, 11 in w."
IDPI	*Dots Per Inch.* Stores dots per inch setting of the digitizer used to produce the file, such as "300."
IENG	*Engineer.* Stores the name of the engineer who worked on the file. If there are multiple engineers, separate the names by a semicolon and a blank. For example, "Smith, John; Adams, Joe."
IGNR	*Genre.* Describes the original work, such as, "landscape," "portrait," "still life," etc.
IKEY	*Keywords.* Provides a list of keywords that refer to the file or subject of the file. Separate multiple keywords with a semicolon and a blank. For example, "Seattle; aerial view; scenery."
ILGT	*Lightness.* Describes the changes in lightness settings on the digitizer required to produce the file. Note that the format of this information depends on hardware used.
IMED	*Medium.* Describes the original subject of the file, such as, "computer image," "drawing," "lithograph," and so forth.
INAM	*Name.* Stores the title of the subject of the file, such as, "Seattle From Above."
IPLT	*Palette Setting.* Specifies the number of colors requested when digitizing an image, such as "256."
IPRD	*Product.* Specifies the name of the title the file was originally intended for, such as "Encyclopedia of Pacific Northwest Geography."
ISBJ	*Subject.* Describes the contents of the file, such as "Aerial view of Seattle."
ISFT	*Software.* Identifies the name of the software package used to create the file, such as "Microsoft WaveEdit."

Chunk ID	Description
ISHP	*Sharpness.* Identifies the changes in sharpness for the digitizer required to produce the file (the format depends on the hardware used).
ISRC	*Source.* Identifies the name of the person or organization who supplied the original subject of the file. For example, "Trey Research."
ISRF	*Source Form.* Identifies the original form of the material that was digitized, such as "slide," "paper," "map," and so forth. This is not necessarily the same as IMED.
ITCH	*Technician.* Identifies the technician who digitized the subject file. For example, "Smith, John."

Device Independent Bitmap (DIB) File Format

The Device Independent Bitmap (DIB) format represents bitmap images in a device-independent manner. Bitmaps can be represented at 1, 4, and 8 bits per pixel, with a palette containing colors represented in 24 bits. Bitmaps can also be represented at 24 bits per pixel without a palette and in a run-length encoded format. This documentation describes three types of DIB files:

- Windows version 3.0 device-independent bitmap files

- OS/2 Presentation Manager version 1.2 device-independent bitmap files

- RIFF device-independent bitmap files

The Windows 3.0 and Presentation Manager 1.2 DIBs are similar, so they are discussed together.

Overview of DIB Structure

Windows 3.0 and Presentation Manager 1.2 DIB files contain the following sequence of data structures:

- A file header

- A bitmap information header

- A color table

- An array of bytes that defines the bitmap bits

The following sections describe each of these structures.

Bitmap File Header

The bitmap file header contains information about the type, size, and layout of a device-independent bitmap (DIB) file. In both the Windows 3.0 and Presentation Manager 1.2 DIBs, it is defined as a **BITMAPFILEHEADER** data structure:

```
typedef struct tagBITMAPFILEHEADER {
    WORD    bfType;
    DWORD   bfSize;
    WORD    bfReserved1;
    WORD    bfReserved2;
    DWORD   bfOffBits;
} BITMAPFILEHEADER;
```

The following table describes the fields.

Field	Description
bfType	Specifies the file type. It must consist of the character sequence BM (WORD value 0x4D42).
bfSize	Specifies the file size in bytes.
bfReserved1	Reserved. Must be set to zero.
bfReserved2	Reserved. Must be set to zero.
bfOffBits	Specifies the byte offset from the **BITMAPFILEHEADER** structure to the actual bitmap data in the file.

Bitmap Information Header

The **BITMAPINFO** and **BITMAPCOREINFO** data structures define the dimensions and color information for Windows 3.0 and Presentation Manager 1.2 DIBs, respectively. They are defined as follows:

Windows 3.0 DIB	Presentation Manager 1.2 DIB
``typedef struct tagBITMAPINFO {
{
BITMAPINFOHEADER bmiHeader;
RGBQUAD   bmiColors[1];
} BITMAPINFO;```	```typedef struct _BITMAPCOREINFO
{
BITMAPCOREHEADER   bmciHeader;
RGBTRIPLE   bmciColors[1];
} BITMAPCOREINFO;```

These structures are essentially alike, and this section discusses them simultaneously. Each field name for the Windows **BITMAPINFO** structure is followed by the corresponding field name for the Presentation Manager **BITMAPCOREINFO** 1.2 structure, in parentheses.

The following table describes the fields.

Windows Field (PM Field)	Description
bmiHeader (**bmciHeader**)	Specifies information about the dimensions and color format of the DIB. The **BITMAPINFOHEADER** and **BITMAPCOREHEADER** data structures are described in the next section.
bmiColors (**bmciColors**)	Specifies the DIB color table. The **RGBQUAD** and **RGBTRIPLE** data structures are described in "Bitmap Color Table," later in this chapter.

Information Header Structures

The **BITMAPINFOHEADER** and **BITMAPCOREHEADER** structures contain information about the dimensions and color format of Windows 3.0 and Presentation Manager 1.2 DIBs, respectively. They are defined as follows:

Windows 3.0 DIB	Presentation Manager 1.2 DIB

```
typedef struct tagBITMAPINFOHEADER{
{
    DWORD   biSize;
    DWORD   biWidth;
    DWORD   biHeight;
    WORD    biPlanes;
    WORD    biBitCount;
    DWORD   biCompression;
    DWORD   biSizeImage;
    DWORD   biXPelsPerMeter;
    DWORD   biYPelsPerMeter;
    DWORD   biClrUsed;
    DWORD   biClrImportant;
} BITMAPINFOHEADER;
```

```
typedef struct tagBITMAPCOREHEADER
{
    DWORD   bcSize;
    WORD    bcWidth;
    WORD    bcHeight;
    WORD    bcPlanes;
    WORD    bcBitCount;
} BITMAPCOREHEADER;
```

Because these structures are essentially alike, except for the added fields in the Windows 3.0 structure, this section discusses them simultaneously. Each field name for the Windows structure is followed by the corresponding field name for the Presentation Manager structure, in parentheses.

Common Fields The following fields are present in both the Windows 3.0 and Presentation Manager 1.2 formats:

Windows (PM) Field	Description
biSize (bcSize)	Specifies the number of bytes required by the BITMAPINFOHEADER structure. You can use this field to distinguish between Windows 3.0 and Presentation Manager 1.2 DIBs.
biWidth (bcWidth)	Specifies the width of the DIB in pixels.
biHeight (bcHeight)	Specifies the height of the DIB in pixels.
biPlanes (bcPlanes)	Specifies the number of planes for the target device. Must must be set to 1.
biBitCount (bcBitCount)	Specifies the number of bits-per-pixel. See "Interpreting the Color Table," later in this section, for more information.

Windows Fields The following fields are present only in the Windows 3.0 BITMAPINFOHEADER structure:

Field	Description
biCompression	Specifies the type of compression for a compressed bitmap. It can be one of the following values:

Value	Meaning
BI_RGB	Specifies that the bitmap is not compressed.
BI_RLE8	Specifies a run-length encoded format for bitmaps with 8 bits-per-pixel. The compression format is a two-byte format consisting of a count byte followed by a color-index byte.
BI_RLE4	Specifies a run-length encoded format for bitmaps with 4 bits-per-pixel. The compression format is a two-byte format consisting of a count byte followed by two word-length color indexes.

See "Windows 3.0 Bitmap Compression Formats" later in this document for information about the encoding schemes.

Field	Description
biSizeImage	Specifies the size in bytes of the image.
biXPelsPerMeter	Specifies the horizontal resolution in pixels per meter of the target device for the bitmap. An application can use this value to select a bitmap from a resource group that best matches the characteristics of the current device.
biYPelsPerMeter	Specifies the vertical resolution in pixels per meter of the target device for the bitmap.
biClrUsed	Specifies the number of color values in the color table actually used by the bitmap. Possible values follow.

Value	Result
0	Bitmap uses the maximum number of colors corresponding to the value of the **biBitCount** field.
Nonzero	If the **biBitCount** is less than 24, the actual number of colors which the graphics engine or device driver will access.
	If the **biBitCount** field is set to 24, the size of the reference color table used to optimize performance of Windows color palettes.

If the bitmap is a "packed" bitmap (that is, a bitmap in which the bitmap array immediately follows the **BITMAPINFO** header and which is referenced by a single pointer), the **biClrUsed** field must be set to 0 or to the actual size of the color table.

See "Interpreting the Color Table," later in this section, for more information on how this field affects the interpretation of the color table.

Field	Description
biClrImportant	Specifies the number of color indexes that are considered important for displaying the bitmap. If this value is 0, then all colors are important.

Bitmap Color Table

The color table is a collection of 24-bit RGB values. There are as many entries in the color table as there are colors in the bitmap. The color table isn't present for bitmaps with 24 color bits because each pixel is represented by 24-bit RGB values in the actual bitmap data area.

Color Table Structure

The color table for Windows 3.0 and Presentation Manager 1.2 DIBs consists of an array of RGBQUAD and RGBTRIPLE structures, respectively. These structures are defined as follows:

Windows 3.0 DIB	Presentation Manager 1.2 DIB
```typedef struct tagRGBQUAD { BYTE rgbBlue; BYTE rgbGreen; BYTE rgbRed; BYTE rgbReserved; } RGBQUAD;```	```typedef struct tagRGBTRIPLE { BYTE rgbtBlue; BYTE rgbtGreen; BYTE rgbtRed; } RGBTRIPLE;```

Because these structures are essentially alike, this section discusses them simultaneously. Each field name for the Windows **RGBQUAD** structure is followed by the corresponding field name for the Presentation Manager **RGBTRIPLE** structure, in parentheses.

Order of Colors

The colors in the table should appear in order of importance. This can help a device driver render a bitmap on a device that cannot display as many colors as there are in the bitmap. If the DIB is in Windows 3.0 format, the driver can use the **biClrImportant** field of the **BITMAPINFOHEADER** structure to determine which colors are important.

Field Descriptions

The **RGBQUAD (RGBTRIPLE)** structure contains the following fields:

Windows (PM) Field	Description
rgbBlue (rgbtBlue)	Specifies the blue intensity.
rgbGreen (rgbtGreen)	Specifies the green intensity.
rgbRed (rgbtRed)	Specifies the red intensity.
rgbReserved (no PM equivalent)	Not used. Must be set to 0.

Locating the Color Table

An application can use the **biSize** (**bcSize**) field of the **BITMAPINFOHEADER** (**BITMAPCOREHEADER**) structure to locate the color table. Each of the following statements assigns the pColor variable the byte offset of the color table from the beginning of the file:

```
// Windows 3.0 DIB
pColor = (LPSTR)pBitmapInfo + (WORD)pBitmapInfo->biSize

// Presentation Manager 1.2 DIB
pColor = (LPSTR)pBitmapCoreInfo + (WORD)pBitmapCoreInfo->bcSize
```

Interpreting the Color Table

The **biBitCount** (**bcBitCount**) field of the **BITMAPINFOHEADER** (**BITMAPCOREHEADER**) structure determines the number of bits which define each pixel and the maximum number of colors in the bitmap. Its value affects the interpretation of the color table.

The **biBitCount** (**bcBitCount**) field can have any of the following values:

Value	Meaning
1	The bitmap is monochrome, and the color table contains two entries. Each bit in the bitmap array represents a pixel. If the bit is clear, the pixel is displayed with the color of the first entry in the color table. If the bit is set, the pixel has the color of the second entry in the table.
4	The bitmap has a maximum of 16 colors. Each pixel in the bitmap is represented by a four-bit index into the color table.
	For example, if the first byte in the bitmap is 0x1F, then the byte represents two pixels. The first pixel contains the color in the second table entry, and the second pixel contains the color in the 16th table entry.
8	The bitmap has a maximum of 256 colors. Each pixel in the bitmap is represented by a byte-sized index into the color table. For example, if the first byte in the bitmap is 0x1F, then the first pixel has the color of the thirty-second table entry.
24	The bitmap has a maximum of 2^{24} colors. The **bmiColors** (**bmciColors**) field is NULL, and each three bytes in the bitmap array represent the relative intensities of red, green, and blue, respectively, of a pixel.

Note on Windows DIBs

For Windows 3.0 DIBs, the **biClrUsed** field of the **BITMAPINFOHEADER** structure specifies the number of color indexes in the color table actually used by the bitmap. If the **biClrUsed** field is set to 0, the bitmap uses the maximum number of colors corresponding to the value of the **biBitCount** field.

Bitmap Data

The bits in the array are packed together, but each line of pixels, or scan line, must be zero-padded to end on a LONG boundary. Segment boundaries can appear anywhere in the bitmap, however. The origin of the bitmap is the lower-left corner.

Windows supports run-length encoded formats for compressing 4- and 8-bit bitmaps. Compression reduces the disk and memory storage required for the bitmap. "Windows 3.0 Bitmap Compression Formats," later in this chapter, discusses compression formats for the bitmap data.

Examples of DIB Files

The following example is a FileWalker text dump of a Windows 3.0 DIB. This is a four-bit, 16-color bitmap:

```
Win3DIBFile
        BitmapFileHeader
                Type        19778
                Size        3118
                Reserved1   0
                Reserved2   0
                OffsetBits  118
        BitmapInfoHeader
                Size            40
                Width           80
                Height          75
                Planes          1
                BitCount        4
                Compression     0
                SizeImage       3000
                XPelsPerMeter   0
                YPelsPerMeter   0
                ColorsUsed      16
                ColorsImportant 16
        Win3ColorTable
                Blue    Green   Red   Unused
[00000000]      84      252     84    0
[00000001]      252     252     84    0
[00000002]      84      84      252   0
[00000003]      252     84      252   0
```

```
[00000004]        84     252     252    0
[00000005]       252     252     252    0
[00000006]         0       0       0    0
[00000007]       168       0       0    0
[00000008]         0     168       0    0
[00000009]       168     168       0    0
[0000000A]         0       0     168    0
[0000000B]       168       0     168    0
[0000000C]         0     168     168    0
[0000000D]       168     168     168    0
[0000000E]        84      84      84    0
[0000000F]       252      84      84    0
          Image

          .
          .                                            Bitmap data
          .
```

The following example is a FileWalker text dump of a Presentation Manager 1.2 DIB. This is an eight-bit, 256-color bitmap:

```
OS2DIBFile
        BitmapFileHeader
                Type        19778
                Size        409454
                Reserved1   0
                Reserved2   0
                OffsetBits  794
        BitMapCoreInfo
                Size        12
                Width       555
                Height      735
                Planes      1
                BitCount    8
        OS2ColorTable
                Blue    Green   Red
[00000000]        0       0       0
[00000001]      248     248     248
[00000002]      240     248     248
        .
        .                                              Color entries
        .
[000000FD]       48      48      56
[000000FE]      176      24      40
[000000FF]      252     252     252
          Image

          .
          .                                            Bitmap data
          .
```

Windows 3.0 Bitmap Compression Formats

Compression of 8-Bit-Per-Pixel DIBs

When the **biCompression field** is set to BI_RLE8, the bitmap is compressed using a run-length encoding format for an 8-bit bitmap. This format uses two modes:

- Encoded mode
- Absolute mode

Both modes can occur anywhere throughout a single bitmap.

Encoded Mode

Encoded mode consists of two bytes. The first byte specifies the number of consecutive pixels to be drawn using the color index contained in the second byte.

Also, the first byte of the pair can be set to zero to indicate an escape that denotes an end of line, end of bitmap, or a delta. The interpretation of the escape depends on the value of the second byte of the pair. In encoded mode, the second byte has a value of 0 to 2.

The following table shows the meaning of the second byte:

Second Byte	Meaning
0	End of line.
1	End of bitmap.
2	Delta. The two bytes following the escape contain unsigned values indicating the horizontal and vertical offset of the next pixel from the current position.

Absolute Mode

Absolute mode is signalled by the first byte set to zero and the second byte set to a value between 03H and FFH.

The second byte represents the number of bytes that follow, each of which contains the color index of a single pixel.

Each run must be aligned on a word boundary.

The following example shows the hexadecimal values of an 8-bit RLE bitmap. Under "Expanded Data," the two-digit values represent a color index for a single pixel.

Compressed Data	Expanded Data
03 04	04 04 04
05 06	06 06 06 06 06
00 03 45 56 67 00	45 56 67
02 78	78 78
00 02 05 01	move 5 right and 1 down
02 78	78 78
00 00	end of line
09 1E	1E 1E 1E 1E 1E 1E 1E 1E 1E
00 01	end of RLE bitmap

Compression of 4-Bit-Per-Pixel DIBs

When the **biCompression** field is set to BI_RLE4, the bitmap is compressed using a run-length encoding format for a 4-bit bitmap. This format uses two modes:

- Encoded mode
- Absolute mode

Encoded Mode

In encoded mode, the first byte of the pair contains the number of pixels to be drawn using the color indexes in the second byte.

The second byte contains two color indexes, one in its high-order nibble (that is, its low-order four bits) and one in its low-order nibble.

The first of the pixels is drawn using the color specified by the high-order nibble, the second is drawn using the color in the low-order nibble, the third is drawn with the color in the high-order nibble, and so on, until all the pixels specified by the first byte have been drawn.

Also, the first byte of the pair can be set to zero to indicate an escape that denotes an end of line, end of bitmap, or a delta. The interpretation of the escape depends on the value of the second byte of the pair. In encoded mode, the second byte has a value from 00H to 02H.

Absolute Mode

In absolute mode, the first byte contains zero, the second byte contains the number of color indexes that follow, and subsequent bytes contain color indexes in their high- and low-order nibbles, one color index for each pixel.

Each run must be aligned on a word boundary.

The end-of-line, end-of-bitmap, and delta escapes valid for BI_RLE8 also apply to BI_RLE4.

The following example shows the hexadecimal values of a 4-bit RLE bitmap. Under "Expanded Data," the one-digit values represent a color index for a single pixel.

Compressed Data	Expanded Data
03 04	0 4 0
05 06	0 6 0 6 0
00 06 45 56 67 00	4 5 5 6 6 7
04 78	7 8 7 8
00 02 05 01	move 5 right and 1 down
04 78	7 8 7 8
00 00	end of line
09 1E	1 E 1 E 1 E 1 E 1
00 01	end of RLE bitmap

RIFF DIB File Format (RDIB)

The RDIB format consists of a Windows 3.0 or Presentation Manager 1.2 DIB enclosed in a "RIFF" chunk. Enclosing the DIB in a "RIFF" chunk allows the file to be consistently identified; for example, an "INFO" list can be included in the file.

The "RDIB" form is defined as follows, using the standard RIFF form definition notation:

```
<RDIB-form> →   RIFF ( 'RDIB'              // RIFF header
                    data( <DIB-data> )) // Bitmap data in DIB format
```

The <DIB-data> format is defined in "Device Independent Bitmap (DIB) File Format," earlier in this chapter.

Musical Instrument Digital Interface (MIDI) File Format

The MIDI file format represents a Standard MIDI File, as defined by the MIDI Manufacturers Association. A MIDI file contains commands instructing instruments to play specific notes and perform other operations.

The specifications for MIDI and MIDI files can be obtained from the following organization:

International MIDI Association (IMA)
5316 W. 57th Street
Los Angeles, CA 90056
(213) 649-6434.

RIFF MIDI (RMID) File Format

The "RMID" format consists of a standard MIDI file enclosed in a RIFF chunk. Enclosing the MIDI file in a "RIFF" chunk allows the file to be consistently identified; for example, an "INFO" list can be included in the file.

The "RMID" form is defined as follows, using the standard RIFF form definition:

```
<RMID-form> →  RIFF ( 'RMID'              // RIFF header
                      data( <MIDI-data> )) // Standard MIDI File
                                           // data
```

<MIDI-data> is equivalent to a Standard MIDI File.

Multimedia Movie File Format (RMMP)

The Multimedia Movie File Format (RMMP) contains animation data for the Multimedia Movie Player. Movie files can be authored on the Macintosh using MacroMind Director, a multimedia authoring tool. A Multimedia Movie Convertor utility, which runs on the Macintosh, can convert the Director file to RMMP format. After the converted file is transferred to the PC, it can be played using the Movie Player. RMMP files generally have an .MMM filename extension.

The movie file format was developed over time by MacroMind, Inc. and does not necessarily represent an ideal file format for the generalized storage of animation data. Rather than attempt to develop such a format, Microsoft chose to support MacroMind Director, a stable, established authoring tool, as the animation authoring tool for the Multimedia Extensions. Vendors wishing to provide multimedia Windows playback capabilities for their own animation authoring tools should create their own Windows playback engine.

This section provides an overview to the movie file format, but it does not attempt to fully explain every data structure. This documentation is not intended to facilitate the creation of utilities for converting other animation file formats to Movie File format; it describes only the basic structure and contents of the movie file. Refer to *Inside Macintosh* for information on the Macintosh data structures used in movie files.

Movie File Structure

The movie file format is based on RIFF, but it is in essence a Macintosh format. The animation objects are Macintosh data structures, and much of the integer byte ordering is represented in Motorola format. The Movie Player converts the byte ordering when it loads the file.

The file contains a table of contents chunk (with chunk ID "CFTC") that lists the animation structures in the file. The animation structures are stored in their own chunks and immediately follow the "CFTC" chunk. Expressed in RIFF notation, the movie file format is as follows:

```
RIFF <ckSize>( 'RMMP'
                <cftc-ck>                 // Table of contents chunk
                <ver-ck>                  // Version chunk
                <mcnm-ck>                 // Macintosh name chunk
                <animation chunks>… )     // Score, cast members, etc.
```

Expressed in RIFF notation, an animation chunk is formatted as follows:

```
<ckID:FOURCC><dwSize:DWORD>(   <dwResID:DWORD>    // Resource ID number
                               <ResName:BSTR>     // Resource name
                               <ChunkData> )      // Resource data
```

The animation chunk fields are described in the following table:

Field	Description
ckID	Chunk ID of the animation element.
dwSize	Size of animation element.
dwResID	Resource ID number. The resource ID number identifies the animation element within a group of elements of the same resource type. For example, a series of four "dib" chunks might be numbered 0x401, 0x402, 0x403, and 0x404. In the same file, there might be a "stxt" chunk numbered 0x401.
ResName	Resource name. This is a variable-length string with a BYTE string-length prefix and no terminating NULL character. Since the **ResName** field has variable length, the starting position of the **ChunkData** is variable. This field is word-aligned, and a pad byte might appear at the end of the field.
ChunkData	Animation resource data. The chunk data is word-aligned, as is the entire animation chunk.

The **dwSize** and **ResID** fields are represented in Intel integer byte-ordering format. Unless otherwise noted, other integer data is represented in Motorola byte-ordering format.

The following section lists the chunks that can reside in a movie file. "Structure of Selected Movie File Data Chunks," following the next section, describes some of the animation structures in detail.

Summary of Movie File Data Chunks

The following chunks can occur in a movie file:

Chunk ID	Description
Information Chunks	
'cftc'	Table of Contents chunk. Contains a series of table of contents entries identifying the type, size, index value, and location of each data element within the movie file. The "cftc" chunk is described in the next section.
'ver '	Identifies the version of the movie file. The table of contents chunk referencing the "ver" chunk duplicates the "ver" data chunk; the file version number resides in the **dwUniqueID** field of the chunk. You can use the **mmpGetFileInfo** or **mmpGetMovieInfo** functions to retrieve the file version number.
'mcnm'	Contains the original Macintosh filename for the movie file. You can use the **mmpGetFileInfo** or **mmpGetMovieInfo** functions to retrieve the Macintosh filename. The filename resides in the chunk **ResName** field.
Cast Resource Chunks	
'pict'	Contains a Macintosh PicHandle resource. The Movie Player does not support Macintosh QuickDraw PICT structures and ignores "pict" chunks during playback.
'clut'	Contains a Macintosh "clut" color resource table. The "clut" header fields and table data value fields are removed, and each table entry is stored as a six-byte RGB value.
'snd '	Contains a Macintosh format 2 "snd" sound resource.
'scvw'	Contains a "vwsc" score chunk, which is a section of the score copied to the cast. This chunk is only used during authoring.
'dib '	Contains a Windows DIB, minus the palette information. The "dib" chunk is described in the next section.
'stxt'	Contains styled text information, including header and string size information, the text string, and a Macintosh StScrpRec style-scrap record.

Chunk ID	Description
Movie Resource Chunks	
'vwcf'	Contains movie configuration information. You can use the **mmpGetFileInfo** or **mmpGetMovieInfo** functions to retrieve the information stored in this chunk.
'vwcr'	Contains the array of cast records.
'vwsc'	Contains the movie score. The movie score is delta-encoded to save space.
'vwlb'	Contains frame label information. The frame-label structure is described in the next section. You can use the **mmpGetInfo** function to access the label information.
'vwtl'	Contains pixel patterns used for filling in quick-draw shapes.
'vwtc'	Contains SMPTE time-code information for movies with locked tempos.
'vwfm'	Contains font mapping information for the movie.
'vwac'	Contains script channel text for the movie. The script-channel chunk data begins with a two-byte command count value, followed by a series of action-entry structures. The action-entry structure is described in the next section. You can use the **mmpGetInfo** function to access the script-channel information.

Structure of Selected Movie File Data Chunks

This section describes some of the movie-file data chunks listed in the previous section. It does not describe all the structures; instead, it describes those likely to be useful to a movie player application.

CFTC Table of Contents Entries

The "cftc" chunk identifies the contents and location of the other data chunks in the movie file. The CFTC chunk can be defined as follows (using RIFF notation):

```
<CFTC-ck> →    cftc( <CFTC entry>… )

<CFTC entry> → struct {
                   FOURCC ckID;
                   DWORD  dwSize;
                   DWORD  dwResID;
                   DWORD  dwOffset;
               }
```

The <CFTC entry> fields are described in the following table:

Field	Description
ckID	Chunk ID of the animation element stored in the file.
dwSize	Size of the animation element.
dwResID	Resource ID number of the animation element.
dwOffset	Byte offset of animation element from start of file.

All integer values in the CFTC chunk are in Intel format.

Windows Bitmap (DIB) Chunk

The "dib" chunk contains a Windows bitmap, minus the palette. The data portion of this chunk begins with a Windows **BITMAPINFOHEADER** structure, followed immediately by the bitmap data. When appropriate, the bitmap data is run-length encoded into Windows RLE format.

The following RIFF notation shows the format of the DIB chunk:

```
<DIB-ck> → dib(    <dwResID:DWORD>
                   <ResourceName:BSTR>
                   <dibHeader:BITMAPINFOHEADER>
                   <BitmapData:BYTE>… )
```

All integer data in the "dib" chunk is in Intel format. The fields in the "dib" chunk are described in the following table:

Field	Description
dwResID	Unique sequence number
ResourceName	Resource name string
dibHeader	Windows BITMAPINFOHEADER structure.
BitmapData	Bitmap data

Label-List (VWLB) Chunk

The "vwlb" chunk contains the label list for the movie file. A label is a textual string assigned to a frame. The Movie Player provides two functions, **mmpGetInfo** and **mmpSetInfo**, that allow you to get and set the label-list information. See Chapter 3, "Function Directory," for descriptions of these functions.

The following RIFF notation show the format of the "vwlb" chunk:

```
<VWLB-ck> → vwlb ( <dwResID:DWORD>
                   <ResourceName:BSTR>
                   <LabelCount:WORD>
                   <LabelRecord:LREC>…
                   <LabelText:CHAR>… )

<LREC> →    struct {
                WORD   wFrameNumber;
                WORD   wTextOffset;
            }
```

The fields of the "vwlb" chunk are described in the following. All integers, with the exception of the **SeqID** field, are in Motorola format.

Field	Description
dwResID	Unique sequence number.
ResourceName	Resource-name string.
LabelCount	Count of labels stored in the file.
LabelRecords	Series of LREC label records identifying the location of the label text and the associated frame number. The chunk contains **LabelCount**+1 label records; the last record in the array has **wFrameNumber** set to zero, and the **wTextOffset** value points beyond the end of the **LabelText** area.
LabelText	Label text stored in packed format. Each label is terminated with a character value 0x0d.

The fields of the LREC structure are described in the following. All integers are in Motorola format.

Field	Description
wFrameNumber	Frame number associated with label
wTextOffset	Offset of label text from start of the LabelText field.

Action-Code (VWAC) Chunk

The "vwac" chunk contains the script-channel text (action entries) for the movie. The Movie Player provides two functions, **mmpGetInfo** and **mmpSetInfo**, that allow you to get and set the label-list information. See Chapter 3, "Function Directory," for descriptions of these functions.

The following RIFF notation shows the format of the "vwac" chunk:

```
<VWLB-ck> → vwac (  <dwResID:DWORD>
                    <ResourceName:BSTR>
                    <ActionCount:WORD>
                    <ActionRecord:ACREC>…
                    <ActionText:CHAR>…     )

<ACREC> →  struct {
                BYTE    chMenuItem;
                BYTE    wActionCode;
                WORD    wTextOffset;
           }
```

The fields of the "vwac" chunk are described in the following. All integers, with the exception of the **SeqID** field, are in Motorola format.

Field	Description
dwResID	Unique sequence number.
ResourceName	Resource-name string.
ActionCount	Number of action codes stored in the chunk.
ActionRecord	Series of ACREC action-code records. The chunk contains contains **ActionCount**+1 action-code records; the last record in the array has **chMenuItem** set to zero, and the **wTextOffset** value points beyond the end of the **achText** area.
ActionText	Action-code text stored in packed format, without terminating characters between action-code strings.

The fields of the ACREC structure are described in the following. Integers are in Motorola format.

Field	Description
chMenuItem	Menu item number from script-channel window.
wActionCode	Not used by Movie Player.
wTextOffset	Offset of action-code text from start of ActionText field.

Palette File Format (PAL)

The Palette File Format (PAL) represents a logical palette, which is a collection of colors represented as RGB values. The PAL format is defined as follows:

```
RIFF ( 'PAL' data(<palette:LOGPALETTE>) )
```

LOGPALETTE is the Windows 3.0 logical palette structure, defined as follows:

```
typedef struct tagLOGPALETTE {
    WORD    palVersion;
    WORD    palNumEntries;
    PALETTEENTRY    palPalEntry[];
} LOGPALETTE;
```

Fields for the **LOGPALETTE** structure are described in the following table:

Field	Description
palVersion	Specifies the Windows version number for the structure.
palNumEntries	Specifies the number of palette color entries.
palPalEntry[]	Specifies an array of PALETTEENTRY data structures that define the color and usage of each entry in the logical palette.

The colors in the palette entry table should appear in order of importance. This is because entries earlier in the logical palette are most likely to be placed in the system palette.

PALETTEENTRY Structure

The **PALETTEENTRY** data structure specifies the color and usage of an entry in a logical color palette. The structure is defined as follows:

```
typedef struct tagPALETTEENTRY {
    BYTE    peRed;
    BYTE    peGreen;
    BYTE    peBlue;
    BYTE    peFlags;
} PALETTEENTRY;
```

Fields for the **PALETTEENTRY** structure are defined in the following table:

Field	Description
peRed	Specifies the intensity of red for the palette entry color.
peGreen	Specifies the intensity of green for the palette entry color.
peBlue	Specifies the intensity of blue for the palette entry color.
peFlags	Specifies how the palette entry is to be used.

Rich Text Format (RTF)

The Rich Text Format (RTF) is a standard method of encoding formatted text and graphics using only 7-bit ASCII characters. Formatting includes different font sizes, faces, and styles, as well as paragraph alignment, justification, and tab control.

RTF is described in the *Microsoft Word Technical Reference: For Windows and OS/2*, published by Microsoft Press. To order a copy of the *Technical Reference*, call Microsoft Press at 1-800-MSPRESS.

Waveform Audio File Format (WAVE)

This section describes the Waveform format, which is used to represent digitized sound.

WAVE Form Definition

The WAVE form is defined as <WAVE-form> as follows. Programs must expect (and ignore) any unknown chunks encountered, as with all RIFF forms. However, <fmt-ck> must always occur before <data-ck>, and both of these chunks are mandatory in a WAVE file.

```
<WAVE-form>    →   RIFF(   'WAVE'                    // Form type
                           <fmt-ck>                  // Waveform format
                           <data-ck> )               // Waveform data

<fmt-ck>       →   fmt(    <wave-format>             // WaveFormat structure
                           <format-specific> )       // Dependent on format
                                                     //  category

<wave-format>  →   struct {
                       WORD     formatTag;           // Format category
                       WORD     nChannels;           // No. channels
                       DWORD    nSamplesPerSec;       // Sampling rate
                       DWORD    nAvgBytesPerSec;       // For buffering
                       WORD     nBlockAlign;          // Block alignments
                   }

<PCM-format-specific> →
                   struct {
                       WORD     nBitsPerSample;       // Sample size
                   }

<data-ck> →        data( <wave-data> )
```

WAVE Chunk Descriptions

The chunks contained in the WAVE form definition are described in more detail in the following table:

Chunk ID	Description
fmt	This chunk contains **<wave-format>**, which specifies the format of the data contained in **<data-ck>**. The **<wave-format>** chunk contains a structure consisting of the following fields:

Field	Description
wFormatTag	A number which indicates the WAVE format category of the file. The content of the **<FormatSpecific>** field of the 'fmt' chunk, and the interpretation of data in the "data" chunk, depend on this value. The valid values for **<wFormatTag>**, and a description of each WAVE format category, is given in the next section.
nChannels	The number of channels represented in **<data-ck>**, such as, 1 for mono or 2 for stereo.
nSamplesPerSec	The sampling rate (in samples per second) that each channel should be played back at.
nAvgBytesPerSec	The average number of bytes per second that data in **<data-ck>** should be transferred at. If **<wFormatTag>** is WAVE_FORMAT_PCM, then **<nAvgBytesPerSec>** should be equal to the following formula $$nChannels{\times}nBitsPerSecond{\times}\frac{nBitsPerSample}{8}$$ Playback software can estimate the buffer size using the **<nAvgBytesPerSec>** value.
nBlockAlign	The block alignment (in bytes) of the data in **<data-ck>**. If **<wFormatTag>** is set to WAVE_FORMAT_PCM, then **<nBlockAlign>** should be equal to the following formula $$nChannels{\times}\frac{nBitsPerSample}{8}$$

Chunk ID	Description
	Playback software needs to process a multiple of **<nBlockAlign>** bytes of data at a time, so that the value of **<nBlockAlign>** can be used for buffer alignment.
FormatSpecific	This field consists of zero or more bytes of parameters. Which parameters occur depends on the WAVE format category— see "WAVE Format Categories" below. Playback software should be written to allow for (and ignore) any unknown **FormatSpecific** parameters that occur at the end of this field.
data	This chunk contains **<wave-data>**, the actual waveform audio data. The format of **<wave-data>** depends on the **<wFormatTag>** value stored in the "fmt" chunk—see "Wave Format Categories" below.

WAVE Format Categories

The format category of a WAVE file is specified by the value of the **<formatTag>** field of the "fmt" chunk. The representation of data in the "data" chunk, and the content of the **<FormatSpecific>** field of the "fmt" chunk, depend on the format category.

wFormatTag Value	Format Category
WAVE_FORMAT_PCM (value 1)	Pulse Code Modulation (PCM) Format

The following sections describe the different format categories.

Pulse Code Modulation (PCM) Format

The "data" chunk contains samples represented in pulse code modulation (PCM) format. For WAVE files in this category, the **FormatSpecific** field of the "fmt" chunk contains a **<PCMFormatSpecific>** structure, which contains a single field, **<nBitsPerSample>**. This field specifies the number of bits of data used to represent each sample of each channel. If there are multiple channels, the sample size is the same for each channel.

In a single-channel WAVE file, samples are stored consecutively. For stereo WAVE files, channel 0 represents the left channel, and channel 1 represents the right channel. The speaker position mapping for more than two channels is currently undefined. In multiple-channel WAVE files, samples are interleaved.

The following diagrams show the data packing for a 8-bit mono and stereo WAVE files:

Sample 1	Sample 2	Sample 3	Sample 4
Channel 0	*Channel 0*	*Channel 0*	*Channel 0*

Data packing for 8-bit mono PCM.

Sample 1		Sample 2	
Channel 0 *(left)*	*Channel 1* *(right)*	*Channel 0* *(left)*	*Channel 1* *(right)*

Data packing for 8-bit stereo PCM.

The following diagrams show the data packing for 16-bit mono and stereo WAVE files:

Sample 1		Sample 2	
Channel 0 *low-order byte*	*Channel 0* *high-order byte*	*Channel 0* *low-order byte*	*Channel 0* *high-order byte*

Data packing for 16-bit mono PCM.

Sample 1			
Channel 0 *(left)* *low-order byte*	*Channel 0* *(left)* *high-order byte*	*Channel 1* *(right)* *low-order byte*	*Channel 1* *(right)* *high-order byte*

Data packing for 16-bit stereo PCM.

Data Format of the Samples

Each sample is contained in an integer i. The size of i is the smallest number of bytes required to contain the specified sample size. The least significant byte is stored first. The bits that represent the sample amplitude are stored in the most significant bits of i, and the remaining bits are set to zero.

For example, if the sample size (recorded in **<nBitsPerSample>**) is 12 bits, then each sample is stored in a two-byte integer. The least significant four bits of the first (least significant) byte is set to zero.

The data format and maximum and minimum values for PCM waveform samples of various sizes are as follows:

Sample Size	Data Format	Maximum Value	Minimum Value
One to eight bits	Unsigned integer	255 (0xFF)	0
Nine or more bits	Signed integer i	Largest positive value of i	Most negative value of i

For example, the maximum, minimum, and midpoint values for 8-bit and 16-bit PCM waveform data are as follows:

Format	Maximum Value	Minimum Value	Midpoint Value
8-bit PCM	255 (0xFF)	0	128 (0x80)
16-bit PCM	32767 (0x7FFF)	−32768 (−0x8000)	0

Examples of WAVE Files

The following PCM WAVE file has a 11.025 kHz sampling rate, mono, 8 bits per sample:

```
RIFF('WAVE' fmt(1, 1, 11025, 11025, 1, 8)
        data( <wave-data> ) )
```

The following PCM WAVE file has a 22.05 kHz sampling rate, stereo, 8 bits per sample:

```
RIFF('WAVE' fmt(1, 2, 22050, 44100, 2, 8)
        data( <wave-data> ) )
```

The following PCM WAVE file has a 44.1 kHz sampling rate, mono, 20 bits per sample:

```
RIFF('WAVE' INFO(INAM("O Canada"Z))
        fmt(1, 1, 44100, 132300, 3, 20)
        data( <wave-data> ) )
```

Appendix A
MCI Command String Syntax Summary

This appendix provides a summary of the syntax of the MCI command strings. The following command tables are included in this chapter:

- System command set

- Required command set

- Basic command set

- Animation command set

- CD audio command set

- MIDI sequencer command set

- Videodisc command set

- Video overlay command set

- Waveform audio command set

For information on using MCI command strings and descriptions of the commands, see Chapter 7, "MCI Command Strings."

About the Command Tables

Each command table has a Command column and an Arguments column. The Command column contains the MCI commands available for a device type. The Arguments column contains the options available for each MCI command. For example, the following table contains the MCI commands all devices support:

Command	Arguments
capability *device_name*	{**can eject** | **can play** | **can record** | **can save** | **compound device** | **device type** | **has audio** | **has video** | **uses files**}
close *device_name*	
info *device_name*	[**product**]
open *device_name*	[**alias** *device_alias*]
	[**shareable**]
	[**type** *device_type*]
status *device_name*	[**mode** | **ready**]

Each command also has a **notify** and **wait** flag that does not appear in the tables. These flags can be added to any command.

The following conventions are used in the previous example and for the other MCI command tables:

Type Style	Used For
Bold	A specific term intended to be used literally. When used in the command column, it represents the MCI string command. When used in the arguments column, it represents a flag. For example, the **capability** command and the **can play** flag must be typed as shown.
Italics	Placeholders for information you must provide. The MCI command or flag associated with the information must precede it. For example, to use the alias words for the *device_name* with the **capability** command, type "capability words can play."
|	Divider for mutually exclusive arguments. When multiple arguments are separated by this symbol, only one of them can be used for each command. For example, the items in the list **can eject, can play, can record, can save, compound device, device type, has audio, has video, uses files** are mutually exclusive and you must select only one to use with the **capability** command. (Do not type the | with the argument.)
{ }	Required argument. You must include an argument enclosed by braces. For example, you must use one of the arguments **can eject, can play, can record, can save, compound device, device type, has audio, has video, uses files** with the **capability** command. (Do not type the braces with the argument.)
[]	Optional argument. For example, the **alias, type** and **shareable** flags are optional for the **open** command. You can use any combination of these flags. You can also use optional argruments with a required argument. (Do not type the brackets with the argument.)

MCI System Command Set

The following table summarizes the MCI system commands. These commands are interpreted directly by MCI. System commands also support **notify** and **wait** as optional flags. You can add either or both of these flags to any system command.

Command	Arguments
break *device_name*	{**off** | **on** *virtual key code*}
sound *sound_name*	
sysinfo *device_name*	{**installname** | **name** *index* | **name** *index* **open** | **quantity** | **quantity open**}

Required Command Set

The following table lists the commands recognized by all devices. Extended commands can add other options to these commands. Required commands also support **notify** and **wait** as optional flags. You can add either or both of these flags to any required command.

Command	Arguments
capability *device_name*	{**can eject** | **can play** | **can record** | **can save** | **compound device** | **device type** | **has audio** | **has video** | **uses files**}
close *device_name*	
info *device_name*	[**product**]

Command	Arguments
open *device_name*	[**alias** *device_alias*]
	[**shareable**]
	[**type** *device_type*]
status *device_name*	[**mode** | **ready**]

Basic Command Set

In addition to the commands described previously, each device supports a set of commands specific to its device type. Although these commands are optional for a device, if a command is used it must support the options listed in this table as a minimum set of capabilities. Basic commands also support **notify** and **wait** as optional flags. You can add either or both of these flags to any basic command.

Command	Arguments
load *device_name*	{*file_name*}
pause *device_name*	
play *device_name*	[**from** *position*]
	[**to** *position*]
record *device_name*	[**from** *position*]
	[**to** *position*]
	[**insert** | **overwrite**]
resume *device_name*	
save *device_name*	[*file_name*]
seek *device_name*	{**to** *position* | **to start** | **to end**}

Command	Arguments
set *device_name*	[**audio all off** | **audio all on** | **audio left off** | **audio left on** | **audio right off** | **audio right on** | **video off** | **video on**] [**door closed** | **door open**] [**time format milliseconds** | **time format ms**]
status *device_name*	{**current track** | **length** | **length track** *track_number* | **mode** | **number of tracks** | **position** | **position track** *track_number* | **ready** | **start position** | **time format**}
stop *device_name*	

Animation and Movie Player Command Set

Animation and movie players support the following set of commands. These devices also support **notify** and **wait** as optional flags. You can add either or both of these flags to any animation command.

Command	Arguments
capability *device_name*	{can eject | can play | can record | can reverse | can save | can stretch | compound device | device type | fast play rate | has audio | has video | normal play rate | slow play rate | uses files | uses palettes | windows}
close *device_name*	
info *device_name*	[file | product | window text]
open *device_name*	[alias *device_alias*]
	[nostatic]
	[parent *hwnd*]
	[shareable]
	[style child | style overlapped | style popup]
	[type *device_type*]
pause *device_name*	

Command	Arguments
play *device_name*	[**fast** | **slow** | **speed** *fps*]
	[**from** *position*]
	[**reverse**]
	[**to** *position*]
	[**scan**]
put *device_name*	{ **destination** | **destination at** *destination_rectangle* | **source** | **source at** *source_rectangle* }
realize *device_name*	{**background** | **normal**}
resume *device_name*	
seek *device_name*	[**to** *position* | **to start** | **to end**]
set *device_name*	[**audio all off** | **audio all on** | **audio left off** | **audio left on** | **audio right off** | **audio right on** | **video off** | **video on**] [**time format milliseconds** | **time format ms** | **time format frames**]

Command	Arguments
status *device_name*	{**current track** | **forward** | **length** | **length track** *track_number* | **media present** | **mode** | **number of tracks** | **palette handle** | **position** | **position track** *track_number* | **ready** | **speed** | **start position** | **time format** | **window handle**}
step *device_name*	[**by** *frames*] [**reverse**]
stop *device_name*	
update *device_name*	[**at** *update_rect*] [**hdc** *hdc*]
where *device_name*	{**destination** | **source**}
window *device_name*	[**handle** *window_handle* | **handle default**] [**state hide** | **state iconic** | **state maximized** | **state minimize** | **state minimized** | **state no action** | **state no activate** | **state normal** | **state show**] [**text** *caption_text*]

CD Audio Command Set

CD audio devices support the following core set of commands. CD audio devices also support **notify** and **wait** as optional flags. You can add either or both of these flags to any CD audio command.

Command	Arguments
capability *device_name*	{**can eject** | **can play** | **can record** | **can save** | **compound device** | **device type** | **has audio** | **has video** | **uses files**}
close *device_name*	
info *device_name*	[**product**]
open *device_name*	[**alias** *device_alias*] [**shareable**]
pause *device_name*	
play *device_name*	[**from** *position*] [**to** *position*]
resume *device_name*	
seek *device_name*	[**to** *position* | **to start** | **to end**]

Command	Arguments
set *device_name*	**[audio all off | audio all on | audio left off | audio left on | audio right off | audio right on | video off | video on]** **[door closed | door open]** **[time format milliseconds | time format ms | time format msf | time format tmsf]**
status *device_name*	**{current track | length | length track** *track_number* **| media present | mode | number of tracks | position | position track** *track_number* **| ready | start position | time format}**
stop *device_name*	

MIDI Sequencer Command Set

The MIDI sequencer supports the following set of commands. MIDI sequencers also support **notify** and **wait** as optional flags. You can add either or both of these flags to any MIDI sequencer command.

Command	Arguments
capability *device_name*	{**can eject** | **can play** | **can record** | **can save** | **compound device** | **device type** | **has audio** | **has video** | **uses files**}
close *device_name*	
info *device_name*	[**product**]
open *device_name*	[**alias** *device_alias*]
	[**shareable**]
	[**type** *device_type*]
pause *device_name*	
play *device_name*	[**from** *position*]
	[**to** *position*]
record *device_name*	[**from** *position*]
	[**to** *position*]
	[**insert** | **overwrite**]
save *device_name*	[*file_name*]
seek *device_name*	[**to** *position* | **to start** | **to end**]

Command	Arguments
set *device_name*	[**audio all off** | **audio all on** | **audio left off** | **audio left on** | **audio right off** | **audio right on** | **video off** | **video on**] [**master MIDI** | **master none** | **master SMPTE**] [**offset** *hmsf_value*] [**port** *port_number* | **port mapper** | **port none**] [**slave file** | **slave MIDI** | **slave none** | **slave SMPTE**] [**tempo** *tempo_value*] [**time format milliseconds** | **time format ms** | **time format smpte 24** | **time format smpte 25** | **time format smpte 30** | **time format smpte 30 drop** | **time format song pointer**]

Command	Arguments
status *device_name*	{**current track** | **division type** | **length** | **length track** *track_number* | **master** | **media present** | **mode** | **number of tracks** | **offset** | **port** | **position** | **position track** *track_number* | **ready** | **slave** | **start position** | **tempo** | **time format**}
stop *device_name*	

Videodisc Command Set

Videodisc players support the following set of commands. Videodisc devices also support **notify** and **wait** as optional flags. You can add either or both of these flags to any videodisc command.

Command	Arguments
capability *device_name*	{**can eject** | **can play** | **can record** | **can reverse** | **can save** | **compound device** | **device type** | **fast play rate** | **has audio** | **has video** | **normal play rate** | **slow play rate** | **uses files**} [**CAV** | **CLV**]
close *device_name*	
escape *device_name*	{*command_string*}
info *device_name*	[**product**]
open *device_name*	[**alias** *device_alias*] [**shareable**]
pause *device_name*	
play *device_name*	[**fast** | **slow** | **speed** *fps*] [**from** *position*] [**reverse**] [**scan**] [**to** *position*]
resume *device_name*	
seek *device_name*	[**reverse** | **to** *position* | **to start** | **to end**]

Command	Arguments
set *device_name*	[audio all off | audio all on | audio left off | audio left on | audio right off | audio right on | video off | video on] [door closed | door open] [time format milliseconds | time format ms | time format frames | time format hms | time format track]
spin *device_name*	[down | up]
status *device_name*	{current track | disc size | forward | length | length track *track_number* | media present | media type | mode | number of tracks | position | position track *track_number* | ready | side | speed | start position | time format}
step *device_name*	[by] *position* [reverse]
stop *device_name*	

Video Overlay Command Set

Video overlay devices supports the following set of commands. Video overlay devices also support **notify** and **wait** as optional flags. You can add either or both of these flags to any video overlay command.

Command	Arguments
capability *device_name*	{**can eject** | **can freeze** | **can play** | **can record** | **can save** | **can stretch** | **compound device** | **device type** | **has audio** | **has video** | **uses files** | **windows**}
close *device_name*	
freeze *device_name*	[**at** *rectangle*]
info *device_name*	[**product | file | window text**]
load *device_name*	[*file_name*]
	at *buffer_rectangle*
open *device_name*	[**alias** *device_alias*]
	[**parent** *hwnd*]
	[**shareable**]
	[**style** *style_type* | **style child** | **style overlapped** | **style popup**]
	[**type** *device_type*]

Command	Arguments
put *device_name*	{**destination** | **at** *destination_rectangle* | **frame** | **frame at** *frame_rectangle* | **source** | **source at** *source_rectangle* | **video** | **video at** *video_rectangle*}
save *device_name*	[*file_name*]
	at *buffer_rectangle*
set *device_name*	[**audio all off** | **audio all on** | **audio left off** | **audio left on** | **audio right off** | **audio right on** | **video off** | **video on**] [**time format milliseconds** | **time format ms**]
status *device_name*	{**current track** | **length** | **length track** *track_number* | **media present** | **mode** | **number of tracks** | **position** | **position track** *track_number* | **ready** | **start position** | **time format** | **window handle**}
unfreeze *device_name*	[**at** *freeze_rectangle*]
where *device_name*	{**destination** | **frame** | **source** | **video**}

Command	Arguments
window *device_name*	[**handle** *window_handle* | **handle default**]
	[**state hide** | **state iconic** | **state maximized** | **state minimize** | **state minimized** | **state no action** | **state no activate** | **state normal** | **state show**]
	[**text** *caption_text*]

Waveform Audio Command Set

Wave audio devices support the following set of commands. Wave audio devices also support **notify** and **wait** as optional flags. You can add either or both of these flags to any wave audio command.

Command	Arguments
capability *device_name*	{**can eject** | **can play** | **can record** | **can save** | **compound device** | **device type** | **has audio** | **has video** | **inputs** | **outputs** | **uses files**}
close *device_name*	
cue *device_name*	[**input** | **output**]
delete *device_name*	[**from** *position*]
	[**to** *position*]

Command	Arguments

info *device_name*	[**file**
	  | **input**
	  | **output**
	  | **product**]

open *device_name*	[**alias** *device_alias*]
	[**buffer** *buffer_size*]
	[**shareable**]
	[**type** *device_type*]
pause *device_name*	
play *device_name*	[**from** *position*]
	[**to** *position*]
record *device_name*	[**from** *position*]
	[**to** *position*]
	[**insert** | **overwrite**]
save *device_name*	[*file_name*]
seek *device_name*	[**to** *position* | **to start** | **to end**]

Command	Arguments
set *device_name*	[**alignment** *block_alignment*]
	[**any input**]
	[**any output**]
	[**audio all off** | **audio all on** | **audio left off** | **audio left on** | **audio right off** | **audio right on** | **video off** | **video on**]
	[**bitspersample** *bit_count*]
	[**bytespersec** *byte_rate*]
	[**channels** *channel_count*]
	[**format tag** *tag* | **format tag pcm**]
	[**input** *device_number*]
	[**output** *device_number*]
	[**samplespersec** *sample_rate*]
	[**time format milliseconds** | **time format ms** | **time format bytes** | **time format samples**]

Command	Arguments
status *device_name*	**{alignment** **| bitspersample** **| bytespersec** **| channels** **| current track** **| format tag** **| input** **| length** **| length track** *track_number* **| level** **| media present** **| mode** **| number of tracks** **| output** **| position** **| position track** *track_number* **| ready** **| samplespersec** **| start position** **| time format}**
stop *device_name*	

Manufacturer ID and Product ID Lists

This appendix provides lists of the manufacturer and product IDs currently used with the multimedia Extensions. This list will grow as more manufacturers create products for Windows with Multimedia.

To get a current list of manufacturer and product IDs for the multimedia Extensions, and to register new ones, request a *Multimedia Developer Registration Kit* from the following group:

> Microsoft Corporation
> Multimedia Systems Group
> Product Marketing
> One Microsoft Way
> Redmond, WA 98052-6399

Multimedia Extensions Manufacturer IDs

The current manufacturer IDs for the Multimedia extensions are as follows:

Constant Name	Value	Description
MM_MICROSOFT	1	Drivers developed by Microsoft Corporation

Multimedia Extensions Product IDs

The current product IDs for the Multimedia extensions are as follows:

Constant Name	Value	Description
MM_MIDI_MAPPER	1	Microsoft MIDI Mapper
MM_SNDBLST_MIDIOUT	3	Sound Blaster MIDI output port
MM_SNDBLST_MIDIIN	4	Sound Blaster MIDI input port
MM_SNDBLST_SYNTH	5	Sound Blaster internal synthesizer
MM_SNDBLST_WAVEOUT	6	Sound Blaster waveform input port
MM_SNDBLST_WAVEIN	7	Sound Blaster waveform input port
MM_ADLIB	9	Ad Lib-compatible synthesizer
MM_MPU401_MIDIOUT	10	MPU401 MIDI output port
MM_MPU401_MIDIIN	11	MPU401 MIDI input port
MM_PC_JOYSTICK	12	IBM Game Control Adapter

Index

PROGRAMMING WINDOWS,™ 2nd ed.

Charles Petzold

This is *the* Microsoft-authorized guide to writing applications for Windows 3 for both new and seasoned Windows programmers. Now completely updated and revised, this thorough resource is packed with tested programming advice, scores of new sample programs, and straightforward explanations of the Microsoft Windows programming environment. New chapters detail virtual memory, multitasking, Dynamic Data Exchange (DDE), Multiple Document Interface (MDI), and Dynamic Link Library (DLL).

**950 pages, softcover   7 3/8 x 9 1/4 $29.95
Order Code: PRWI2**

Contents:

Section One: A Windows backgrounder.

Section Two: Working with input from the keyboard; using the timer; using the mouse; using child window controls.

Section Three: Understanding memory management; working with icons, cursors, bitmaps, and strings; working with menus, accelerators, and dialog boxes.

Section Four: Introduction to GDI; drawing graphics; manipulating graphical information with bits and metafiles; working with text and fonts; using printers.

Section V: Dynamic Data Exchange (DDE); Multiple Document Interface (MDI); Dynamic Link Library (DLL).

Index.

Microsoft® Windows™ Multimedia Programmer's Library

(See back cover for more information)

**MICROSOFT® WINDOWS™
MULTIMEDIA
PROGRAMMER'S REFERENCE**

**MICROSOFT® WINDOWS™
MULTIMEDIA
PROGRAMMER'S WORKBOOK**

**MICROSOFT® WINDOWS™
MULTIMEDIA
AUTHORING AND TOOLS GUIDE**

To order, call 1-800-MSPRESS or mail this order form:*

Quantity	Order Code	Title	Price	Total Price
_____	WIGUPR	Microsoft Windows Guide to Programming	$29.95	$_____
_____	WIPRRE	Microsoft Windows Programmer's Reference	$39.95	$_____
_____	WIPRTO	Microsoft Windows Programming Tools	$24.95	$_____
_____	PRWI2	Programming Windows, 2nd ed.	$29.95	$_____
_____	MMPRRE	Microsoft Windows Multimedia Programmer's Ref.	$27.95	$_____
_____	MMPRWO	Microsoft Windows Multimedia Programmer's Workbook	$22.95	$_____
_____	MMAUGU	Microsoft Windows Multimedia Authoring and Tools Guide ...	$24.95	$_____

SUBTOTAL $_____

SALES TAX CHART
Add the applicable sales tax for the following states: AZ, CA, CO, CT, DC, FL, GA, HI, ID, IL, IN, IA, KS, KY, ME, MD, MA, MI, MN, MO, NE, NV, NJ, NM, NY, NC, PA, OH, OK, RI, SC, TN, TX, VA, WA, WV, WI.

SHIPPING
One book	$2.50
Two books	$3.25
Each additional book	$.75

Sales Tax $_____

Shipping $_____

TOTAL $_____

BHE

NAME _____

COMPANY (if applicable) _____

STREET (No P.O. Boxes) _____

CITY _____ STATE _____ ZIP _____

DAYTIME PHONE _____

CREDIT CARD NUMBER _____ EXP. DATE _____

CARDHOLDER SIGNATURE _____

PAYMENT:

☐ Check/Money Order (U.S. funds)

☐ **VISA** VISA (13 or 16 digits)

☐ MasterCard (16 digits)

☐ American Express (15 digits)

**FOR FASTER SERVICE CALL
*1-800-MSPRESS***

(8AM to 5PM Central Time)
and place your credit card order. Refer to campaign **BHE**.
All orders shipped RPS or UPS.

No P.O. Boxes please. Allow 2–3 weeks for delivery.

* In Canada, contact Macmillan Canada, Attn: Microsoft Press Dept., 164 Commander Blvd., Agincourt, Ontario, Canada M1S 3C7   416-293-8141

In the U.K., contact Microsoft Press, 27 Wrights Lane, London W8 5TZ